BABY BOOM OR BUST

Chronicles of Audacity Across Six Decades

JOHN T. HOWARD,
GRAYING BABY BOOMER

GLEEFUL CURMUDGEON PRESS

Gleeful Curmudgeon Press LLC

Publisher's Cataloging-in-Publication data

Names: Howard, John T., author.

Title: Baby boom or bust: chronicles of audacity across six decades / John T. Howard.

Description: Indianapolis, IN: Gleeful Curmudgeon Press, 2021.

Identifiers: LCCN: 2021913155 | ISBN: 978-1-7362820-0-7 (paperback) | 978-1-7362820-1-4 (ebook) | 978-1-7362820-2-1 (audiobook)
Subjects: LCSH Howard, John T. | Broadcasters--United States--Biography. | Baby boom generation--Biography. | Baby boom generation--Humor. | Indiana--Biography. | Indiana--History--20th century. | BISAC BIOGRAPHY & AUTOBIOGRAPHY / Personal memoirs
Classification: LCC PN1990.72 .H69 2021 | DDC 791.4402/8092--dc23

Events described in this book are true. The names of many characters and places have been changed to protect the privacy of subjects. Some events and locations have been combined to enhance story continuity.

First Edition

Cover design by Darko Bovan

Content Editors: Joshua Lisec, Howard Lovy, Made in the USA

Now, do I think the baby boomers tend to be self-absorbed? I do.

-P.J. O'Rourke

The baby boomers have dropped the ball on their burden of responsibility.

-Meghan McCain

The baby boomers are the most spoiled, most self-centered, most narcissistic generation the country's ever produced.

-Steve Bannon

A lot of baby boomers are baby bongers.

-Kevin Nealon

TABLE OF CONTENTS

PROLOGUE

THE BOOMER JOURNEY

Why would an average guy born smack-dab into the middle of the post-WWII baby boom write a memoir? Who does this guy think he is? Is the story *that* unique, especially for a baby boomer? Why would anyone beyond family and friends even care?

Because this book is not just *a* baby boomer's autobiography; it is potentially *the* autobiography of baby boomers. Wholly unauthorized, of course. *Baby Boom or Bust* attempts to explain how sex, drugs, and rock and roll defined, or at least road mapped, a generation. As a result, this work is (loosely) laid out according to these most obvious if not important life aspects for once youthful boomers. Besides, no one else in my demographic category has bothered, and we're starting to die off. Why not me, right now?

Tales that follow are not that different from other boomers', and many stretch boundaries of decency. Almost anyone else born between 1946 and 1964 could spin equally compelling yarns. This is merely my collection. It captures times, places, and events spanning the 1950s through today. In many cases, my story is cringeworthy; in others, it's too much information. Still, if this is as entertaining to read as it was to experience and then write, we will all end up happy.

This romp through the past joins the Ike era and continues beyond high school and college during the time of Richard Nixon, Vietnam, and Watergate. A fourteen-year career of near fame in small, local radio markets followed. It was a golden time for that medium before today's group-clustered, unimaginative corporate radio. There was also deviant behavior that went with the territory. That radio career ended abruptly, as most do. Closed doors opened new ones in corporate America. Adventures in broadcasting technology spanned another twenty-eight years, several companies, travel to all fifty states and all but the coldest continents.

The journey also examines a darker side fueled by narcissism, depraved misogyny, and a disproportionately large ego, only without all the money and power. Three beautiful wives participated along with three children and an amazing supporting cast of diverse characters. Many names have been changed to protect otherwise innocent souls who either vanished or might litigate.

Do-overs in life are not possible. While additional maturity would have been nice, little might have changed had other opportunities popped up.

My mother and father were in some ways as different as night and day. The original John T. grew up in Washington, Indiana. That small, rural southern Indiana town was notable in its day as a regional Baltimore and Ohio Railroad maintenance facility, ideally located halfway between St. Louis and Cincinnati.

Dad's home birth occurred in 1929 toward the younger end of a total herd of twelve children. I met all of them except one. Charles

II was an airborne gunner inside the ball turret of a B-17 bomber that got shot down over Germany during the Second World War. The family still mourns his loss. Howards are prolific breeders, and the surviving eleven were fruitful and multiplied. Several first cousins roam America whom I have never met. Most Howards left their hometown hamlet for distant states from coast to coast.

Grandfather Charles Howard was a proud man. His job at the B&O Railroad was eliminated during the Great Depression. Pride prevented the acceptance of any public assistance. He felt dollars should be earned honestly, no matter what. Charlie took whatever work came his way, ultimately settling in as janitor for the church and schools of St. Simon Parish. Grandpa also eventually succumbed to Parkinson's disease. At the time, I did not understand why he always frowned a scowl or why he shook.

Grandma served spaghetti for dinner one evening. It was scarfed down in short order by several visiting young cousins. Grandpa tried, but none of the pasta remained on shaking cutlery long enough to make it to his mouth. It was simultaneously horrifying but oddly entertaining to young kids. We learned years later that is precisely what he intended. After rug rats were safely tucked into bed, grandpa ate fried chicken with grandma. A hearty sense of humor lay under a gruff exterior aided by an occasional careful sip of bourbon. He always managed to find his mouth accurately with that. Grandpa used grandkids as television remote controls to switch between prime-time Westerns and adjust set-top rabbit ears as required.

Mother Eileen grew up two generations beyond Irish immigrants that emigrated to the Midwest, attempting escape from extreme persecution in and around Boston. The Sullivan family even dropped a leading O' from the front of their surname to minimize rampant ethnic prejudice of the day. Her father was a heavy industry man with Crucible Steel of Pittsburgh. He was one of five golf-playing, hard-drinking brothers. A lone sister became a nun. In terms of relative affluence, Mom perhaps married someone from the other side of the tracks. Their love remained strong, resulting in my four other great siblings. We believed it was a perfect union.

Dad lived through a nasty bout of rheumatic fever as a young child that irreparably damaged the bottom of his heart. His fondness as an adult for unfiltered Pall Malls, standard Midwestern meat and potato diet, and prodigious amounts of Wiedemann or Stroh's beer usually consumed inside his local Knights of Columbus hall, did not enhance his health metrics. He began suffering heart attacks in the 1970s. Cardiologists encouraged him to give up cigarettes, improve his diet, and cut beer consumption to just one per day. Dad sort of complied. Winston Lights replaced Pall Malls. He threw a few green vegetables onto his plate. He also saved daily beers for one weekend night to consume all at once. Dad's sense of humor was sharp, and he was universally loved in town. Fellow Knights elected him Grand Knight posthumously.

A rubbery steak dinner inside a Terre Haute, Indiana, joint in the fall of 1977 marked the last time we ever talked in person. He was proud of my accomplishments and told me so. Dad was just back from Long Island, New York. He traveled there to say goodbye to his oldest brother, Ernie, then in the final stages of a terminal illness. Life is short, he cautioned. Dad's demise came suddenly just a week later. He reached the bottom step of the choir loft in St. Simon church. He craved a smoke and snuck downstairs during communion. A local nurse and family friend accompanied him, also for a nicotine fix. She thought the funny face he made as he hit the floor was a gag right up until his color turned gray. Nurse Colleen grabbed a cardiologist from a rear pew. Resuscitation efforts commenced immediately. Dad was in the emergency room of the local hospital before Mass ended. In reality, he died before being carried from the church. Seventy miles northwest, I signed on to the airwaves of WBOW-AM in Terre Haute, rolling the song *My Little Town* by Simon and Garfunkel. My sister Maureen dialed the station hotline during that first song with news that pierced like a bullet. It changed the course of our lives forever.

Dad and I forged a strong bond too late as adults. At least he lived long enough to hold my first child. My father remains a large part of who I am. He unwittingly handed down his colorful ways. For example, Dad was always reluctant to explain why he needed fifty stitches in his behind. At eighteen, he plopped down on a concrete wall, forgetting the whiskey bottle inside his back pocket. His lips also remained sealed about why the Navy forced him out in his first year. It was actually his heart condition, but he created a myth about rampant carousing and drinking that was far more exciting. That helps explain his legend in Washington, Indiana.

I dedicate this work to Dad and to Mom, the saint who put up with him all those years. They both endured the hardships I brought upon the family but ended up proud parents anyway. Perhaps by the end of this book, you will learn more about our new nation of elders. We're the group you're now supposed to respect, if you dare.

Above all, always remember to respect your elders, OK?

Part I: SEX!

CHAPTER 1

PINK HATS AND PEE-PEES

Any potential loss of virginity comes down to technicality or semantics. It's difficult to determine what counts, but in terms of pure mechanics, my own could be considered jettisoned at age four and barely a half. The experience is also my earliest childhood memory.

The Howards were new residents of a hastily sprouted postwar National Homes neighborhood inside the suburban Indianapolis hamlet of Lawrence. In the late 1950s, that suburb provided starter housing for new boomer families. Dads went away to work. Moms kept houses cleaned, food prepared, and kids in line. A house across the street featured the McDougals, also Catholic, and prone to even more effusive procreation. Mr. and Mrs. McDougal eventually became the proud parents of eight. Bear in mind that mass-produced homes of the day contained just three bedrooms and one bathroom. In the Howard abode, Mom and Dad occupied one bedroom in the front of the house. Three Howard brothers shared one small room across the hallway while two sisters shared another next door. Any attempt to determine how the McDougals lodged ten people inside

1,300 square feet remains difficult. Logic suggests the kids surreptitiously observed enthusiastic carnal activity from unsuspecting parents. One of their daughters, Nadine, who was my age, must have witnessed them more than once. Perhaps they believed she was sleeping.

On the Fourth of July weekend 1958, Nadine and I were playing under her backyard swing set. In the middle of my dissertation about which type of stick is best suited for digging up ant hills, Nadine announced out of the clear, blue sky she would become my "wife."

"John," she ordered, "we're going to get married."

"OK," I said, thinking she was no longer interested in insect habitat destruction. "What do we need to do?"

"We need a priest."

At that moment, our neighborhood chum named Alan hopped over Nadine's fence to play.

"Hey, Alan!" Nadine waved.

"Hi," Alan said.

"You're going to be the priest so we can get married." Nadine took my stick and grabbed my hand.

"OK." Alan shrugged and turned up his white shirt collar to form an impromptu priestly vestment. Our families all went to Mass together.

"Where do we get married?" I asked. "Where's the church?"

"Over there." Nadine pointed to a tunnel of rose bushes by the back fence.

Alan crawled under the arch while Nadine and I marched down

our wedding aisle—the dandelion-covered lawn. Instead of pronouncing us man and wife, Alan simply said, "You are married now," then thoughtfully added, "May the Lord be with you." He hopped the fence, mounted his bike, and peddled off to find some other preschool pursuits. His exit was Nadine's cue to suggest acting married.

Nadine informed me that because we were married, "we have to take our clothes off and kiss." My reply—"Do we *have* to?"—was the last time I ever uttered those words in any similar situation. Nadine's proposal reminded me of the one time I caught my parents naked in the act a few days prior. I assumed they were fighting, so I got scared and dashed back to bed. Nadine, however, was apparently a student of her parents' carnal activities, including both detailed mechanics and subtle nuance. She led me by the hand into the rose bush tunnel. She took off our clothes, sat down cross-legged together, and made an awkward attempt at smooching. *Where're my sticks?* I thought, bored already.

Nadine pointed to her anatomy and stated, "Kiss me on the chest and then on my pink hat." I wanted to get back to my ant hills, so I followed her instructions. Even young kids knew that a "pink hat" referred to a vagina, and it wasn't a big deal.

"Now I will kiss you on your pee-pee at the same time."

At that age, I was still learning to count to ten, a far cry from sixty-nine. While involuntarily sniffing around her bare behind, more or less lodged in my face, what she did on the other end felt really good. The sticks could wait.

Nadine announced we would conclude our marital play-acting with something that sounded very strange.

"Get on top of me and go in and out of my butt with your pee-pee."

It made more sense to avoid the butt and aim instead for the pink hat.

Shortly thereafter, I found myself experiencing proto-coitus with an erection as girthy and stout as the last inch of a #2 pencil. There was no finishing, just unsatisfied curiosity. Nadine took off, hastily clothed, to tend to her plastic dolls by the swing set. It seemed weird that she then attempted to breastfeed Sweet Sue and Tiny Tears. So weird, I forgot all about the ants. Tonka trucks and more dirt in my own backyard beckoned.

The only other time Nadine and I waded into adult married play-acting territory occurred less than a year later.

"John, will you help me cut this hair off my dollies?"

Feeling sorry for cute little Tiny Tears, I asked, "Why?"

Nadine produced a bottle of mucilage.

"So we can both have hair," she said.

"We already have hair."

"I mean on my pink hat and your pee-pee."

"But I don't want glue or doll hair on my pee-pee."

"But—but—we're married. You're supposed to listen to me."

At that moment, I realized many females might have a crazy streak. My intent before Nadine pulled out the glue was to watch *Clutch Cargo* in black and white on a boxy Philco from the safety of my living room floor.

"We're not married anymore," I huffed.

"But Johnnyyyyy . . . "

I turned and walked away.

Whether the first instance of young children mimicking mom and dad can be officially considered loss of virginity depends on subjective definitions. I was inside young Nadine and rocking the pink hat, but otherwise oblivious to any sensations or emotions that would come storming in years later. Both our families moved away from Lawrence in the middle of the 1960s, thwarting any chance to see what we might have become as teenagers.

Chapter 2

Getting Naked on Purpose

Nadine evolved into a typical boy-avoiding little girl as we left toddlerhood for the elementary years. No further mention of pink hats, pee-pees, or marital play-acting ever came up again. Still, our "relationship" remained vivid in my impressionable young mind for years afterward. The experience Nadine and I shared amounted to a teaser trailer for a movie I knew I'd get to watch all the way through someday. That day came sooner than expected.

Birthday number ten occurred in 1964. Alan down the street (the same Alan who officiated the rosebush wedding) turned ten the day after I did. His mother threw a joint birthday party for us and invited other neighborhood kids. Alan had a big sister named Caroline, who was thirteen going on twenty-five.

Shortly after blowing out ten candles, popping open gifts, and consuming cake, I found myself inside her bedroom (impressed that it was all her own) with two other kids my age, Ricky and Ellen. We took turns with my new paddleball.

Without warning, Caroline proclaimed, "I have a present for you, too, John," stood up, and proceeded to take off all her clothes. Our eyes got as big as the paddle. This felt like trouble.

So, what's the present? I thought.

Caroline had hints of emerging breasts and an inkling of hair other than on her head. Until that moment, my erections had mostly been random, involuntary, and meaningless. This one felt purposeful.

Ellen, that friend everyone has who is up for anything, also got naked. She was as much a little girl as I was a little boy.

How big a sin is this? I thought. *Will this make me go to hell? I'm just a kid—I'll take my chances. Besides, this is WAY more interesting than sticking paper donkey tails on a wall.*

I joined the clothing drop adventure. Ricky, eyes still wide, scrambled off the bed, said, "I have to leave now," without looking back, and slammed the door on his way out.

All three remaining birthday celebrants wormed under the covers in case Ricky decided to tattle. The last thing we needed was Alan's mother bursting through the door. Some of the neighborhood mothers were guzzling cocktails, no doubt discussing important issues of the day (and Jackie Kennedy).

What followed can best be described as a hands-on anatomy lesson. Caroline insisted on showing us every nook and cranny.

"My pink hat bleeds every few weeks, and that means I am becoming a woman," she said. This was the first I ever heard of periods.

The lesson got personal when Caroline and Ellen began simultaneously fondling my naked body. My bewilderment turned into fascination when Caroline saddled up. Ellen continued feeling her way around.

Our adventure came to an abrupt halt when Alan's mom bellowed our names.

"CAROLINE! ELLEN! JOHN! What are you doing?"

She opened the door to find three fully-clothed kids (from the waist up) under Caroline's covers.

"Mooooooom . . . we're playing a game," Caroline said matter-of-factly.

"You should be playing with all your friends. They'll feel left out."

I simply wanted to know the name of that game. Was virginity lost? Or re-lost? A matter of interpretation. A ménage à trois before becoming a teenager? Semantics.

CHAPTER 3

FORMAL SEX EDUCATION

Grades 1 through 6 were spent within glazed cinder block school walls at St. Lawrence parish. Habited nuns, Franciscan priests, and lay teachers ensured both good grades and lockstep deportment. That's right. Deportment. It was graded on report cards. The Catholic school cliche of knuckles rapped with a ruler was entirely accurate. Aside from reading, writing (including precise cursive—Lord help lefties who took more than their share of abuse from the servants of Jesus), and arithmetic, grade school threw four memorable curve balls.

Third grade was led by a nun whose name was lost to time. All the nuns dressed alike and kept identically regimented schedules. Class start and end times, recesses, lunches, and bathroom breaks were enforced to the minute. At three pre-designated times every day, boys lined up in the hallway and marched to the restroom. It contained ten urinals, ten sinks, and four toilets. The nun opened the door so that ten boys could enter, and ten others could leave until all boys answered nature's call. One day, I simply did not have to pee at the designated time. I just stood at the floor-length urinal without unzipping. Then, in unison with the other nine, handwashing motions were repeated until the door opened for our single-file departure back to class.

But the boy who'd stood at the urinal beside mine felt obliged to inform the good sister that "Johnny didn't go potty, Sister."

Sister Mary Perv flipped out.

"Little Mr. Howard here did not empty his bladder at the time he was supposed to, and that is not a good thing," she announced as soon as class resumed. Little Mr. Howard was forced to stand face-first in a corner for thirty minutes in front of the class for the transgression of a dry bladder.

I have had a chronic nail-biting habit for as long as I can remember. The problem bothered fourth-grade matron Mrs. Renner, who one day stopped class to inform me (and all other uniform-wearing fourth graders) that "nail-biting will eventually lead to your horrible deaths." When fingernails were swallowed, she continued, "they do not digest and eventually a large ball is formed inside your bodies that has to be removed by cutting open your stomachs." Her warning was not over. "If you swallow chewing gum, it is also not digestible and makes the ball of bitten nails inside you much worse." Mrs. Renner piled it on. "The same goes for snot, and it's poison." Her attempts to scare me into unbitten nails failed, and no surgery is imminent decades later. We were a class of rebels. Many youthful peers continued occasional chewing of gum and reckless consumption of boogers, undaunted by fear.

Mrs. Renner was also teaching with an iron fist the afternoon of November 22, 1963, following lunchtime recess. The school PA system, used only in the morning and at the end of the school day, crackled to life.

"The father of our country, President Kennedy, has been assassinated in Dallas, Texas," the school principal said. At the time, I thought the word "assassination" meant a symbolic death. Had the president's character been assassinated? I knew there had to be a chance JFK lived on.

What happened next made no sense. Prayers were uttered and Mrs. Renner broke down. School was dismissed. Every adult in sight openly wept. For the next four days, my parents, especially mom, were not themselves. Three local TV network affiliates carried only assassination coverage from sign-on to sign-off. There were no cartoons and no Mickey Mouse Club. Just sad grownups. The local independent station simply left the air for a couple of days.

During the funeral procession, military drummers tapped a somber cadence behind a horse-drawn casket. This nine-year-old decided to keep time by thumping fingers on the coffee table. Not long after, the back of Mom's hand reached my cheek with an intensity not previously experienced.

"Show some respect, Johnny!" she shouted. "This is serious." *What happens to John-John and Caroline*, I wondered silently. It was too early to ask mom about it. *Kids are supposed to grow up with dads.*

Her mood soured further as we watched Lee Harvey Oswald die on live television. The Kennedy assassination was my first "Where were you?" moment. Four days in November 1963 changed the life trajectory of an entire generation.

Elementary school proved traumatic when JFK was killed, yet it also accelerated my mysterious journey through sexuality. Shortly before sixth-grade ended, Father Cyril J. Conan, an aging priest with a gruff exterior and gentle heart, offered upper elementary children our first formal sex education. His means of delivery, a clacking 16-millimeter film from a noisy but trusty Bell & Howell, explained biological functions. How babies are made, what menstrual cycles are, when bodies change, and other clinical aspects added clarity to previous experiences not yet fully grasped. Anatomical graphics and illustrated mechanics in the movie were nowhere close to controversial. The Dick and Jane version contained merely hints of Dick.

Although we understood in theory what the eloquent narrator described, morals remained cloudy. On the do's and don'ts of sexual activity, Father Conan offered an analogy. He likened men and women to stoves.

"Men," he said, "approach intimacy like gas stoves. Turn them on, and they get immediately hot. Turn them off, and they cool just as quickly. Women, on the other hand, are like electric stoves. When turned on, it takes a long time for them to warm up. It also takes an equally long time to cool off when the heat is removed."

That brief lecture turned out to be the most practical sexual advice I've ever received. Once put into practice much later and following several years of knob-turning practice, I'm left wondering how Father Conan knew that—and why he shared it with sixth graders.

CHAPTER 4

PARENTS COMING OF AGE

Sexual freedom in the United States increased dramatically during the 1960s. By '64, nearly four million American women were taking a new drug called "the pill." Its clinical use was menstrual cycle regulation; the unspoken benefit was pregnancy prevention. Such sexual freedom was not limited to liberated young women. The public later learned that our recently assassinated President enjoyed the benefits *a lot* before his sudden departure. Catholic clergy condemned the prescription as a mortal sin.

A house down the block provided residence for a couple with no children. That was odd for Lawrence, Indiana. Husband Cyrus was a retired Army Sergeant. He returned from Eastern Europe with a young bride named Marta. Cyrus worked for Western Electric, a Bell System telephone factory. Just about every household telephone in America originated from Western Electric. Choice was limited to the color black in either wall mount or desk models.

Cyrus was a neglectful redneck with a drinking problem. Marta was lovely but lonely. An ocean and half a continent separated her from home and family, and her husband was absent up to fourteen hours a day. He worked first shift, then ate supper at a nearby watering hole with work buddies.

Given easy birth control availability, raging hormones, and opportunity, youthful Marta became hot to trot. Indianapolis was once home to Drake Refrigeration, a large appliance repair company. Their boxy repair van fleet featured namesake ducks mounted to cab roofs. Duck eyes lit up and moved up and down whenever vans were in motion. The tin fowl also quacked. The faster the truck, the faster lit eyes moved and the faster ducks quacked. That marketing proved effective.

Mom and her friends often discussed the frequency with which Drake Refrigeration visited Cyrus and Marta's. The same repairman made service calls a few times every week. I didn't understand why that poor lady had so much difficulty with brand-new appliances. Mom informed Mrs. McDougal one day that "Marta must need her pipes reamed again." Years passed before I grasped what Marta and the Drake repairman were up to—and why neighborhood husbands seemed enamored with her, much to the chagrin of their stay-at-home Gladys Kravitzes.

One bright spring day in 1962, my minor sniffles before sunrise convinced Mom to keep me home from school. All symptoms predictably vanished by the time school let out that afternoon. Skipping school precluded outdoor play. To enforce the sentence, Mom locked the screen door. The deadbolt was impossible to reach unassisted for someone my height.

Justine McDougal, Nadine's younger sister, heard of the predicament from my meddlesome little sister Maureen. Justine stood on the front porch after school making faces, pointing, and laughing. "Ha-ha-ha-ha-HAA-HAA!" Her taunts welled my anger.

"Come outside and get me," Justine hissed in a sing-songy tone. Once I had enough, I charged across the living room, palms extended, toward the typically flimsy aluminum door. Flimsy right up until Mom locked it, which youthful rage made me forget.

My arms burst through the glass, followed by the rest of me. As I somersaulted onto my back, jagged shards sliced open my chin, neck, and left shoulder.

Justine ran away screaming. I hardly felt scratched. My main worry was the trouble I'd be in for breaking the glass. Until I saw the blood. A puddle. A big puddle.

"I'M BLEEDING!" I screamed.

Mrs. McDougal bounded over from her front yard, scooped me up, unlocked the door through the shattered glass, and rushed me inside. Mom, hearing commotion after her bath, hastily dressed and joined her friend. At the kitchen sink, both attempted to stop the bleeding while extracting glass from gaping wounds.

"What are we going to do?!"

Mom and Mrs. McDougal discussed calling an ambulance but ruled it out. It would take half an hour for Lawrence's volunteer rescue squad to arrive. Little Johnny could wind up dead. They had to get to Community Hospital right away, but families only had one car, which Dad drove to work. That left one option: The Drake Refrigeration van in front of Cyrus and Marta's.

Through hazy, blood-splattered pain, I saw Marta wearing a bathrobe. She had probably been taking a nap. The repairman buttoned up his shirt as he left Marta's house. Must have been a tough repair job if he had to take his shirt off. Vision grew cloudy as Mrs. McDougal shouted, "We have an emergency next door." The repairman and Marta gave each other quick glances of disappointment.

He saw my slumped body in Mom's arms. Every other day he looked cocky, like Chuck Conners. On that day, he was wide-eyed and eager to help. His van had one seat for the driver. He turned an empty plastic milk crate upside-down where the passenger seat would go.

"I hope you can make do, ma'am."

Off we screamed toward Community Hospital with Mom balancing herself using elbows, knees, and occasionally her head while cradling me.

The lit eyes of the duck on top rotated like fruit in a slot machine. Combined with continuous quacking, the van took on an almost demonic appearance with high quacking decibels. A cop who stopped us for traveling 75 mph in a 30-mph zone yelled all the way to the window of the van until he saw Mom holding a wounded little boy.

"Follow me and keep up," was the officer's directive.

High speed resumed with a police escort. Sirens, a quacking duck, and a profusely bleeding child probably amazed those who got out of the way.

Four hours and sixty-four stitches later, I enjoyed ice cream served aboard Grandma's couch. The doctor let the entire family know I was lucky to be alive. One jagged piece nearly penetrated my jugular vein, so the family treated me like a king. The aching lasted weeks.

CHAPTER 5

INFORMAL SEX EDUCATION

In January 1966, my father's employer downsized him—his boss literally handed Dad a pink slip. This was two decades before layoffs became corporate America standard practice. My dad spent years establishing a healthy trucking logistics career and wanted to pick up where he left off. As it turned out, Dad found a remarkably similar job in his hometown of Washington, Indiana. To him, the rural community 120 miles from suburban Indianapolis also offered a more wholesome place to raise children—a midwestern Mayberry.

Our family set off for greener pastures and virtuous neighbors on Memorial Day. As a big city girl, Mom was uneasy about the change of pace. Dad reassured her the family would fare better in the long term.

We relocated to 107 East Flora Street, a ramshackle relic of a rental property. Gene Wood, an old classmate of my father's and a one-man Washington-chamber of commerce, welcomed us the week we moved. He brought bear hugs, sweet treats, and one of his many daughters, Ellen, who was my age. She seemed cordial but bored. Being dragged to meet a stranger simply because we were the same age explains that. I was gratified to meet a pretty girl who would share classrooms with me.

Far more frequent visitors were my dad's sister's family—Aunt Patty, Uncle Don, and their daughter Lynn, also my age, who would always remain close to my heart. Dad was the eighth of twelve children reared by Charles and Frances Howard. Patricia was number eleven.

Over the summer, Lynn escorted me around town to meet other future classmates. Her concierge guidance coincided with my exit from boyhood and entrance to hormonal volatility. That's why I noticed how attractive her friends were. Instead of seeing girls as potential playmates, my concept of "play" changed. Dad and Mom noticed these changes and decided to have "the talk."

Their awkward lecture began with standard birds and bees analogies. Then my dad stumbled into a cryptic description of sexual mechanics, interjecting the absolute necessity of love, responsibility, and marital commitment.

"The whole point, son, is the creation of life. There are a lot of potential dangers if you're just looking for fun, including nasty diseases like syphilis and gonorrhea . . . *and* unmarried pregnancy."

The most confusing part was his description of passing seeds from my penis into a vagina to fertilize an egg, which might create bastard child John T. III. I couldn't get past the "seed" part.

"Dad, precisely how big are these seeds? Are they like watermelon seeds? A cherry pit? All that disgusting, pulpy orange stuff inside a cantaloupe? And they are going to . . . *shoot out the end of my penis?!*"

"Well . . . to tell you the truth, Johnny . . . it's not a bad thing, trust me . . . don't worry."

I feared *any* type of seed would hurt. I couldn't even fathom a sesame seed. I was skeptical. I had not yet experienced this "seed-passing" for myself. Masturbation was a vague concept, often accompanied by dire warnings about blindness and palm hair. As far as I can tell, those fears remain unfounded.

One summer night at the decrepit Howard barn, my cousin Lynn brought a group of seventh-grade female classmates with her for dinner. During the gathering, one pretty classmate after another excused herself to our lone bathroom upstairs. My turn finally arrived after the dinner party departed. We all guzzled too much lemonade.

The toilet at 107 was as dilapidated as the rest of the house. Efficient disposal of any waste, solid or liquid, was impossible without multiple flush attempts. When I flipped up the seat, I saw blood in the water. In the wastebasket beside the sink was a discarded sanitary napkin, also bloody. What began as surprise turned into lust.

Important caveat: Although I claim roots from southern Indiana near Kentucky, areas long stereotyped as filled with incestuous hillbillies, I've never experienced the slightest desire to sleep with *any* female cousin. My only thought was that the blood originated from the vagina of a pretty young new friend, *not* Lynn's. She didn't even visit the worn-down, cracked porcelain potty. I think. All her friends would have begun bleeding. They were becoming women, and my penis should have found its way into all those vaginas except the one that belonged to my cousin.

As I stood at the toilet doing my business, the contents of my right hand became rigid as a pole. Users of feminine hygiene products were now potential girlfriends. Sudden self-stroking came far too naturally. It didn't take long. *This is it*, was my only thought. Seeds passed. They were messy. Dad never mentioned specifics about color, viscosity, or volume. Or the mess. But it did *not* hurt. It was as far removed from pain as possible. It felt great! I cleaned and polished glass and porcelain until my mirrored reflection sported a broad smile.

From that evening forward, sexual fantasies exploded in the privacy of my mind. My alternative universe starred every good-looking, hiked-up plaid skirt-wearing Catholic schoolgirl. They all did very nasty things. When I wasn't riding my bike or figuring out how to get in trouble, I spent junior high years blasting away at the bedroom ceiling. Finding a girl with similar hormonal proclivities and eagerness to partner up for real remained a formidable challenge.

During the summer before high school, THE Summer of Love, that girl was Nicky Traylor. Washington had relatively large public junior and senior high schools but much smaller Catholic elementary schools with one high school. Students from each tended to herd separately. High school is chaotic enough, but trying to assimilate into cliques established in childhood proved traumatic. One of the few places I felt part of the "in" crowd was Allen Field, just up the street from the Howard barn. Townsfolk showed up for baseball games in high numbers. There, I met Nicky. She was overly friendly and aware I was still the newest kid in town. Washington was the kind of burg where everyone knew everyone else—and everything about them. On the rare occasion they didn't, they needed to find out. One such person was Nicky, who came out of nowhere and sat next down beside me on the grass during the seventh-inning stretch.

I assumed she attended the public high school since I'd never seen her before.

"Where you from?" she asked before introducing herself. "And how'd you get so handsome?"

Who the hell is this girl?

"Hello, gorgeous."

She smiled. And winked.

"Nicky Traylor."

"JT," I said, trying to be cool. JT was less grade-school-sounding than Johnny.

"JT what?"

"JT Howard."

"What do you like to do, JT Howard?"

"It all depends...."

Nicky's accent was distinctively Southern, accentuated by blonde hair more yellow than shiny on a short frame. Given my raging hormones, her cute, twangy words sailed right out my other ear. I paid more attention to her chest, which seemed large for our age. Casual chit-chat continued into the eighth and then ninth innings.

The Allen Field baseball diamond sat at the base of a large hill. Sloped areas contained seating around home plate and toward first and third bases. Dusk became darkness as the game ended. Nicky and I reclined on the left-field hill. Alone. Conversation seemed deep, and she did most of the talking. Without warning, Nicky grabbed my hand. Shortly after, she pulled my head toward hers and kissed me squarely on the lips, complete with her tongue. Moonlight seemed to make our sudden friendship awkwardly romantic, but Nicky complained about humidity. SHE REMOVED HER JEANS.

I was Mr. Stud in my bedroom with an overactive right hand and vivid imagination, but this was new territory. I was a trembling bundle of confused nerves. My own jean removal with one free hand was awkward. Nicky knew her constellations and pointed them out with her free hand. Her other hand found its way back to mine. I sat there with knees to chin attempting to conceal hormonal changes poking around my Fruit of the Looms. *How Can I Be Sure* by the Rascals looped inside my head.

Nicky leaned in for a second kiss. She positioned herself between my legs with her back against my chest. The moment of truth. I recalled Father Conan's gas and electric stove analogies. Mine was ready to melt steel. I hugged Nicky from behind and felt my first actual live breasts but felt uneasy about doing it right. My worries dissipated when she turned around, pushed me toward the slope of the hill, and climbed aboard. Kissing resumed, and she rubbed her pelvis against mine. Erection concealment was no longer possible, nor did it matter. It was sort of positioned in the right place, but two layers of cotton made things challenging.

Another horny teenager trick became suddenly obvious at that moment. If the erection suddenly found its way out of the flap of my tighty-whities, and somehow the bottom of her panties got pushed to one side, some interesting things might happen. Mission accomplished. But only for a few milliseconds. Nicky realized there were no longer two cotton layers between us. I was inside her. Bulging eyes and cold sweat gave me away.

Nicky rolled over, grabbed her jeans, and pulled a condom out of the back pocket.

"If we're going to make love, you need to put this on."

"Yes, ma'am."

Off came the undies. Rubber deployment reached nearly half shaft when I stopped cold. Suddenly, the entire baseball field lit up. Someone pulled the lever on the power box behind home plate that operated all the spotlights. Near-pitch blackness to high noon on a cloudless summer day was instantaneous.

"Time to split, JT," Nicky sort of whispered even though her mouth was wide open.

We grabbed our duds and scurried off to nearby woods where, mood ruined, we agreed to try again sometime. Once re-clothed, Nicky offered a kiss and bid adieu. By the next morning, my right arm looked as if it had been stolen from Popeye following ravenous spinach consumption.

The search around town for her lasted days. Finally, a week later, Nicky reappeared at Allen Field for a game. She was also holding hands with a man-sized boy. Nicky introduced him to me as her boyfriend "Moose." I was disappointed but not devastated. She talked way too much for me, and there was no way the new kid in town intended to run afoul of someone known as Moose. There were plenty of other pretty girls in Washington, and JT Howard was about to turn on the charm.

CHAPTER 6

FLESH-AND-BLOOD GIRLFRIENDS

"Please, please, please just let me see. It will be something I never forget. You are sooooo beautiful."

"John, you are not even allowed in my house, and we can't go to yours."

"Do you have a Polaroid?"

"John, that's sleazy."

The object of my incessant pleading was Darlene, a neighbor up the street and one of my very first flesh-and-blood girlfriends. I was fourteen years old.

She was proud of our relationship and considered us a steady couple. We kissed a lot. "Practice makes perfect," she often noted. Darlene's mother discouraged the relationship at every turn. "You will NOT date a Catholic boy, Darlene," she sneered. I can only assume Mrs. Woodman voted for Nixon (not the very Catholic JFK) in 1960.

Alone time was challenging, but very late one night, Darlene at last succumbed to a repeated request to see her naked. I had devised an evil plan worthy of James Phelps, my very own Mission Impossible.

"Darlene, you take showers in the basement, right? What if I happened to look into your basement window around 9 tonight?

"I don't know, John. Seems risky."

"Just take a chance. It's only a few seconds."

At 9 p.m. that night, it was time for her shower. As I sat on the ground in front of the window, the only things I forgot were binoculars and a box of popcorn.

The window glass was cloudy and the light inside was dim. Darlene dropped her towel, turned like a model, and entered the shower. Curiosity was satisfied in a very brief gander.

Maybe it was this non-Catholic girl, or maybe it was the times, but my brain occasionally pondered subjects other than sex. Suspicion about Catholic dogma that seemed increasingly like propaganda nagged inside. The United States was mired in Vietnam. Antiwar sentiment was feverish. Few trusted any authority. Thoughts about love (but mostly sex) were calming. If I was ever going to become intimate with a female and claim non-virginity honestly, solicitation of a partner from the public-school system was necessary. Catholic girls did not give anything up, at least not to Catholic boys.

For example, take a nice, uniformed Catholic girl I knew back in junior high school: Becky Newsom. We passed notes in school, held hands in church and spelled out messages of love on our palms when I was not being an altar boy, something she found charming.

Becky seemed eager for me to make the first move. I drew her close and asked as romantically as possible: "Are you ready?" She nodded affirmatively and closed her eyes. Kissing began. It was sweet but methodical. I was not an aggressor and did not want to push anything.

Several days later, some vague extracurricular activities became the excuse to get together. It was Saturday, so there were no uniforms or curfews. Becky sported a striking yellow dress that zipped all the way down the front. It accentuated her slim, ironing board figure. She was as tall as I was.

We found our way into a teacher lounge. It was empty because there were no teachers that day. As an added safety measure, we decided to share intimacy inside a locked closet. Once alone, isolated, and presumably safe, there was no questioning readiness. Kissing gave way to roaming hands, which found the dress zipper. A slow descent followed. Wandering hands and warm flesh excited me on entirely new levels.

My shirt came off, and skin-to-skin contact was electric. Becky even managed a couple of brushes to sensitive areas that were probably accidental. Our tryst ended by mutual consent after we decided treading in those areas should wait a few years. Our romantic relationship cooled, but memories of absolute sweetness remain. Becky helped me feel accepted.

One year on Flora Street, complete with its coal-fired stove, bad plumbing, and splinter inducing wood floors, was enough for Mom and Dad. They happily surrendered the rental. A much better and more functional two-story house at the base of the 2nd Street hill on the south side of Washington was purchased. Not long after we departed Flora, the house at 107 became a flat spot in a field after it fell in on itself. Our new location led to many great new friends throughout the neighborhood. Lifelong memories began in that more upscale residence, including one that featured black and white portable television on the front porch that flickered Neil Armstrong stepping onto the moon in the summer of 1969.

But the memory of Darlene, and her shower show, remains among the most vivid. A few weeks later, my parents and siblings made a trip north to Indianapolis. Darlene and I took full advantage of the empty Howard house. Experimentation with hands, mouths, and reproductive organs was taken to exciting new levels. It was the very first time I ever uttered the words "just the tip, *pleeeaaase?!*"

Comfy beds or the couch were not allowed. She feared the consequences. As a result, all carnal action occurred on the uncomfortable living room floor. Loud shag carpeting failed to provide adequate cushioning but tickled while mostly naked. "Just the tip" gave way to just an inch or two, and eventually every last one.

Darlene decided we should at least wear underwear, but the sliding panty trick soon took ominous turns. She needed to wait, and my quest for unquestioned virginity expulsion was thwarted again.

Mutual defiance of the no-Catholic dating mandate forced Darlene's mom to put her foot down. Our relationship was ended forcefully. Advancement sexually remained a work in progress.

CHAPTER 7

CARS, STARS, AND ABJECT FRUSTRATION

An ill-fated high school adventure became the first of three times in my life I found myself running as fast as possible while evading bullets whizzing past my head. All three involved sex and automobiles.

As a teenager of driving age with raging hormones in 1970, two unrelenting pursuits became nearly obsessive. Girls and a car. Raw passion with someone else was not yet meant to be. I did earn a freshly minted Indiana driver's license, and therefore had to obtain a car immediately. The Howard parents were not well to do. Catholic school attendance required tuition and seven Howard family members had to eat. Dad's cardiac issues forced mom into the workforce.

Employment for money began in 1967. Aunt Patty managed the downtown Western Union office. I washed windows and swept up telegram strip remnants. Simultaneous jobs were balanced at Williams Pharmacy, the Indiana theater, and its companion East 50 Drive-In all through high school. That allowed not only paying my own way but also buying a car. My first vehicle was a turd-brown

1953 Plymouth Cranbrook, located and retrieved from the overgrown property of an elderly lady. She had not driven anything for at least ten years. The asking price was $35. The spinster simply wanted it removed permanently from her garage.

My high school best friend Joe Buck was quite gifted mechanically. He managed to crank it over and move it to the Howard garage. Joe worked engine wizardry on what he called, "A piece of shit L-head 6-banger with a three on the tree." He continued his critical evaluation. "John, you'll buy as much oil as gas for this turd. It's a shame we can't find a slant 6 to slam in there, but that would take a lot of work." A few spark plugs, belts, hoses, and used tires (investment in rehabilitation of the vehicle exceeded its sale price) enabled the clunker to spin like a wobbly top. It could have used considerably more cosmetic work. The Cranbrook indeed contained what we referred to as a self-changing fluids system. Pay from the Indiana theater and East 50 Drive-In was cash inside a brown envelope every Friday. The first chore after work was a trip to the local Clark station. The dark brown beast got filled with gas ($.36 a gallon, same as a pack of Tareytons), oil, brake, and radiator fluids. It seemed convenient and efficient.

The state of Indiana legislated mandatory auto inspections, primarily to prevent junk cars like mine from being driven. When a car was rejected, it could be driven for thirty days with a large red rejection sticker on the windshield. Indiana expected the time to be used for repairs and re-inspection. There was a three-strikes-and-out rule for failed vehicles. That is what happened to Cranbrook. Counting cheating, the Plymouth was driven for nearly a year.

Cranbrook highlights: It was one of two such antiques in

Washington. The other was also owned by a high school kid, but he restored and tuned his machine to a pristine, nearly showroom condition. Given our age and proclivities, both Daniel Mangus and I knew racing them on a rural country road was inevitable. My preparation consisted of splurging for Sunoco 260, then the highest octane that could be purchased when people still chose leaded or unleaded gas.

"Cheatin' fucker," Danny snarled before our best of three sprints atop a makeshift quarter-mile along Edwardsport Road. "Prepare for an ass whoopin,' little Johnnie."

The first two late-night county road races were lost in rather dramatic fashion. No third race was necessary.

"Good race, man," I conceded.

"No, it wasn't, little Johnnie. You got your ass whooped." Adding insult to injury, Daniel grabbed his girlfriend and stuck his tongue down her throat during a victory kiss. I coughed due to toxic smoke sputtering from the tailpipe of my forlorn Cranbrook.

The list of 1953 Plymouth flaws was lengthy. Although the interior was spacious with comfortable bench seating, there was no way the chosen chariot of an aspiring non-virgin was ever going to cause any female to swoon with moist desire. If I was lucky, just minor chuckling would ensue. If not, looks that telegraphed disgust were inevitable. The old cloth seats smelled of formaldehyde and body odor.

The Cranbrook had to go. It was being driven illegally, polluting the earth, and keeping virginity intact. How did a teenager dispose of a crappy Plymouth? By strapping in and driving off a small cliff into a pile of other junk cars at the salvage yard.

That was fun, but mom and dad would never have approved.

My next vehicle was an object of beauty. A light green, long, sleek 1962 Pontiac Catalina. Those cars were never factory equipped with manual transmissions, but another friend named George Reisens modified the automatic transmission so that a four on the floor with a trendy Hurst shifter came along with.

George was a year or two out of high school. He called a trailer on the edge of Washington home. Reisens possessed a fondness for young ladies still in their final years of high school. George invited me over one night with hints of frolicking among the opposite sex. His latest girlfriend was accompanied by a beautiful young woman named Becky Sloan, blessed with sandy blonde hair and piercing blue eyes. I was suddenly a bit smitten. George and his lady friend soon disappeared to the comfort and privacy of the bedroom in the back. It was not long before moaning derived of youthful, passionate writhing echoed through veneered paneling inside the tenuously moored structure. My thought, not shared with Becky, was *...when in Rome...*

Many women referred to me as a good kisser. That skill likely resulted from being the only available option. Most extra-base attempts were consistently rebuffed.

"No."

"John, no."

"I told you NO."

That became a maddening theme in my young life. My friends ended up with sluts, but I got saddled with their chaste, pure-as-driven-snow besties.

The young ladies obviously did not understand what they were missing.

My Pontiac, though beautiful, was prone to ongoing mechanical issues. That was understandable considering a shade tree mechanic unnaturally rigged a manual transmission that led directly to a ripple effect of other major issues. Shortly after high school I eventually traded it straight up for a pale yellow 1969 Opel Kadett GT Wagon. Driving a European import seemed glamorous before later realizing that in Europe, Opel was considered a cheap brand.

The lemon-yellow foreign car was primary transportation through a year or so of college. Frequent trips during and after high school were a couple of dance halls near Jasper, Indiana. A preferred venue was The Rustic. Depending on the band, a joint called The Calumet was also highly attended. Both venues allowed high school kids inside after paying cover charges, but both were adult clubs. Beer and spirits were sold to those over twenty-one. Thwarting purchases by underage kids was expected, but blind eyes were generally turned toward those who drove it in and consumed outside in their parking lots. The Rustic and Calumet were relatively remote, and noise never presented problems. Both also provided easy pickings for college students.

The rural clubs boasted reputations for being places where teenagers with cars could park and smooch without fear of being arrested. Joe Buck, the engine wizard best friend who previously brought the Cranbrook back from the dead, made the journey with me one Friday night. He picked up an eager companion from Oolitic, Indiana. She also brought a friend, Delores Schwartz, whose innocent good looks belied her stodgy sounding name. We immediately hit it off as dancing and sipping of beverages not legally accessible continued.

Joe and Oolitic's finest eventually suggested we retreat to the Opel.

"Gimme the keys," he ordered.

Joe immediately lowered the rear seats to a flat position. Makeshift installation of a cardboard barrier between the front seat and the now unfolded back seats followed. He was not subtle about it.

Delores had a slight underbite that made for spectacular kissing. That was as far as it went up in the front seat.

Having hands repeatedly moved from the vicinities of intimate areas became annoying. Distinct sounds of flesh making passionate contact on the other side of the cardboard were accompanied by musky scents and audible moaning. Hijinks were accentuated by steady up and down movement atop the worn shocks of the Kadett.

All of that forced potential introspection about my dating choices. Why did I keep getting stuck with potential nuns, something Delores actually became a few years later? I was never going to compete with Jesus as a potential boyfriend.

It was all merely youthful tribulation. My feeling was that if you were going to get that close, it should absolutely be by mutual consent. A hand was always available. Besides, being rebuffed while barely out of high school was bound to be temporary.

As an added bonus, my dental hygiene was spectacular. Bad breath tended to ruin physical romance.

Noble intent and lack of action did not stop trouble.

Another great high school friend was Mike McKlain. He also nurtured a palpable hankering for young ladies. The daughter of a prominent local farming magnate lived in nearby Odon, Indiana. Paula Garland was strikingly beautiful. Her status included prom queen, cheerleader, and involvement in every conceivable community and school activity. The queen liked Mike. She also had a best friend with a great and excessively corn-fed personality. The four of us found our way upstairs to a hayloft shortly after dusk one starry Friday night. It felt safe inside the main barn on the farm that was her home.

Mike and Queen Paula retreated to a darkened corner. Personality and I discussed current affairs in more granular detail than in any semester of school. Any sort of contact with her, sexual or otherwise, was out of the question. I felt no chemistry, although she seemed eager to try anything and dropped hints about it between deep conversation topics.

"What's your take on the suspension of the Cambodian National Assembly by Prime Minister Lon Nol, its effect on democracy, and whether such a strategy will be effective against the Khmer Rouge?" I diverted while silently contemplating whether getting blown by someone I considered unattractive would be OK.

We eventually (and possibly mercifully) heard noisy footsteps, muffled cursing, and the loading of shells into a shotgun. Mike and I looked at each other with terrified wide eyes.

What the hell?!

We made a beeline for an open rear ventilation shaft dead center in the upper portion of the barn. Being fully clothed and wearing athletic shoes proved useful for me. As the first shots rang out, Mike attempted to dress while running. As I later learned for myself a few years later, you can do one or the other, but not both simultaneously.

We counted at least six shots on the way down a wooded hill, encountering sharp underbrush, various unknown members of the animal kingdom, and a barbed-wire fence. Bullets striking trees less than five feet from our noggins inevitably led to personal reflection about life choices.

"HOLY SHIT, that one was close!" Mike, bringing up the rear, wondered aloud. "Are we going to friggin' die right here?!"

We survived and doubled back to the car parked down the road in Personality's driveway. Mike declared that in the future he would seek a frisky partner with a father not so enamored of the Second Amendment. We also decided to clear of Odon, having previously spent a night in its tiny jail for possessing over-twenty-one beverages prematurely.

CHAPTER 8

TRUE YOUNG LOVE

Everybody has a first real love, and they never permanently leave your consciousness. Some young lovers live happily ever after together. Most go forward along entirely divergent paths, and that's how it worked out with Janice Richards.

Janice also hailed from a large family of meager means. Her rural southern Indiana landscape was dotted with farms. Their property still contained a functional outhouse. She was wholesome, beautiful, and smart; destined to go on to bigger and better things. Janice had long brown hair that perfectly framed an angelic face. A favorite photograph shows her smiling broadly from a large pile of leaves snapped one crisp fall day in Indiana. I was utterly smitten almost from the time we met. That approach to courting included brand-new romantic gestures. Instead of being completely consumed by sex and loss of innocence, it went deeper. Proactive gestures of kindness, fawning, and surprise gifts became important. The relationship mattered and opened new emotional doors. It felt like *love*.

We also remained curious about sex. The attraction we felt seemed mutual, and it was not long before careful steps into the realm of passionate affection began. We made out wherever and whenever we could. That was not as easy as it sounds. Both of us worked, participated in activities at different schools, and attempted to make limited time together count. Being alone together was difficult. Family homes were always filled with people. The Pontiac could be parked along country roads after dark, but meddling yokels were always nosey. Bouncing around inside a parked car also felt sleazy given the self-perceived purity of our mutual young love.

A preferred post-date location was a very private wooded area next to the White River. Under moonlight and in the Pontiac, we usually stopped just short of all the way. Everything else was fair game and fully exploited. We included hands, mouths, and anything goes a few seconds at a time, "*just to see what it feels like.*" Nude anatomy sessions after dark were thrilling and dangerous.

"No, we shouldn't."

"Yes, we should."

"OK...no, wait. I don't know. I love you…"

Breathy panting always accompanied desperate words as sweat flowed freely.

Our relationship eventually reached the point at which we decided official consummation of it was what we wanted. It had to be not just perfect, but filled with romance and meaning. Janice also began taking the pill, which meant no clumsy condoms. Using them seemed akin to eating a juicy and well-marbled steak through a baggie.

Our only dilemma was pinpointing the right time and spot. We considered a room in one of a handful of local motels. Given our youthful age, too many questions might get asked. Washington was small. People gossiped because there was not much else to do. Janice's dad was prone to excessive nips from the bottle and also had an affinity for the Second Amendment.

We decided the most romantic place would be atop a levee next to our newly beloved White River. It was near those banks we had already done everything but. We soon found ourselves completely naked on a humid July night atop a soft, quilted blanket. A bottle of cheap wine was already screwed open. The night was cloudless. Just enough illumination was provided by a full moon. For a few precious moments, the visual perfection was stunning. Janice and I were about to make sweet, passionate love.

Our time had arrived. We were naked and sweaty. The river slowly flowed, and water lapping rocks added a romantic soundtrack. Foreplay became more urgent, but not because we were overcome with passion.

Janice and I suddenly realized we were slapping our own naked flesh. Hard. We failed to consider that mosquitos and other various no-see-ums also preferred slowly flowing rivers in the humidity of summer for their own breeding. Hugs became pushbacks so more six-legged creatures could be dispatched.

Dammit, go for it. It won't take long at this point.

"John, we have the rest of our lives."

"You're right," I said, whacking another winged insect.

"But what if we, uh cocooned?"

That was a really bad idea given temperatures in the high 80s and even higher humidity.

Contact with poison ivy was also made somewhere along the way. There was no choice. We were going to try again very soon, only with adequate precautions for Mother Nature.

Getting dressed in the car was entertaining because both of us appeared to have the measles from head to toe. Explaining that would be difficult. A few days passed before clothing came off in the back seat again. Between acne, bites, scratches, rashes, and calamine lotion, we resembled mimes with leprosy. I even had bites under my scrotum. Scratching was embarrassing. Janice remained the most beautiful lady I had ever seen.

We decided our next best opportunity would be the rear bench seat of the Catalina, in plain sight, tackled head-on. What better place than the local drive-in movie theater? The lot was filled with like-minded youth anyway. Because I worked at the East 50, I knew all its nooks and crannies.

The darkest corner in a distant row was selected. The freshly laundered quilt from the riverbank was arranged so the spacious rear of the car took on a homey feel, devoid of green Naugahyde and glaringly abundant chrome.

Mackenna's Gold illuminated the night, but inside the Pontiac it was nice and dark. Janice and I ignored Omar and Gregory, and embraced completely naked. There were no hungry arthropods for a change. Janice and I worked ourselves into animalistic frenzy, and the moment of truth arrived. The last remnants of her nearly completed period should not have been an impediment, but the possibility of blood on the quilt was a deal killer for her.

"This was my great grandmother's quilt," she cautioned. "It's a family heirloom."

Undaunted, I got dressed and proceeded to the concession stand supply building. A large roll of commercial butcher paper came off a shelf inside. Fifteen feet or so was hastily ripped from the roll. An old black blanket from the trunk was also grabbed before jumping back into the car.

The back seat was covered by neatly arranged layers of an old quilt, butcher paper doubled over about six times, and the old blanket onto which we could have slaughtered a cow. Anything we were about to do would neither have mattered nor affected the slick vinyl underneath. That could easily have been wiped off anyway.

Once again, our young love was about to be unofficially consummated. In I slid, very slowly, savoring every single millimeter. About four inches in, wide eyeballs began rolling upward into my skull. Janice began softly cooing. It felt better than I ever possibly imagined.

That was also the precise moment Dwight Mason, a developmentally challenged man-child employed by benevolent theater owner Karl Kalvin to maintain law and order at the drive-in, decided to wield his brand of long metal flashlight justice. He rapped back end against the glass and immediately followed with several hundred lumens from its business end.

Dwight's pronunciation of my name always sounded like it began with a cheeky series of Gs instead of just one capital J.

"Now Gggggggohn, are you up to no good back there?"

"Dwight, get the fuck away from here right now." The rapid manner in which my manhood was withdrawn from heaven did not feel as great as it did going in.

"Gggggggohn, you said a very bad word and you are naked. I'm telling Karl."

"Dwight, get the FUCK out NOW." Dwight indeed got the fuck out. Janice became uneasy. Actually, Janice flipped out.

"NOW WHAT ARE WE GOING TO DO, JOHN!?" Her tone turned decidedly unromantic.

Thwarted again, we hit the highway.

The perfect moment never arrived, at least not for a few years, so we routinely settled for almost. Even post-prom night trysts proved impossible. Her mother caught us on the family couch very late one night following post-prom. She merely offered a suggestion. "You should leave before pop gets home."

Janice met me another day after a visit to her doctor. The diagnosis sounded grim: "I have a form of stenosis not caused by normal aging, which may or may not be permanent." It sounded a lot worse than it was. I wanted to comfort Janice in her time of need using all the selfish teenage logic that could be mustered. What better way to do that than to get naked in the Catalina?

The only viable location under sunlight seemed to be a remote cemetery on the outskirts of Washington. Oak Grove may have been creepy, but it featured rolling hills and abundant, shady trees. We decided not to take any chances outside the vehicle, partly due to being outside in broad daylight but mostly out of respect for the deceased. Best not to disturb those reposed eternally under verdant grass. Soon we were naked again in the back seat, reaching the moment at which Janet began guiding me in with a free hand.

Gentle encouragement of her soft fingers suddenly became a full-fisted death grip. Her eyes lit up and I felt metal on the back of my skull. I turned and found myself staring into both barrels of a shotgun. Janice continued clutching my shriveling manhood, which began to throb from a dreadful combination of blue balls and vise-like fingers.

The caretaker of the cemetery, a scraggly, bearded fellow with more gum than teeth, began threatening us. "I'm a-gonna call the law and then your parents, ya little shits!"

He demanded our names. "Dwight Mason," I stammered. Janice became Nancy Traylor, only because those were the first names that popped into my head.

Deliverance guy continued waving his shotgun while lecturing with tenuous literacy. His grammar was hard to follow, included high decibels, and repeatedly violated the commandment about the Lord's name. Janice began sobbing. Her hand was still attached to what was left of purpled manhood. Anger welled inside.

Revenge was eventually extracted from two private mafia-like enforcers/juvenile delinquents, George and Joey Miller, fellow troublemakers from high school. A few days after the shotgun incident, the orthodontics-challenged rifleman suddenly found his car temporarily disabled, and parts of his home in need of cosmetic repair.

Not long after, Janice began acting strangely. Distant. Remote. Unavailable for dates. Gossip had her dating someone from her school I naturally considered uncouth. He was a rotund, prematurely bearded guy who, although friendly, stole my one true love. Worse, his family owned a vacant commercial building in town where they could enjoy all sorts of privacy. It was devastating. Janice eventually told me what was going on. Then I was inconsolable. It was one thing to be thwarted from the type of pleasure I could feel with someone I loved, but losing a love that felt that powerful became unthinkable.

THIS is what a broken heart feels like.

Slowly but surely, and with college on the horizon, time healed wounds. New life chapters materialized. I was a year ahead of Janice in high school and barely graduated following four years of mischief. Sixteen entire semesters were spent laying waste to the good Sisters of Providence and most everyone and everything else at Washington Catholic High School.

The senior class totaled 36 students. Any of them who wanted to attend college received some sort of scholarship or grant. Anyone except me. I spent four years solidly atop Principal Sister Joseph Louise's shit list. That forced two years of self-financing at Vincennes University, a junior college twenty miles away that created an outstanding broadcasting program. It is where I fell into suddenly diligent study habits. The predicament was entirely my fault; long-term thought in high school was not yet possible.

Janice graduated with honors and set off for Indiana University in Bloomington. We lost touch as new lives began and remained that way for a couple of years.

One day, out of the blue, Janice's mother called my parents' home. I happened to be there that day.

Janice was involved in a bad car accident on the way back to her dormitory after a concert. All passengers were seriously hurt. She spent days in the hospital dealing with traumatic injuries and multiple fractures. Once released, Janice convalesced at her childhood home. Mrs. Roberts hinted that Janice wanted to see me.

I was dumbfounded. Should I? My heart still felt broken. The unselfish part of my conscience wanted to help in any way I could. I never stopped loving her.

Seeing Janice after the accident was rough. She was immobile, uncomfortable, and mostly encased in plaster. The glow of her skin was pale. She had a hollow look. Through it all, she remained the most beautiful young woman in the world. I became smitten all over again.

Renewed visits to the Richards house were steady and frequent. I tried bringing small gifts she could enjoy. Seated next to her bed, I held her hand, brushed her hair, or simply discussed life after high school. I was very proud of what she began accomplishing in Bloomington, where she was anxious to return. I wished I could join her.

Janice became increasingly mobile over time and was able to free herself of various chunks of plaster and metal. That led to noticeable mood improvement. The warmth of love returned. Although it did not feel completely mutual, her words and actions felt just like a few years prior.

Near the end of her recuperation, we found ourselves completely alone in her house. Dad and mom were away at work and everyone else was in school. That realization harkened back to our prior quest for the perfect opportunity. Perhaps it had finally arrived.

Talking gave way to kissing and kissing gave way to deeper passion. The primary impediment was clothing. It was difficult for her to either remove or add it. Her private parts were mostly encased in plastic or plaster. Access to them was not designed for play, but rather waste elimination.

The prognosis did not look good until she suggested "Let's give it a go, John."

Are you sure?" I asked, pondering logistics.

Janice cooed "I miss your touch."

Encouragement like that was all I needed. Her touch was missed more than she could ever possibly know. Finally, after careful positioning, removal of the wastegate, then makeshift foreplay, it was then or never. Once again, a gentle hand guided me lovingly toward the ultimate prize.

Being inside her brought nirvana. Hindsight revealed that remaining motionless would have been a perfect choice, and I may have attempted it for a second or two. During actual intercourse, however, it is natural not to stay in one place, but to move in then out then in again and out again and so on until nature takes an inevitable course. Mechanics aside, moving into and out of that orifice feels best when not compromised by hardened plaster. The former had warm, velvety elasticity; the latter contained jagged edges and zero give.

Approximately three lustful thrusts were all that was possible until the bottom of my shaft rapidly transformed into a bloody pulp. Not wishing to risk permanent injury, not to mention hard-to-launder stains, Janice and I again decided to wait a while. Her healing was progressing nicely. She would soon be back to normal. Since she was in college, alone time was certainly possible.

My own college experience featured rapid, conclusive expungement of every last vestige of sexual naivety. Despite recently active hedonism, my longing for Janice continued. After graduation from VU and working my first post-college job, Janice contacted me with an invitation to a party being thrown at an off-campus house in Bloomington. I could not arrive quickly enough. My buddy Carl Nettle from work was enlisted as a wingman. We met Janice and a friend in Bloomington over burgers, then toured her dorm. She looked as beautiful and glowing as ever, and a feeling of love that never really left rushed back.

The party wasn't bad but seemed sedate for a young college crowd in a known party town. I knew no one except Janice and Carl. Strangers seemed more eager to socialize with folks they already knew. Janice stayed mostly unavailable but telegraphed an occasional look or wink. She seemed particularly fond of someone to whom no introduction was offered.

Hopes of utopian sleeping arrangements were dashed a few pointless hours in. My original intent was to spend an entire night in an actual bed together with Janice to finally cement our bond. The last time I ever laid eyes on her, she was moving from one room to another wearing very little clothing. She glanced slightly my way, then vanished.

"Carl, we are leaving, like, right now."

He looked confused. "What? Why?"

My eyes screamed what my mouth couldn't. *I need to get as far away from here as I can. We're done. FOREVER.*

Carl got the message. We didn't say a word the entire two-hour return trip home. It all just needed to be put in the past.

CHAPTER 9

GOODBYE FOR GOOD, INNOCENCE

My college experience was nontraditional. Paying for it depended on jobs at the Indiana Theater, East 50 Drive-In, and Williams Pharmacy simultaneously, at least for a while. All were located just twenty miles from school. Dorm or frat life was never in the cards. A fair amount of time was spent on campus and lodging other than my parents' house was secured. It was a single second-floor room rented atop the residence of an elderly woman. Space was shared with a stoner buddy named Louie Heitzenberg, which made it affordable.

We also endured a communal bathroom with a ham radio operator living down the hall. Mr. Peters became progressively annoyed with Louie. Wafts of pot smoke and excessive volume from loud bands such as White Witch drifted his way nearly continuously. The lower floor owner had hearing difficulties and remained oblivious. It was a place of my own. Sort of.

Normal days usually included two conversations. Mr. Peters always caught me walking down the hall, usually in my underwear. "John, PLEASE get that useless son-of-a-bitch to turn that noise down. I lost another good radio buddy the other night. He's from Nova Scotia, and we had a hard enough time hearing each other without all that loud crap."

"I'll do what I can, Mr. Peters."

Louie was usually propped up clumsily on his couch/bed. His eyes were always red, even through half-open slits. "Louie, when are you going to give me your part of the rent money so I can pay old Mrs. DeLong?"

"Awww, man. Don't bum me out. My dad says a check is on the way. Any day, JT. Any day."

Louie had a gregarious friend named Lori from his hometown of Otwell, Indiana. She befriended a shy but bubbly young lady from northern Indiana named Shelly Scott. Shelly's voice was high and squeaky, and she sort of sang as she spoke. The way she warbled "JT" pegged the adorably cute scale. Shelly and I became close quickly—a steady couple almost from the first day we met. Dates were squeezed in whenever possible.

Shelly was a diligent student, the youngest daughter of a disciplinarian school administrator. She and Lori shared a dorm room. Shelly's college experience included the freedom of being on her own for the first time in her young life. Lori fell into the borderline slut category. She enjoyed the company of numerous young men inside the restricted dormitory. That made Shelly available for dates a lot because access to her room revolved around the sexual exploits of Lori. Since I also worked at least forty hours every week, Shelly often tagged along to the theater where she sat quietly in the office doing homework while Lori pointed her spread legs skyward back at the dorm.

Shelly and I took in a movie and ordered pizza one Saturday afternoon. We spotted a note from Lori on Shelly's bedpost. "Bobby and I are going up to Chicago and we'll be back sometime Monday."

Though we danced around the subject of sex, it was never possible in my room because Louie was *always* there, stoned all day, and consuming food scraps when not passed out. I do not recall him ever attending any class. Not one. Not ever. That room was not the place for intimacy, although we could have gone for it. Louie's "far outs" and affirmative head nodding would have been interesting, but neither of us desired an audience

We could never consider that room a den of passion unless Louie was gone and we thoroughly disinfected it first. He got thrown out a few months later. Louie set a wall on fire with a portable camping burner after smoking himself to sleep. He forgot about the Jiffy-Pop and failed to consider the flammability of dirty laundry piled nearby. Mr. Peters repeated screams of "FIRE!" even woke up Mrs. DeLong. "LOUIE! LOUIE! ARE YOU IN THERE?" As smoke thickened, Mr. Peters kicked in the door and blasted away with a fire extinguisher.

Louie, now even more ghostly looking while coated in fire retardant, woke up. "Mr. Peters, this is a genuine bummer."

"Now look here you lazy bastard. You have spent the last few months disrupting this entire house, and your time here is up. I'm going to go talk to Gertie downstairs, and if you are smart you will start packing, like right this minute!"

"Mr. Peters, this is way too heavy. You should try some of this," holding up a half-smoked joint.

Gertie sent Louie packing after inspecting smoke damage and a badly charred wall. I got to stay because the rent was paid and I volunteered to repaint the room and reside alone without any loud music. "I *promise*, Mrs. DeLong."

Shelly's empty dorm room was all hers for an entire weekend. Talk about opportunity! Sweet nothings were whispered, and clothing dropped to the floor. She was radiant. Although short in stature, her body was perfect. An untouched virgin. Shelly remained reluctant to remove her glasses.

"Be gentle," she warned. It all seemed very sexy at the time.

"We have all weekend," I said, turning on the charm.

From late Saturday afternoon until our first classes early Monday morning, every shred of doubt about the potential or remaining innocence of either one of us was permanently removed, all aboard the comfort of an actual bed behind a locked door. A cycle of intimacy, showering and repeating continued unabated for blissful hours. Shelly was a sweet young lady who quickly formulated thoughts of wedded bliss.

Marriage was a theoretical concept for which I was completely unprepared, and even if some enlightenment nudged its way into me, was Shelly the right one? Now that self-assigned status as a stud was established, the endless possibility of additional pleasures with a variety of young ladies remained appealing.

Shelly and I remained a couple focused on school and jobs, and squeezed in intimacy when possible. Narcissistic tendencies, however, began to surface. During one six-month period, girls with pronounced underbites were recruited. I convinced myself, with no scientific evidence, that they would be much better fellators. Shelly steadfastly refused to even experiment with that.

Now that I was a college guy and not a high school guy, finding research subjects with underbites willing to risk bumping their noggins on the bottom of a steering wheel was easy. My own private science needed resolution. No conclusive evidence one way or the other emerged, but the sample size was adequate.

I got creative with income generation by selling spiked pot to college students. Fewer hours were required for my movie and drug store jobs. That freed up additional time for pleasures of the flesh. Shelly was my official girlfriend through two years at Vincennes University.

Shelly also seemed consumed with good grades and matrimony. "John, we should talk about what we're going to do when we graduate. I love you. You love me. Should we get married?"

I wanted to date around. *Best to get it out of my system*, I selfishly rationalized while plotting counter-arguments to marriage.

Shelly's parents were nice but old-fashioned. "Nice to meet you, Mr. and Mrs. Scott," I fibbed, wondering about sleeping arrangements. They looked suspicious. The only nod to contemporary life in their home was a gigantic Amana Radarange, one of the first commercially available microwave ovens. It cost them several thousand dollars. Shelly enjoyed cooking hamburgers in it.

There was an older sister I met just once who was mostly estranged from her parents. Diana Scott's circumstances seemed suspicious. It was the first time a potential in-law family was evaluated, and I remained unsold on the concept.

I overheard Mr. and Mrs. Scott in another room. "He seems like a creep," Arthur offered. "Now Art, we don't know him yet. He is courteous and seems OK."

"I don't know. I don't think I trust him."

Great first impression, idiot.

Shelly found civil service work with the state of Indiana in Indianapolis immediately following graduation. I was the first in my broadcasting class to secure professional employment. A postgraduate job took me to the rural Indiana town of Crawfordsville. That small town contained a daytime AM radio station. I worked board shifts and read the news on their newly launched FM station.

The Opel did not make it. I failed to realize that instead of merely keeping the oil full, it should also be changed every few thousand miles. Its last memorable trip was to southern Indiana from Indianapolis. The lemon Kadett made it as far as the last hill before Worthington, Indiana along state Highway 67, where the engine exploded. As a yellow hood flew over the windshield, smoldering parts littered the highway. Acrid smoke filled the air. It was stone dead. I called dad from a farmhouse down the road, and he arranged towing the seized Opel from the spot where it died. It landed eventually in the same junkyard that contained rusting remains of the Cranbrook. Shelly rescued me in her powder blue and highly dependable 1967 VW bug, then sold it to me cheap after her parents bought her a brand-new Ford Pinto. That was her reward for graduating with honors.

Shelly moved to a very nice apartment in Indianapolis. Visiting from Crawfordsville was easy and frequent. I looked forward to intimacy because it felt great. She remained pretty in her uniquely quirky way. Visits to local malls became opportunities for her pointed questions. In jewelry stores, it was, "Which rings do you like the best?"

Bridal boutiques led to the modeling of wedding dresses and questions like "How does this one look?"

My guard was up. The world was not yet conquered. I had considerable uncertainty as to whether spending years with a civil servant who was completely unadventurous in bed, with all the emotion and reciprocation skills of an inflatable sex doll, would constitute a wise choice. The best things she had to offer besides an endearing personality and big boobs were expertly prepared microwave hamburgers.

Shelly never touched me below the waist. The second carnal activity concluded, she quickly lumbered out of bed and into the bathroom. Douching herself into a refreshed state of purity took a while. I often intentionally tempted fate by wiping myself clean on her side of the bed linens as she splashed around in the bathroom. That was about the only thing that drove her into a moaning frenzy. Very few aspects of our relationship constituted a recipe for any HAPPY lasting relationship, so I ended it. Shelly's heart broke in much the same way mine did with Janice. Remorse was palpable, but not enough to continue the relationship. Guilt followed for years.

CHAPTER 10

ALTERNATIVE LIFESTYLES

An eccentric young teacher named Marius Winston pranced happily through Washington Catholic High School every day. He was flamboyantly gay well before many of us were even aware that lifestyle existed. The only things we knew about gay folks back then were mostly just dismissive, often crude epithets passed down by elders in rural Indiana.

The only sexuality I ever considered was my own, and I was enamored permanently to females. Societal outcasts and eccentrics, however, became best friends. I was drawn toward those whose lifestyles deviated from anything considered normal by judgmental locals.

More than one person of authority encountered at Washington Catholic carried dark baggage. Me and two other notoriously unruly heathens were not above exploiting such people for our own entertainment. The gang included first cousins George and Joey Miller, the same guys who exacted revenge on the cemetery hillbilly, plus me. George was known as "Elmo," though the specific reason why will never be known.

I assumed a smooth-talking mafia don persona.

Elmo, Joey, and I enjoyed dragging our innocently goofy friend B.A. along in our shenanigans. B.A. also worked his way through school in a blue-collar fashion. Armed with a freshly minted Indiana driver's license, he fell into a gig delivering pizzas. We fancied ourselves practical jokers and talked Marius Winston into allowing a visit after hours at his apartment in an old Victorian mansion for some pizza.

"Come on, Mr. Winston ... it'll be a hoot!"

Marius redecorated his portion of the grand home on the ground floor in Victorian-era style. One of the subjects he taught was French, so it was British Victorian from around 1850 or so, only with decidedly French twists. All of it was garish and tacky.

A second bedroom contained not a bed, but a padded table. On the mostly red-velvet-papered walls hung handcuffs, whips, chains, leather, and other tools that required more vivid imagination than we had as teenagers. Vague, harpsichord-ish music wafted from unseen speakers. Marius answered the door wearing furry thongs and a leopard-skin robe.

"Come right on in, boys!"

The centerpiece of the living room was a giant aquarium. There were no fish and it was not filled with water. It was the usual resting place for a fully mature female yellow ball python that was over five feet long. It had free run of the place that evening.

Elmo, Joey, and I sketched out an elaborate practical joke on the way over. We remained committed despite red flags from the moment of our arrival.

Getting Marius to participate, we feared, might be problematic.

"It's play-acting," I said. "We all have specific roles. B.A. will go nuts."

Elmo added, "B.A. falls for anything." Joey grunted and asked Marius, "Got any beer?"

"NO!" Marius snapped.

The plan was to order a pizza, then request that B.A. deliver it. When he arrived with the pie, the house would be completely dark. We intended to make it sound as if an orgy was in progress, complete with moaning, groaning, and thumping. B.A. would get invited in with the pizza, and then encouraged to join in. He would be directed toward the lurking, unseen python. At that point, the lights would get flipped on so that everyone could watch hilarity ensue.

"OK boys, I'm all in, but give me plenty of notice." Mr. Winston was cautious.

B.A., pizzas in hand, proved a tough sell. "Come on guys ... what is going on?" B.A. was suspicious. We eventually talked him over to where we believed the python was, waited for any sound of possible disrobing, and then hit the switch well in advance of the planned moment of truth.

The python was nowhere to be found, but Marius was flat on his back laying atop his robe, furiously masturbating, wearing a glove that looked like feathered chenille. Whoops. That turned out better than the snake plan but put Marius in a decidedly compromised state. He was not happy.

"The party's over, boys, and it's time for all of you to hit the road.

Go home and do something normal, like homework, for a change." Marius had strange ideas about normal.

Given the general quirkiness of his personality, domicile, reptilian roommate, and lifestyle proclivities, we decided it would be all business with him from that moment forward. Even at that age, we figured nothing experienced there constituted an acceptable teacher/student relationship.

We learned even more later. After Marius departed Washington at the end of the school year, he faced difficult times with family and others in mostly isolated southern Indiana. Marius Winston took his own life a few years later. That saddened all of us because we genuinely admired folks otherwise labeled freaks. Sadly, he was not the only teacher who eventually chose suicide.

Some folks through the years have occasionally assumed I am gay. I try to dress well and can be very fastidious about where things go and how they are organized. I have never bothered correcting a hereditary gap in my front teeth that causes lisping. I have always been steadfastly heterosexual, but many of my best friends in life are not. I never saw anything wrong with that.

One of the few times a fellow male aggressively pursued same-sex pleasures occurred during college. The Vincennes University broadcasting program employed a brilliant technical person as Head Engineer, a potentially unfortunate title used to describe the most knowledgeable technical person in a station. Many of those people are now bestowed more flowery titles such as CTO, CIO, or IT Professional. The Head Engineer was often the most important person in the building because they were directly responsible for keeping stations on the air. It was a perfect title.

B. Wylie Stanton was one of the best ever. He had the chiseled physique and long blondish locks of a California surfer. Ladies thought he was hunky. Wylie even owned a rare, limited-edition American muscle car that always turned heads: a souped-up Camaro. With a *wing*. He could make just about anything work, including obsolete, hand-me-down equipment with which VU's college stations barely made do.

Wylie's house was a technical marvel for its day, filled with gadgetry that affected everything from the telephone to the way doors opened and closed. He was also an avid photographer and videographer before actual videotape existed on a mass scale. Some of his prized possessions included footage he shot at a rock festival held over Labor Day weekend in 1972 outside Evansville, Indiana. Bull Island was positioned to be as big as or bigger than Woodstock. The ill-fated event did draw hundreds of thousands of people, along with similar weather and behavior. Subject matter captured on film by Wylie included many young folks naked in the Ohio River and occasionally up to no good. That was fascinating both technically and aesthetically for me, and he was happy to share.

Technical services Wylie offered were also in high demand by just about every commercial radio station within a couple hundred miles. He took off, usually after hours, to some far-flung local station in a rural, remote location. He saved their days and then got paid handsomely for his efforts. As a broadcasting major who wanted to learn from the best, I eagerly accepted an invitation to join him on an after-hours jaunt to a radio station in Danville, Illinois.

I learned something new about Wylie on the way back. Idle chatting about school turned carnal. Wylie asked about my girlfriend

Shelly. He was particularly interested in the physical mechanics of sex we were having. With any luck at all, that would also occur upon my return from Danville. I refrained from kissing and telling, figuring something that intimate should probably be kept between the two directly involved.

Answers remained vague, but Wylie kept pressing. "How hard do you get?" "How long is it when you put it in?" What seemed even more unusual was his selection of back roads he was taking to get back. Wylie was persistent. Finally, he stopped, pulled his pants down, and asked "Do you mind if I take care of myself?" There did not seem to be a choice. "Have fun," I urged as casually as possible under the circumstances. Most of the time, it does not take men very long.

Wylie continued: "Join in, John . . . it's a great night!" He *really* wanted to see the thing that was pounding Shelly.

Get out of the car now and wait for this guy to blow a load. Maybe not. There are no houses in sight anywhere. It's late. Look out the window. Oh ... he's done.

What seemed like an eternity didn't take long. Wylie wiped himself off. The return trip continued uneventfully and as if nothing had happened. I remained creeped out for a long while.

Over forty years later at an old-timer reunion, a former administrator at the college relayed a story about the precarious financial situation of the college television station during the early 1970s. Every sudden but regular emergency that required not only expertise but cash always seemed to get resolved once Wylie intervened. School administrative personnel often fielded emergency requests for tens of thousands of dollars from broadcast leadership.

All were routinely denied, even when request justification included certainties the station would not stay on the air without it. Wylie was chummy with the school accountant. The numbers guy invariably found funds for maintenance and repair of Wylie's equipment just in the nick of time. As that story was relayed, a chuckle surfaced with graphic notions about how such wheels got greased.

CHAPTER 11

GOING WAY TOO FAR

Shortly before 3 a.m. Sunday morning late in the winter of 1978, *The Things We Do For Love* by 10CC played on radio station Z-96 in Lafayette, Indiana. The man behind the microphone was me, and I had company. I explained to my brand-new rebound girlfriend Rebecca Bosch how the band 10CC chose its name according to an urban legend of the day.

"The average male ejaculation yields about 9 cc of semen. 10 cc is greater than 9 cc, and the band is certain they are just that great."

Emboldened with this knowledge, Rebecca grabbed my crotch with one hand and pulled my ear to her mouth with the other so she could whisper into it. "John, I want to swallow all of it tonight. Right here. Right now."

WAZY played contemporary hits during daylight, the top 40 or so. Focus at night shifted slightly toward a hipper album track sound. Contemplation in the middle of that night included what tracks could be queued up on turntables that would yield at least fifteen minutes for uninterrupted passion. The correct answer was the extended version of Led Zeppelin's *Stairway to Heaven* at seven minutes fifty-five seconds, followed by a live version of Lynyrd Skynyrd's *Free Bird*, clocking in at just over nine minutes. Seventeen minutes to do something extremely unprofessional were created. Violating the format was suddenly acceptable. Those two records were part of a category unofficially labeled "TAS," a crude acronym for long songs played when the person on the air needed to defecate.

Lights were sufficiently dimmed. Control room speakers got turned way down. Rebecca adroitly positioned herself atop the padded bar stool with her back to the control board. Every stitch of her clothing was long gone. It was the perfect height for standing penetration. Rebecca quickly began losing herself in blissful pleasure. She eventually braced herself by placing one leg on the tape deck side of the U-shaped console counter, and the other on the turntable side. She leaned on backward-facing palms of her hands, using her arms for support in front of the console.

Rebecca's vocal enthusiasm got louder a couple of minutes into the song. Neither of us was aware of the LIVE microphone, inadvertently switched on by one of her twitching fingers resting awkwardly near the button. Audio from my headphones laying on the console ensured music was flowing, so I did not notice muted studio speakers.

Stairway to Heaven reached its crescendo. The intricate series of riffs got heavier, and Robert Plant ironically wailed "...a lady we all know, who shines white light and wants to show."

That was the exact point at which Rebecca began the deepest throes of her pleasure-based spasm. In the midst of repetitive "OH GODs" and "FUCK ME HARDERs" broadcasting live at 96.5 FM very early Sunday morning, her left foot made violent contact with the turntable tone arm tracking Zeppelin. The tenuous rod of metal, wood, and wires broke completely free of its mount. On the air, listeners were treated to a horrific "zzzziiiipppppppp" as its needle carved against the vinyl groove and ultimately all the way to the wall behind the spinning hopelessly scratched disc.

My own high decibel "Oh SHIT!" was the last thing listeners heard before the rest of the train wreck toppled off the track.

Reaching behind Rebecca, I hit the start button to start *Free Bird*. At some point during the excitement, Skynyrd became un-queued. The needle was still on the record, only about a minute or so into the song. It took the turntable about half a revolution to reach a full 33 1/3 RPM. An unceremonious early end to *Stairway to Heaven* confirmed neither great nor professional radio that morning.

I sent Rebecca home, then attempted repair to the tonearm. No dice. I subsequently explained (lied) the damage away by claiming the clipboard used to keep track of transmitter readings fell on top of the tonearm during an hourly scribing of technical parameters. Management bought the fabrication, and my ruse was strengthened after no outraged listeners called.

The shoe eventually ended up on the other foot later in my career. On that frigid overnight in rural northwestern Indiana, however, I pondered exactly how that particular adventure came about. All I knew for sure was that my first marriage failed, an uninhibited playmate was now involved, and I desperately clung to a career in grave danger of dying permanently.

How did I get there?!

The 1970s were ending. Suzie, the first Mrs. Howard, was a

small-town saint, but her idea of happily ever after did not mesh with my deeply rooted desire to take radio as far as I could. The decision to end our marriage felt like failure. Wondering "what if" nagged at me, but so did checking out greener grass. Those leaps of faith inspired other occasionally romantic, but frequently lurid, adventures in my third decade of life.

Rebecca Bosh had real girlfriend potential. She worked as lead cashier four or five nights a week at the drive-in theatre I also managed. She supplemented her income from a full-time day job in the medical field.

Rebecca was mostly single, rented an apartment, and graciously offered lodging as marriage to Suzie officially dissolved in a law office. She was also unnaturally beautiful with piercing eyes alternating between shades of lavender and brownish-red. Her hair was white and appeared translucent. Her body was centerfold-worthy. I was convinced that when she cashiered, sales jumped due to visits by males enamored of her beauty and friendliness.

We became certain there was going to be a relationship while closing shop one night. She and I were the only two people left inside its locked gates. Lights in the concession stand were extinguished. As we prepared to lock the doors on the way out, Rebecca whispered, "I need to check the drawer at the cash register. Would you go over there with me?"

The passionate kiss she planted once seated on the stool at the cash register was unexpected. Even more startling was the realization her underwear WAS missing after she also whispered, "I forgot my panties." The skirt followed. She was in complete control and I was helpless.

It was primal in moonlit darkness atop a cash register bar stool. Not very romantic, but not really the point.

Rebecca began spending time in the drive-in office, located inside the structure that supported the screen. I never knew why there was a bed in that office, but it proved useful on several occasions, because Rebecca was completely uninhibited.

Once divorce became final, I became persona non grata in the house Suzie and I shared. Her father even changed the locks.

My full-time radio career was eventually resuscitated. Mike King, operations manager of WCSI in Columbus, Indiana threw a lifeline. I decided to temporarily move in with my aunt on the west side of Indianapolis while searching for a place of my own in Columbus. Aunt Kathy enjoyed the arrangement because she worked during the day. Various chores were tackled every morning before I left for Columbus, and Kathy got to check items off a to-do list. Rebecca visited one morning in an unannounced early morning surprise. I was very happy to see her. Better yet, the house was vacant. It was a bright, sunny day, and was about to get even better.

Cloudless morning sun forced a sudden realization that I had never seen Rebecca completely naked in broad daylight. My mind wandered as I positioned my face between her thighs, fully intending to work what I knew would be magical for her. I did not lack self-confidence, and was arrogantly short on humility. That was also the precise moment the physical, genetic reality of albinism was grasped. In bright sunshine her vagina looked like raw poultry in a meat department display case—the fluffy part of feathers plucked with stems intact.

Most men today who are the age I was during those hormonal exploits expect a mostly or fully hairless vagina. That concept remains completely foreign to many baby boomers, most of whom enjoyed a sexual treat euphemistically called hair pie. I preferred it to apple. Viewing all of the albino merchandise up close in the late 1970s, despite pubic hair you could see right through, was disorienting. For the first time in my young life, I failed to perform despite pleasurable coaxing from Rebecca. My mind twisted something beautiful into a sordid allusion that involved fucking Johnny Winter.

Rebecca was ultimately able to salvage the moment. She mounted atop and began galloping her way toward what promised to be splendidly shuddering bliss, complete with audible references to the Almighty and couched with plenty of nasty chat in between.

"OH JOHN...OH, OH **OH**! RIGHT THERE, RIGHT THERE, **RIGHT THERE**...your beautiful dick ALWAYS finds that spot!"

That's just what I need to hear, darling!

Her climactic moaning peaked, and coincided with entry into the room of my maternal step-grandmother and her recently betrothed Bob, who let themselves into the unlocked side door of the house a few seconds earlier to check up on me. Once they realized what they walked into, their retreat was rapid and silent. Grandma tossed an "I will call you later" into my direction. She did, but not a word was spoken of the naked living room rodeo from then on.

Getting-caught scenarios with Rebecca became more dangerous:

WAZY, overnight in the dead of winter, for example.

Extreme professionalism was my foundation most of the time.

Being on the air was serious. Funny business usually waited until air shifts ended. On that cold winter night, however, when Rebecca urgently whispered "John, I will swallow all of it," probity took a back seat. She decided kneeling under the console, offering pleasure whenever I attempted delivery of aural perfection through the microphone, was a great idea. It escalated from there.

As I cleaned up the remnants of passion run amok in a federally licensed facility, I re-dedicated myself to a full-time career in radio, setting my sites on the Athens of the prairie, WCSI in Columbus, Indiana.

CHAPTER 12

TWO YOKELS AND A PORN QUEEN

Scott McKain is a widely respected speaker and best-selling business author whose friendship dates back to the early 1980s, when and where we shared radio airwaves in Columbus, Indiana. Two things we have in common are small-town Hoosier roots and an occasionally devious pattern of mischief that served us well both on and off the air. Our social visits are rare these days, but even after a few years pass we pick up where we left off. This holds especially true for cutting up.

In 1985, Scott and I whimsically decided: "We should head for Las Vegas and take the wives!" At the time, a large-scale purge of shady figures from hotel and casino businesses was nearly complete. Mega-resort operators began assuming control of the desert oasis. New moguls reshaped both the direction and appearance of the Strip. Las Vegas today is very different than even thirty-five years ago. Despite the transformation, great meals could still be found for very little money in the 1980s. Show pricing along the Strip remained reasonable and was accessible to nearly everyone.

Scott's late wife, Sheri, and my second wife, Stevie, shared being tall, blonde, smart, and obsessively successful. Both were forces of nature. Sheri and Stevie also possessed innocence that wound up being tempered over what became a memorable weekend.

We decided to attend a comedy revue at the old and long-departed Riviera. The show was highly recommended and featured both up and coming new talent and established acts. The only one I remember was Joan Rivers, and even then, every morsel of her set was completely forgotten almost immediately. Not one of the acts was forgettable. An enthusiastic audience enjoyed the entire show. Scott and I, however, were severely distracted.

We discreetly slipped twenties to the doorman as we entered the room. The uniformed pro led us directly to a circular, very high backed, red velvet upholstered booth in front and slightly left of the stage. It seemed unusually intimate and mostly enclosed, except for a surprisingly open view of the stage. The booth was also specifically designed to comfortably accommodate six people. There were four of us and the show was sold out. We sat boy-girl-boy-girl style. I was at the end. Just before the curtain rose, the doorman seated two other occupants inside what we concluded was already a cool lair. The guy slid in first and sat next to Sheri. He could have been a mobster or any one of a variety of other stereotypes characterized by an exaggerated, permed head of unnaturally curly hair, a shiny shirt unbuttoned to mid-chest complete with gold chains underneath, lots of rings on both hands, and an equally bright blazer, meticulously tailored from only the finest synthetic fabrics. The lady with him was dressed head to toe in a tight-fitting, entirely neon pink jumpsuit with faux fur at the neck, sleeves, and ankles. The top was open and provided ample, seemingly intentional cleavage.

Less than three seconds transpired before Scott and I realized, more or less simultaneously, who was seated with us. We simply looked at each other and smiled knowingly, both astonished and wide-eyed. Our thoughts were identical. Grins we sported might have been something our wholesome wives referred to as "shit-eating."

Be cool. Scott had the same thought. We were already sweating.

Marilyn Chambers was in the booth with us. That name may not resonate with generations beyond boomers, particularly after her untimely passing in 2009. During the 1970s and 1980s, however, Marilyn was arguably the most famous pornographic film actress in the world. She was different than every other female porn star because she somehow retained a wholesome, girl-next-door beauty no normal person would have ever associated with pornography. Marilyn Chambers became notorious in the classic adult films *Behind the Green Door* and *Insatiable.*

Pornography today seems run of the mill compared to older films that at least attempted to mimic cinematic art. Chambers became embroiled in mainstream scandal as her pornography career exploded. She was the first big-name Caucasian pornographic actor to have sex with a black man on camera. An even bigger and more significant bit of societal ignominy involved laundry soap. Outside graphic adult films, her day job involved being the model featured on the front panel of each and every box of Ivory Snow detergent. Labels featured broadly smiling Marilyn Chambers holding a happy infant, and all of those boxes occupied shelves of every grocery store in America. Average housewives did not handle that revelation well.

There was no chance Scott or I would remember a single thing that occurred on stage. Sheri and Stevie remained completely oblivious. Once house lights dimmed and performers inspired laughter, the mischievous boys from Indiana had palpable difficulty NOT gazing at Marilyn. Worse, she knew that we knew who she was and decided to screw around with us (figuratively) throughout the entire show.

Marilyn winked occasionally and offered plenty of smiles. Our tense and sweaty phase intensified after she began playing footsies under the table. Her angle to Scott was probably a bit more challenging, but at one point the toes of her right foot made it almost all the way up the inside of my right leg. Oblivious to the show, consumption of alcohol became feverish.

The show mercifully ended about ninety minutes later. Our party of six meandered outside to the valet stand. Although Scott and I were grown men, we were reduced to giggling school girls on the verge of peeing our britches. Marilyn remained as cool and pure as Ivory Snow. Her chauffeured vehicle arrived quickly. As she entered its back seat following her escort, she turned to Scott and me. In full view of both Sheri and Stevie, Ms. Chambers slowly waved, then blew exaggerated kisses directly at both of us.

Milliseconds later, the first predictable questions from spouses erupted.

"Who was THAT!?"

There was no reason to lie. "Marilyn Chambers."

Blank stares. No Internet or YouTube existed yet. A few days later, VCRs and video rental places with back rooms were patronized solely for their educational enlightenment. During plot highlights of *Behind the Green Door*, the innocent jaws of our relatively innocent and sheltered wives slackened nearly to ground level.

Eyeballs bulged from their sockets. Their reactions made an entire evening more entertaining than the show we paid for.

CHAPTER 13

FLEETING FLASHERS

I rarely minded being nude in intimate situations with, say, lovers. I have even gone commando in public a few times, from beaches in the Caribbean to streaking once in a larger group when that act was popular during the early 1970s.

Flashing was never given a second thought. I always thought it was just something perverted dirty old men in trench coats might do to unsuspecting folks.

One afternoon my wife, Stevie, welcomed a high school best friend and college roommate to our house, along with her husband. Janie and Brian Watson were equally young and fun-loving, and the four of us soon began enjoying all sorts of adventures together. There was no sexual chemistry outside our marriages. Janie, once a high school cheerleader, and her husband gained a few pounds each in their blissfully betrothed state. It happens a lot. Oddly and without warning one day, Janie and I determined we enjoyed flashing one another in completely innocent ways.

We hiked through a state park, but there were no restrooms were near our remote vantage point. We did have seclusion and acres of forest, so none of us worried about it. Male urination is not complicated in such situations. You find a tree, duck behind it, whip it out, and let 'er fly. I did not announce my intention while wandering away, but after my stream began a safe distance from the others, Janie suddenly appeared from around a tree several yards ahead. Instead of turning away or being embarrassed, I waved at her with one free hand, and also with what was in my other hand, spray and all. Her laughter echoed through the trees with multiple decibels.

Turning back was never an option from that point forward. Creative flashing popped up whenever the other person least expected it, and the more public or risky the better. Our goal was always to one-up the other. Janie and Brian were getting ready to move into a new house. She tried grabbing a box on a shelf but couldn't reach it. I volunteered to grab it using a nearby stool. I retrieved the box and turned around to hand it over. Almost at her eye level, she came face to face with little John. Laughter ensued. Spouses always recognized the laughter and rolled their eyes.

All of us were scheduled to attend a formal function that required fancier clothing than any of us possessed. Day trips to local department stores turned arduous. Brian and I found adequate duds quickly. The ladies' search turned into a day-long scavenger hunt. Janie carried three nice outfits into a fitting room. Periodically she called for Stevie or Brian to enter and offer opinions. They entered dressing room areas, and Janie appeared in an outfit for which she sought approval. No consensus was reached for any of them. Finally, Janie announced she wanted my neutral opinion and summoned me to the hallway of the dressing room. When I entered, she stepped from the dressing room without one stitch of clothing. She was stark naked. Laughter ensued. Stevie and Brian simply shook their heads back and forth. Janie *won*.

Flashing experiences Janie and I shared were random, meaningless, and fun. No sexual tension ever complicated the delinquency. Neither of us felt perverted or dirty. It was something I never felt inclined to do with anyone else.

More than a decade passed before an identical urge struck with someone else. That impulse constituted palpable, career-threatening danger. Twisted misadventure, however, was exhilarating.

My second career included high-level consulting for large media clients with Jefferson-Pilot Data Services. I became a go-to guy for difficult and challenging projects and spent most of my time on the road. One of the biggest and most important JDS clients was the Post-Newsweek television group. Their stations dotted major markets from Detroit to Houston to Miami and several points in between. The account generated millions of dollars annually but fell into jeopardy. Their contract neared completion and Post-Newsweek was shopping competitors. They felt neglected and openly believed they were saddled with technology rapidly becoming obsolete, unable to meet their basic business needs.

I was recruited internally to step in, assume daily management of the account, and help facilitate the renewal of a long-term contract worth several million additional dollars. The challenge was daunting, but responsibilities were clear. Travel to each location, spend several days with all key stakeholders, document gaps, enhancement requests, current business practices, and determine whether their use of company products was geared for peak performance. More importantly, all aspects were carefully committed to paper, organized, and presented to management and developers from both organizations in language everyone could easily understand. Evaluation began. Each item was made actionable for people in both organizations. As actions were completed, results were tested. Rollouts at each client location were closely managed, along with training and optimization as necessary.

The Post-Newsweek organization then was years ahead of its time in terms of upward mobility for women. The vast majority of senior management people I worked closely with were female, and all were paid well. No one ever worried about being compensated less than men. There was no deviation. Leadership began at the top, which was held for years by the legendary and visionary Katherine Graham. She was one of the most powerful people in media in her day, and definitely the most powerful woman.

Post-Newsweek also appointed a project leader. Tracy Milner was tall, determined, and unafraid to say whatever was necessary. She focused intensely on actual results. Tracy was also a force of nature who tolerated very little nonsense. She tempered intensity with exceedingly fair balance, considering all sides of an argument before passing any judgment. Her sense of humor was also very strong. Our professional relationship began guarded and tenuous but gained strength as trust was established. Working with her was enjoyable, but she could turn frightening on a dime.

Tracy also had a close and loving family. She bragged on all of them often.

One extended client session began with a flight to Miami. There, several Post-Newsweek managers, Tracy, and I were scheduled for a dinner meeting the evening I arrived. Our hotel was nearby, so Tracy suggested, "Why don't you check in, drop off your luggage with bellhops, and not have to worry about lugging it to dinner?" *GREAT idea.*

A young female clerk behind the front desk tapped busily into her terminal as check-in commenced. She was oblivious to the position of her right breast. Unencumbered by any undergarment, it found its way mostly out the side of her very loose-fitting sleeveless blouse. Tracy noticed. I noticed. The clerk eventually noticed as keys were being pressed, and she surreptitiously rearranged her anatomy.

Walking down the block to dinner, Tracy nudged me and quipped, "John, you had an admirer back at the hotel," and winked. My response was a chuckle and an observation that "I enjoyed the show, but she wasn't my type." That was that. Dinner was great. Meetings that followed over the next few days became difficult and often tense.

Tracy was often intimidating, and people had to stay on their toes during meetings. During a morning session on the third day, Tracy carted in a large printout of computer-generated green bar reports used for slicing and dicing inventory and availabilities. It was lifeblood data for television stations. JDS used 11 7/8" X 14" paper generated using a printer the size of a large commercial washing machine. The capability to view data on screens did not yet exist, partially due to the excessive volume of it contained in the reports, and also because large, heavy, tube-riddled workstation screens were simply not yet large enough. Reviewing reports resembled an extreme version of spreading the *Sunday New York Times* out on a floor, then perusing each section.

I was seated to Tracy's right at the end of a long conference table, and large sheets blocked others from seeing much more than our faces above massive printouts. Tracy was articulating points about what the group felt were perceived inaccuracies in the numbers. I casually noticed at one point that the nipple end of her right breast found its way out of her open sleeve, and did not appear to be an accident. Quick movements of her arm sent it back inside as she lowered the report, but I became unnerved. Her grin screamed, "I gotcha!"

Against ALL better judgment, plotting of one-up revenge began. Initial attempts were tame and relatively conservative, and mostly included unzipping my pants and pulling innocuous objects out. Sharpies. Staplers. Framed pictures from her desk. It escalated immediately prior to a large meeting in a conference room that featured an on-screen presentation.

As final preparations were made, Tracy and I faced the screen with our backs to the audience entering the room. "John, do you have the remote?" Unzipping my pants, she expected that the remote would be produced. Nope. This time Little John tumbled out. These were times in which the kind of laughter Tracy and I shared seemed natural, but highly inadvisable given the professional surroundings. The game, however, was officially on, and both of us jumped in.

Related mischief continued randomly and sporadically throughout the eastern half of the United States. Detroit. Houston. San Antonio. Jacksonville. Miami. Each time we fretted about appropriateness but enjoyed the exhilarating danger of surfing the very edge of that envelope. We never deeply discussed it. Flashing was mostly subtle. Horseplay occasionally degenerated into more crude and wildly unprofessional events like mooning contests.

Our competitive spirits were aligned even though no sexual chemistry was ever shared. It was ill-advised competition flashing. We both wanted desperately to "win," but we would be the only people who would ever know or could celebrate it.

Tracy eventually did. Decisively so. We found ourselves in a headquarters conference room in Washington, DC. It was an important meeting with Post-Newsweek senior executives and executive leadership of JDS. Topics included project status, budgets, direction, and decision time frames. It represented the establishment of several critical milestones. An unannounced appearance by their corporate matriarch Katherine Graham, whose retirement had already begun, surprised us. She was engaged in helping others in occasional transitionary roles. Graham had little to no involvement in our project or the company but sat in for much of the meeting.

Tracy always carried a small leather pouch that contained notes referred to in such meetings. She and I were seated across a polished table from one another. The most powerful woman in media since the 1960s, and probably ever, was seated a couple of chairs away from Tracy. Early in the meeting Tracy picked up the pouch, fumbled as she unzipped it, and then dropped it onto the floor. It landed in my vicinity under the table. She looked, pointed, and whispered whether I would mind retrieving it using silent motions.

I stealthily slid off my chair and kneeled to retrieve the pouch. It was not difficult noticing Tracy's hiked up skirt and no underwear. She went full-blown Sharon-Stone-*Basic-Instinct* underneath the hard surface of the table. The same surface the back of my head smacked with unintended force on the way back up. As I handed the pouch back to her my eyes conceded defeat. Nothing I could ever do would top that and remain relatively normal, legal, or ethical, much less professional.

Katherine Fucking Graham is sitting almost next to her. Tracy's got some guts...

The account was saved and renewed for several more years. Millions of dollars continued flowing until well after I departed JDS. Katherine Graham is long gone, and I was saddened to learn Tracy also passed away far too young a few years ago. Despite one distinct aspect of weirdness, the Post-Newsweek adventure became one of the highest points of that career phase. No compulsion to flash anyone occurred prior to Janie or after Tracy.

Did that signal late-blooming maturity? Probably not.

Part II: DRUGS!

CHAPTER 14

GATEWAY DRUGS

I was in seventh grade the first time any significant thought about cannabis hit Washington. Not many locals discussed it. The subject was not verboten; silence was more the result of a stunning lack of knowledge. Older folks in the late 1960s derided beatniks, a term on its way out of popular culture. "Hippies" was more commonly spouted. The phrase "Goddamned long-haired hippies" was heard more than once, usually by someone with a crew cut and a pack of Chesterfields stuffed into a rolled-up sleeve. The English language included words and phrases like "groovy" and "far out" as part of normal conversation, usually with Tommy Chong-like inflection well before he and Cheech Marin came along to parody exactly that. Peace and love styles of the day occasionally ran contrary to an increasing propensity toward civil disobedience. Not only were many high on life but also increasingly high on pot, all while embracing hijinks in our storybook version of middle America.

The stodgy older generation flipped out. Reefer Madness was alive and well. It seems shameful that any first exposure to even the concept was framed by dire warnings about some inevitable succession of addiction that merely began with marijuana, and ended either in a tragic death, mental illness, or other life-ruining side effects. Just like sex or masturbation. Most youngsters saw right through irrational warnings.

Given all the hype, it seemed like something a young rebel might enjoy. So, I did in 1967, between seventh and eighth grades. The Summer of Love was in full swing. Travel to San Francisco with flowers in my hair was not yet possible, so the home of brothers Lonnie and Keith Cline served as the southern Indiana version. Lonnie was a year older than me and Keith a year younger. They were the cool kids, and the vibe inside their oversized and stately old home was mellow. "Hey, JT, wanna get high?" The notion of waving it off occurred to me but subtle, raised eyebrow peer pressure easily won out. It took a lot of hits from that pipe to attain a state of tranquility that seemed anywhere near cool.

As we relaxed into a comfy sofa and became suitably buzzed, the best music I ever heard in my life began playing. Nazz. Todd Rundgren's earliest band. It seemed to touch a musical portion of my brain on an entirely new and brilliant level. Given the freshness of that newly mellow experience, they could have rolled Jimmy Brosch and his polka band and I probably would have gotten off. Listening to Nazz later completely sober did not quite resonate the same way. Early musical wizardry was just more unrefined than Rundgren's more contemporary works, much like junior high school students in the late 1960s.

The first rung of the drug addiction ladder was accomplished before high school began. Washington Catholic High School employed an eclectic mix of faculty. There were nuns, priests, and lay teachers who fell into two primary categories. Either they were working first jobs beyond college, or headed toward (or had passed) retirement. In between were a few who generally carried dark secrets, and none of them ever seemed truly happy about being exiled at WC.

One bright young star there in the early 1970s was recent college graduate Standley Falk. His approach was participative and inclusive. Usual stodginess associated with religious types was not part of Standley's repertoire. His physical features included a beard and long hair. Standley was the closest thing to an authentic hippie in Washington. Class discussions included deep analysis of contemporary issues, including Asian war resistance and presidential improprieties. It was suddenly OK to openly believe a war on the other side of the globe was a really bad idea. No one got in trouble for calling Richard Nixon a crook. A handful of diligent students received after-school mentoring. The passing of a loaded pipe often accompanied homework at the Falk residence. Standley was always supplied and willing to share. He also peppered everyone with, "What do you think about …" questions regardless of subject matter.

One bright summer day, Falk took an entire class on a field trip to downtown Washington. "You are going to rob this bank," pointing at the First Federal building. Standley cleared the fake holdup with the bank beforehand. We were supposed to use the experience to follow the legal steps taken after a robbery as part of a civics exercise. On another occasion, we staged a loose recreation of the Kennedy assassination outside the local courthouse across the street from the high school. A shooter was positioned INSIDE the school library. He wanted students to see the event as members of the media would. "React as if it's your responsibility to tell the entire world what is happening."

It was beyond a normal curriculum, but far more compelling than mandatory Latin classes.

Falk's house sat on the edge of town. His approach outside the classroom was identical to inside, except for pot smoke. Very few students were invited for obvious reasons, but he never allowed anyone to drink alcohol. My best grades in an otherwise unremarkable high school academic career were earned in his classes, but wheels were greased out in the real world.

For me, being high never really felt as inspiring as it did for many. Pre-1970s pot was largely unrefined and exponentially less potent than future pot. The biggest effect it had on me was hunger. I gobbled far too many Big Chefs from the local Burger Chef. That was about as far as the consumption of cannabis went for me. It was not as much fun as beer. Hard liquor was also nixed, having vomited nearly three days of stomach content after slurping a bit too much Old Crow. Classmate parties while parents were away did that. Wine palates of high school students had not progressed much beyond Boone's Farm through the 1970s.

Considering the level of discipline and order otherwise attempted by Catholic faculty, being effectively motivated by and receiving honestly earned good grades from someone so culturally different was amazing. The majority of four years there were otherwise gleefully spent being a mostly disruptive spawn of Satan.

Cannabis became neither a problem nor a gateway for me. Pot got more potent in college. Breathing became labored one smoke-filled night in college. Stoned friends decided the best place for me was a local hospital, where a doctor concluded I was probably allergic to whatever I had consumed.

Verification occurred the following week.

An alarmingly high number of small needles, each containing a small amount of a potential allergen, were stuck into me in a pattern. Results showed allergies to a shocking variety of tree species, cat dander, and THC. Damn it.

CHAPTER 15

DEMONIC POSSESSION, MISDEMEANORS, AND OTHER WAYWARD STRAYING

Washington Catholic High School was already over a century old in the early 1970s when I became the first and only class president ever impeached by the administration. Achievement of that milestone required three years of pathological misbehavior.

I was addicted to the drug of disruption throughout high school. It was an offbeat way of pandering for acceptance. My trusted high school accomplices, Elmo and Joey, were not only enforcers but co-conspirators. A big mystery is how any of us completed four years and left the school upright. Every once in a while, pangs of regret knocked around my hard head. Almost as quickly, the brain inside screamed *SCREW IT! This is FUN!* It made college and professional life better later, so those running the school actually fulfilled their stated missions. Elmo, Joey, and I just never made it easy.

The school administration contained colorful characters. Green Bay ran the show. Sister Joseph Louise was her anointed name. That seemed better than her real name, Thelma Louise. The nickname was bestowed and handed down through several graduating classes. Her temperament was consistently stern. She tolerated no misbehavior, kind of like the famous linebacker Ray Nitschke who inspired the "Green Bay" moniker. In addition to her primary duty as principal, Algebra was her teaching class. It was the only course in which no one did anything except study and behave angelically. "You kids think you won't need algebra? Think again. You will use it all through your adult life if you graduate. You'd best pay attention, study and LEARN IT," she bellowed more than once. It was the most difficult C ever honestly earned.

Father Joe Clauss was the school superintendent. Many priests had pedophilia disorders exposed later in life. Father Clauss was one of them. We were completely unaware of anything like that as students. He was the saint in a bad parent/good parent relationship. Classmates often gossiped that Father Clauss and Green Bay shacked up.

Our nickname for Father Clauss was Papa Joe. Innocent enough, but based on master brewer Papa Joe Griesedieck. That became Papa Joe Greasy Dick because none of us delinquents knew how to spell Griesedieck. We knew how to giggle, though. We also enjoyed whatever beer we could get, which was usually Falstaff, brewed by the Griesedieck family.

Papa Joe was a diplomat who smoothed waters whenever any of us ran afoul of Green Bay, which occurred with alarming frequency. His only potential personal demon, discovered after breaking into his office after hours, was a bottle of opened bourbon in the bottom drawer. That was low on his character flaw list. Papa Joe often lamented "You hoodlums are driving me to drink." Yes, we did.

Calling our behavior bad would understate reality. Most of it was stunningly inappropriate. Specific acts were often incited by dares. Mostly, sheer meanness exploited weaker faculty members.

Horace Broadman was an elderly, hard-of-hearing retired gentleman who lived an hour or so away and commuted to school in a very old van. Accompanying him every day was his equally senior wife, who spent her days inside the vehicle doing needlework. She was occasionally pressed into service when a substitute teacher was needed. Every day, Mr. Broadman wore one of two wool suits he owned. His silver hair, stained by nicotine, was stylishly slicked back. Both suits reeked of cigar smoke. His style was facing the class and delivering lectured material at high volumes to compensate for a lack of hearing. Horace used chalk on a traditional black slate board in a school building originally constructed in 1857. When he did, his entire body spun around. Careful, deliberate, precise cursive writing slowly followed.

Horace's back to the class cued mischief. Simple delinquency, such as the launching of spitballs, was far too lame. One classmate's dad had a job in a steel ball factory. Guess where we secured projectiles? They ranged in size from BB to somewhere between marble- and golf-ball-size. Small balls shot through a straw did not faze Horace. The distance was too great and the wool too thick. Whenever lucky blows resulted in contact with bare skin, he thought it was an insect bite and simply swatted at it. It was more entertaining to hit the back of some unsuspecting classmate's head, and then watch the unlucky soul get in trouble for disrupting class following inevitable yelps and anger.

That grew boring. Much larger steel balls could not be shot through straws but could be flung following a windup and pitch. Whenever a solid steel ball that size made contact with a thick slate blackboard, the sound it created was unique and deafening. Balls of steel did not bounce. They just dropped to the hardwood floor, which created other loud explosions. It also caused Horace to literally jump off the ground every time. One of us offered apologies, claimed it slipped, and then retrieved the ball. The same act was repeated every few days.

Another ignoble goal was getting teachers to storm out of class. Whenever Green Bay showed up, pointing and motioning, then shouting "GET OUT HERE NOW!", we suddenly became models of deportment with our noses in books. *Who, me?* feigning shock. It was important to get issues escalated to Father Clauss. With him, we always found ourselves back in class with fresh sets of chances. Horace was hardened and never left the room.

A grand finale occurred on a day when Elmo, Joey, our friend JB, and a few others came armed with steel balls. Machine-gun-like explosions caused the elderly teacher to forego his cane and sprint from the room. Green Bay heard the commotion from her office and arrived before all the balls could be retrieved. We were busted. Horace finished the year then called it quits for good.

English class was taught by an elderly nun who still preferred full woolen habits, even though most of her contemporaries had begun dressing more casually. Elmo, Joey, and I picked a midsemester day to seat ourselves throughout the room. We rigged up an elaborate sound system in the coat room at the back of the classroom. A recording of an approaching train was borrowed from the local radio station, whistles and all, that eventually crashes. We also incorporated a makeshift spotlight for effect.

About halfway through another mostly boring class, the train began approaching the classroom. Actual tracks used by the Baltimore & Ohio Railroad were six blocks away and ran nowhere near the high school. "Do you hear that!?" Elmo seemed alarmed. Joey looked up and said, "Whuuu?" It got much louder. I flipped the switch for the spotlight. The oncoming, out-of-control train got much louder. Boomers, already familiar with duck-and-cover exercises in school designed to shield us from nuclear annihilation, were prepared to dive under desks on a moment's notice. Just before certain catastrophe, Elmo shouted "DUCK!" and Joey, me, most of the rest of the class, and the good sister hit the floor to escape the carnage.

Green Bay quickly appeared. "COME WITH ME. All three of you. NOW!" she pointed at me, Elmo, and Joey, wagging a finger. Formality was bypassed and we were transported directly to the office of Father Clauss.

"Boys, what is wrong with you? Why do you have to cause so much trouble? Please do me and everyone else in the school a big favor. Cool it. It's not funny anymore. I am not going to be able to vouch for you much longer."

The elderly nun also retired permanently that year.

Halloween in 1970 featured a cool promotion by Burger Chef. Pumpkins were FREE with the purchase of selected meals. That turned out to be a huge marketing miscalculation. We took the pumpkins back to school. Then we removed sports trophies from their cases, established a makeshift bowling alley on the long main hallway, and rolled for orange-hued strikes. Joey, Elmo, and I each got one messy throw before the very tall and strong Athletic Director Larry Dodd, who never had anything to do with students who did not participate in sports, roared up behind us and lifted all three of us by our shirt collars. A bum's rush did not conclude until we were out the front door, across the street, and on the lawn of the neighboring courthouse. His face was beet red, and a giant vein ran vertically down the middle of his forehead. There he growled "If I get my fucking way all three of you are gone for good. You're OUT!" Green Bay was next, silently handing us three-day suspension paperwork.

Two years of aberrant behavior was the norm, and was evidently entertaining. My election as president of the junior class seemed improbable, but we made the most of it. One of the functions junior classes controlled were concessions at high school basketball games.

At that point in history, basketball in Indiana was king. No multiple class system existed to dilute competition. That same vibe inspired the classic movie, *Hoosiers.* Twelve of the fourteen largest high school gymnasiums in the country are located in Indiana. The gym at Washington Catholic was much smaller than others but was always packed for games on two levels that occupied three sides of the old building. One main concession stand occupied space near the main entrance. Lines were always long.

An "aha" moment arrived. "We could harvest a lot more dollars if we set up smaller locations in the gym for concessions. All we'd need to do is pop more corn, keep the dogs rolling, the drinks cold, and shuttle all of it between stands." Logistics were easily accomplished. Convenience made it much easier for patrons to spend their money AND allow time for game watching. Concession revenue that year skyrocketed.

Our personal civics lesson that year included discovering for ourselves how organized crime works on a small scale. Sophisticated accounting practices were not used in managing concessions. We, meaning myself and capos Elmo and Joey, collected all the money from sporting event concessions, and then deposited the vast majority of it into the school concession fund. For all our hard work, however, we treated ourselves weekly. "We need a juicy steak dinner at the New Café," I'd insist. Elmo might suggest "We could use some smokes." Normally quiet Joey's simple hint was typically just, "Beer." The token bit of skim never amounted to much.

After every school year, it was customary for junior classes to present a legacy gift to the school. They were usually mundane. An engraved stone bench, a planted tree, new equipment for the chemistry lab, or similarly charming physical items were common examples. In our case, a small plaque was cast. The real prize, however, was simply handing over more money than had ever been made from concessions. Cold hard cash was what the school needed more than anything else. Being aspiring mafiosi, however, a small portion was withheld to fund alcohol and entertainment for a large party planned for a rural farm east of town at the end of the school year.

The class of '72 included a popular, mostly straight-as-an-arrow member named Jack Fiskus. Jack's uncle owned the farm and planned to be on vacation for a few days that summer. Jack was the pride of not only the class but of the entire town, having formally accepted appointment to West Point after graduation. His gracious offer to host a party for thirty-six underage high school kids and selected others from the public high school made him even more popular.

Elmo and Joey arranged for the underage acquisition of alcohol. A plentiful stash included cases of cheap beer, wine, flavored vodka in screw-top bottles, and sloe gin. Why sloe gin? Urban legend assured certainty that bras and panties would easily slide off after sloe gin was consumed by chaste female classmates. Elmo and Jimmy also knew their hard liquor, and several bottles of top-shelf bourbon were included.

The party quickly became a rousing success. A bonfire bonded classmates, some drinks were consumed, and the night looked promising. Jack failed to inform neighboring farmers beforehand that a party would occur that night, which proved to be a big mistake. The only thing folks in that slice of rural Indiana knew was that Farmer Fiskus was out of town, and mischief was occurring on his land. Calls to law enforcement were predictable, something completely unforeseen by seventeen- and eighteen-year-old teenagers.

The fine deputies of the Daviess County Sheriff Department did their jobs effectively. Using multiple cars, the perimeter of the party scene was quietly surrounded by police vehicles with doused lights. Suddenly, and with a great deal of surprise, spotlights and flashing beacons illuminated the party scene from all directions. There was no place to run or hide because cops had the group flanked. Worse, the party had barely begun.

Partygoers were segregated into two sections. One was reserved for males over age eighteen; the other included anyone under eighteen and all females regardless of age. Jack and I were two of just four over-eighteen males and assumed instigators. The crime scene became a makeshift transportation hub in which angry parents arrived to pick up wayward offspring while glaring at the freshly handcuffed gang of four. All four of us were soon off to the hoosegow.

Following incarceration processing, Sheriff Everett Beasley arrived in an animated foul mood after having been awakened from a deep slumber. His stern lecture preceded a painful ritual.

"You four delinquents are going to take turns dumping all that cheap swill and rotgut crap down this toilet, then I am going back home to bed," Sheriff Beasley harangued loudly in front of a metal commode in an open cell. "You will stay in this cell with the door closed until mommy and daddy bail your sorry little asses out, which hopefully won't be until tomorrow. You will not EVER pull a stunt like this in my county ever again. You got me?!"

All of the top-shelf bourbon was removed and retained by the department as evidence.

Jack was beside himself. Would his military academy appointment get rescinded? The Fiskus family was the first to arrive to bail their child out. They were in tears. The remaining three of us were stuck with tough love parents who took hands-off approaches. "Rot in jail, you little bastards" was the general tenor. Responsibility for bailing me out fell to Uncle Don, who showed up, chuckled, and spent the short ride home repeatedly referring to me as a "dumb ass" this or a "dumb ass" that. "Won't your mom and dad and grandmother be so proud, you dumb ass?" Dad eventually got home from his watering hole at the Knights of Columbus hall, and passed judgement. "You're grounded, you little shit." Mom fought back tears.

Repercussion varied for the newly infamous wayward teenagers. Jack's military academy appointment was quietly smoothed over behind closed doors. The other two also faced groundings. The school year was over, but my formal impeachment proceeding began that weekend. Green Bay relished delivering that news to the entire student body the very first day of my senior year.

"Mr. Howard let down not only this school, but the entire town of Washington. He and his gang brought shame to this institution. That is NOT what we stand for. As a result, Mr. Howard will be stripped of his title permanently. Let this be a lesson to anyone else looking to pull a stunt like this!" I was pronounced guilty, denied legal representation, and no appeal was allowed.

The ceremonial removal of a title by the rotund sister was taken in stride. The school was financially enriched. I provided meaningful extracurricular activities. It was a win-win. Senior year with no official title was spent working, being with Janice, figuring out how to get into college, and a couple of other important projects. The Catholic high school wanted to convert a mostly unused room above a corner of the gymnasium into a chapel. Fancying myself an artist, stained glass patterns were mimicked using contact paper on a bay of large windows in the room.

Another personal goal was shaking up the annual school yearbook. I was appointed editor. Yearbooks at the school resembled thick magazines for decades. All contained snapshots of a few class highlights in sports, academics, and other activities, along with rows and rows of carefully staged class pictures. The last page always thanked a few individual sponsors for support.

Enabled by another odd, eccentric faculty advisor who hailed from the very northernmost polar regions of Michigan, Leon Dysynskie, a grand plan was executed that required spending money to ultimately make money. The school lost money every year printing yearbooks and distributing them for donations. Leon ran interference with Green Bay, and most free time was spent crafting what we intended to be the best yearbook the town and school had ever seen.

Leon's idea of practical joking was ordering pizza that contained anchovies. "Anchovies are the single best topping you can possibly get on a great pizza." He urgently stated that case every time. For all we knew, he meant every word. The rest of us rural Hoosier bumpkins never acquired the taste. His idea of radical journalism during the early 1970s was Playboy magazine. Hugh Hefner's publication began including pubic hair in shots of models adorning their pages. He was obsessed with it. "Just look at her! She is BEAUTIFUL!" This is art, and it should be treated seriously." Given his nerd-like appearance, which was always disheveled, complete with flaky dandruff, teeth that grew in various directions, horn-rimmed glasses, and pocket protectors, that magazine was probably as close as he ever got to a naked woman.

Radically different approaches were taken with *The Cardinal.* We decided it would sport a hard-bound cover. Traditional school pictures were included, but so were alternatives. Elmo and Joey, for example, never had formal pictures taken. Their official class portraits became casual shots leaning against my Catalina puffing cigarettes. It was groundbreaking and cool. I also decided to use an embossed hardcover, varying type styles, art, and short stories to go with some of the pictures. I even managed to talk Green Bay and Father Clauss into posing together, and then applied filters that resulted in a very creative shot.

All of that cost more money than we had in the budget, so Leon and I recruited two students to pound pavement and sell print advertising. Instead of one page in the back to thank sponsors, multiple pages of actual advertising crafted by students occupied the space. We attached a nominal price tag, promising all proceeds would go to the school.

Distribution of the finished product was my last official act in high school. It was well-received in the community, which had never seen anything like it. The venture was profitable and returned the school's investment, along with a sizable surplus that was not skimmed.

Graduation as part of the class of 1972 was improbable, but I made it. My parents were finally proud, and there would be no more angry phone calls from Green Bay.

Chapter 16

A Brief Tenure as Drug Dealer and ~~Destroyer~~ Enricher of Young Lives

The minimum wage during my high school and early college years floated somewhere between $1.15 and $1.30 an hour. Putting in twenty or so hours at the drugstore and twenty or so more at the theater and drive-in netted about fifty bucks a week. That would never fund my lifestyle, college, or a place to live, much less gas and maintenance for a car. Mom and dad had no money to offer. There was a grant or two and a student loan, but funding dreams proved elusive.

Then we found the opium.

Williams Rexall Pharmacy, one of my employers, maintained its primary location in downtown Washington, Indiana. The enjoyable job involved nearly everything. I tackled maintenance, stocking, pricing, cash register duty, and other tasks daily. I even learned how to properly wrap Christmas presents from Becky Newsome, who also worked part time in the store. The single most satisfying part of the job was being a legal drug mule. Most pharmacy customers were elderly shut-ins who could not easily get downtown. As a result, prescribed medications were shuttled to their homes. This freshly licensed driver got paid to drive the store vehicle, an International Harvester Scout, to residences and nursing homes with bags of medication.

Williams occupied a very old building at 2nd and Main with two stories and a rickety wooden elevator, activated by utilizing manually operated ropes and pulleys. The second floor was used for storage of stocked goods before placement on shelves downstairs. One room contained a myriad of pharmaceutical raw ingredients.

Many doctors in town were also increasingly elderly and decidedly old school. A high percentage of prescriptions required pharmacists to mix specific quantities of often-colorful ingredients such as dried, powdered bat wings and such into a pill or liquid form. Mortars and pestles in the pharmacy at Williams were never merely decorative pieces.

A drugstore peer named Morty Ryan was already enrolled at Indiana University in Bloomington. He also worked a few hours a week at the drugstore. One day as we shuttled stock from upstairs onto store shelves below, we happened upon the raw material drug room.

Ice cream shops often display their sweet wares inside glass counters that contain five-gallon buckets of frozen goodness. A bucket just like that was partially hidden in a corner, covered with dust, and squeezed behind some boxes.

"John, you gotta see this!" Morty yelped. The largest letters on the cardboard spelled "opium." Our eyes widened and, in perfect harmony, we both shrieked, "HOLY SHIT!"

The vat was nearly full and had not been used in a very long time.

Morty and I spent the next few days concocting a crude business plan that could put this unused powder to profitable, albeit illegal, use. A plan evolved that seemed brilliant at the time. Young people smoking marijuana in the 1970s needed to purchase a bag, condition the pot by separating seeds and stems, and then roll joints, fill water pipes or concoct other exotic smoke delivery systems. Folks even enjoyed showing off their roach clips. It all seemed crude. The solution to that problem? "What if we sold joints laced with opium, only rolled like regular cigarettes in a pack?"

Pot smokers also felt compelled to take measures that prevented getting caught. Plenty of damp towels at the bottom of doorways, open windows, and elaborate but crude ventilation systems could be observed in many college dormitory rooms. Smoking cigarettes was then perceived as normal, and many young people also enjoyed their Marlboros. Even college professors were known to smoke in class.

The genesis of the idea was to combine the mainstream availability and ease of cigarettes, only with our custom proprietary blend of smokable illegal substances. Neither of us had any idea whether the relatively weak pot of the day laced with powdered pharmaceutical opium would result in any sort of enhanced state of consciousness, but we figured no one would die. If we concocted a way to convey the notion that pre-rolled joints were laced with opium, that marketing message alone might drive up demand and price.

Equipped with a couple of Laredo cigarette rolling machines and as much free time as we could muster, we began experimenting. It was not as easy as it sounds. The blend had to be precise and just the right amount of product was needed. The pot was hand-chopped to mimic tobacco. Our blend was roughly four parts pot, less than one part tobacco (we used a mild cherry blend), and about half part opium. We were also alpha and beta testers of the product. It was difficult to tell whether the opium made any difference, but we actually needed the mild cherry blend to mask the bitterness.

"Smooth," Morty said while nodding his approval.

That literal partner in crime managed to procure several cartons of empty sampler cigarette boxes that held five smokes each. They would normally get distributed as samples with free cigarettes as part of big tobacco marketing efforts. Morty secured a supply big enough to fill the back of the Scout a couple of times. We did not intend to give any product away.

We surreptitiously crafted crude labels using a hijacked school mimeograph machine and Scotch tape. We called it simply "College Blend." The initial price for a box of smokes was $10. It was a huge hit from day one, and demand soon exceeded supply. Word spread. Initial sales were confined to Bloomington, Indiana, but grapevine requests were soon being fielded from Purdue, Notre Dame, and many smaller colleges, even colleges WAY out of state.

Manufacturing the product rapidly became a full-time endeavor. The future looked bright and profitable, and a dent was made in the opium. All the fun lasted less than a year. Although we intended the product to be popular, it all needed to be kept hush-hush no matter what. No trail could ever lead back to us. Demand for, and popularity of, College Blend began messing with our minds. Someone would surely get caught with the product.

Law enforcement, obviously smarter about catching dealers than dealers were about not getting caught, would eventually figure it all out. Pot was pot, but stolen narcotics constituted an entirely different felony class. Potentially dire consequences diverted us from any real cartel-like aspirations.

Before the brief foray into that particular dark side concluded, I managed to pay off my car, all the rent, and finance two years of higher education with no debt. No one got killed or seriously injured, and we may have even provided some enlightenment for youthful minds.

CHAPTER 17

HALLUCINOGENIC BETRAYAL

Uh-oh. A flashback. It's really early in the 1970s, and now appearing at B-movie heaven at the East 50 Drive-In: *The Night of 1,000 Bearded Cartoon Characters*!

Around the time high school began, Dr. Timothy Leary became a vocal proponent of not only world peace and finding an inner self, but ingestion of lysergic acid diethylamide to expand consciousness. His most famous words, "Turn on, tune in, drop out," became lifestyle mapping for rebellious youth of the day. LSD eventually made its way to southern Indiana. Older folks predictably took a scare-the-youth approach, warning of dire consequences involving bad trips. My inclination was simply not to sample it because folks appeared to transform into something oddly disturbing while partaking.

Many days and most evenings during summer months were spent working outside Washington, Indiana at the local drive-in theater. It was a mecca for young families and horny teenagers. The outdoor theater even featured a miniature train that circled the screen structure then tunneled underneath. Little kids loved it and the on-premises playground in front of the large screen. Assigned tasks were plentiful, including painting poles, replacing speakers ripped from painted poles when folks drove off without returning them, rewinding the film, and working in the neon-lit concession stand. Standard fare included continuously popped corn, hot dogs, soda pop, and large boxes of candy.

Customers entered the stand, passed the projection booth, then picked up trays, napkins, plastic cutlery, and straws. Hungry folks inched along a cafeteria-style line to receive goodies. The guy who ran the entire show, Karl Kalvin, sat at the other end manning the cash register. He was an enigma, short in stature, who barely spoke. When he did, it was usually a mumbled whisper. Karl ran both the drive-in and the local downtown movie theater with an iron fist. He knew what he wanted, and his messages were always effectively conveyed.

A concession stand pastime involved guessing how many customers in a row would stretch their necks at odd angles to look at numbers through the glass plate atop the manual cash register used by Karl after he calculated order totals. "At'll be frdrsermsentyfrv cis," he might mumble. Gawking was common.

Karl's grandson Billy operated increasingly antique carbon arc projectors from a booth located off the main entrance to the concession stand. Each movie reel allowed about eighteen minutes of idle time between changes. Projectionists often used that time to refill beverages or grab fresh popcorn. As a young man, the grandson also encountered serious acne issues. Few patrons visited the concession stand while movies rolled. Karl used slow times to occasionally pop zits on Billy's face while seated atop his stool at the cash register.

It was merely an endearing part of that small-town fabric.

I became smitten by a local girl named Darla Klingenfus. Her raven-haired beauty, combined with a large dimple-accentuated smile, big personality, and a body developed far beyond her youth, made such attraction involuntary. She seemed to like me as well. When Darla and any number of her friends made a trek to the drive-in, excuses got concocted for leaving my post inside the concession stand to take care of one thing or another outside.

Love and loads of pollen were in the air one early summer night. My heart was eager but sinuses were clogged. That led to a headache that wouldn't quit. On the first visit to her car, I mentioned the throbbing along with my profound wish for a couple of aspirin. Darla produced a couple of small yellow pills.

"I promise your headache will disappear if you dissolve these under your tongue." She was confident.

"What are these?" I asked. "Um, Anacin, John." It seemed downright heartfelt.

The double-feature that night at the drive-in was *They Call Me Trinity* and *Trinity Is Still My Name*, two spaghetti western comedies that starred Terence Hill. Back inside my post at the concession counter, the relative drudgery of popping corn and filling cups with soda continued uneventfully. Between movies about forty-five minutes later, the patron calorie rush began. I found it odd that every third patron in line or so was a Disney character, either from cartoons or movies. Mickey, Goofy, Donald Duck, Snow White, Jiminy Cricket, even relatively obscure personalities such as Horace Horsecollar made their way through the line and on to Karl with all sorts of delectable snacks in tow.

The transition to genuinely weird began when Uncle Remus bellowed "Uh, hey son, gimme a couple of those hot dogs and a large bucket of freshly popped corn with LOTS a buttah." About twenty minutes remained until feature number two began, and everyone that followed Uncle Remus sported a full beard. Every man, woman, and child, every fellow concession worker, Dwight Mason, Karl, his grandson; EVERYONE was adorned with impressive mats of carefully coiffed facial hair. Even Darla and her friend had beards and giggled excessively through the line.

Even after the second *Trinity* feature rolled, everyone continued sporting beards. Bearded Karl pulled bearded Billy over to the register for additional blackhead grooming. This time when they popped, a spray of rainbows erupted. Just as Darla suggested earlier, I completely forgot about the headache.

It is impossible to remember how the rest of the night went, how I got home, or anything else until the next day. Darla came clean a few days later after school.

"I am soooo sorry if I got you in trouble," she cooed. Her apology was sealed with a kiss that felt sincere.

It was anything but. Telephone conversations in the early 1970s consisted of lying near a corded telephone and chatting away. The second Howard family phone was attached to a wall in the hallway that connected bedrooms. Like most teenagers, I reclined awkwardly on the floor, twirling a cord in my fingers. Darla was on the other end of the line.

A good twenty minutes was spent suggesting we take our friendship to another level.

"I think I am falling in love with you. …

You are already a beautiful woman. … I want to kiss your entire naked body." Voice-cracking, hormone-raging, rapidly-becoming-a-man Johnny was on fire.

Darla did not say much, but courteously allowed me to continue, which I did with reckless abandon. At some point during the twenty-first minute, Moose, the very same large individual who dated Nicky Traylor a few years before, interrupted. His voice was huskier and more menacing. His physical growth spurt was unbridled.

Moose indicated in relatively loud and crude terms that "Just about every fuckin' bone in your scrawny little body will end up broken within one week, you fuckin' idjet, and it'll happen when you least expect it." Darla and a friend giggled in the background. That was my first (but not last) experience with a deceitful member of the opposite sex toying for sport.

Begging for lust quickly shifted to negotiating for my life. Over time, bones remained unbroken. That experience, and many other earlier experiences with females, probably contributed to a mostly cavalier attitude toward them in general. If you fell in love, was laughter supposed to result? There was still much to learn.

CHAPTER 18

500 CHRONIC INTOXICANTS

I got hooked on the Indianapolis 500 in 1959, shortly after turning five. That was the first year I was dragged into the gates for the first weekend of time trials. Racing became my first intoxicant. I begged to go to the race for the next two full years. Finally, in 1961, arrangements were made. Great Uncle Mike was the golf pro at the Speedway course. He arranged tickets for family members as well as police escorts from the home of my grandparents into the track, a protocol that was followed for many years until he retired in 1970.

As a kid in the early 1960s, a red Huffy bicycle became my neighborhood IndyCar. I attached twin checkered flags to the back of the seat, and fastened playing cards to the frame with clothespins. Cards made contact with spokes in the front and back. The faster I pedaled, the louder noise the laminated cards made. My block and the next one became the Speedway oval. My quest for high speed meant ignoring stop signs and many pedestrians. An average run lasted four laps, just like qualifying at Indy.

Legendary track announcer Tom Carnegie proclaimed new track records loudly inside my head every time I ran.

The year 1964 began a golden age. Reliance on burly front-engine racing machines gave way to European influenced formula cars with engines behind drivers. Speeds rose quickly, and innovative designs were encouraged. It was the final year a "traditional" front-engine IndyCar won.

Dad and I were perched inside the second turn during the early laps. Suddenly, a large, black mushroom cloud appeared on the opposite end of the track in the fourth turn. It was surreal, particularly after the smells drifted past. Dad attempted to stand atop a folding wooden camping stool with a canvas seat for a better view. The canvas ripped open, and Dad tumbled to the ground with a stream of cursing brand new to my young ears. Ten-year-old Johnny learned that Jesus Christ's middle name was Fucking, but was corrected a few weeks later by mom. She made me take a hearty bite of soap after I invoked all three names as loudly as dad did after I crashed my bike.

Sadly, two drivers lost their lives in the accident, including one of the most popular in the sport. They called Eddie Sachs the clown prince of auto racing. Dave MacDonald was a talented and fearless rookie. That moment crystallized a realization that participants play for keeps at Indy.

No tickets were available through the family in 1966, but I needed to be there anyway. The creative solution was signing up to sell the Indianapolis Star in the stands. I was already a neighborhood carrier of the paper, so I had dibs. My spot when the green flag waved was close up at the end of the main straightaway.

An illusion of selling newspapers was merely an excuse for admittance. Mom and Dad, who scored tickets, were seated high above in the Paddock Penthouse. A massive pileup erupted on the first lap right in front of where I stood in box seats along the wall. Car parts, fuel, tires, and other debris whizzed past our exposed heads. The legendary A. J. Foyt climbed over the fence less than ten feet from my spot to escape the carnage. Mom's thought, not really knowing where I stood, was that I had certainly been killed. At our designated meeting area following the race, she hugged me as if I had gone missing for years. Dad lamented her extreme nervousness that prevented enjoyment of the race.

"Your mom was a nervous wreck for five hours, Johnny. Next time find us so we know you're OK."

The early 1970s were my final years of high school. The one place in which most teenagers could be found was the infamous former snake pit inside turn one. These days it has been relocated to the opposite end of the track and is now driven by corporate sponsorship. It is nothing like its predecessor. The original snake pit was a hedonistic den of sin where anything went. Underage drinking, drug use, fights, sex in the open, furniture or vehicles on fire, and worse constituted normal activity. Extreme behavior was the norm, but cops generally looked the other way unless serious injuries began occurring. These days, ecstasy and EDM accompanies sweat. It even has a logo. I stay as far away as possible.

A frequent fence-side visitor to the original was the late actor James Garner, a huge fan who found time every year to share fried chicken and a beer or two with locals. The crude phrase "show us your tits" originated in the snake pit. We usually observed more breasts in a day than plastic surgeons see in a year. Celebrities are paraded each May, but many prefer anonymity. They are there because they are also addicted. David Letterman co-owns a racing team. The late Paul Newman kindled interest in auto racing while filming the movie *Winning* there in the late 1960s and later became a successful team owner. Even George Harrison was known to show up incognito.

The year 1973 was the most challenging time many racing fans have ever endured. The weather was horrible all month. It took parts of three days to run the race, which concluded midweek after just 332 miles. Anticipation was high for breaking the 200-mile-per-hour barrier. Drivers came up just short. Still, the 1973 race has often been thought of as cursed. Drivers and crew members suffered multiple injuries and fatalities. It was gruesome—the only time loyalty and enthusiasm for the sport was questioned.

Ernest Hemingway was credited with saying there are only three real sports: bullfighting, mountain climbing, and auto racing. In each of the three, one wrong split-second decision can result in immediate death. That is not what attracts addicted fans. We are far more interested in seeing death or serious injury *cheated*, all while witnessing the envelope that involves staying alive being stretched as far as it will possibly go.

My span of Mays includes seeing most major speed milestones fall, from 150 to the current record of just over 236. The track, constructed in 1909, was designed for maximum speeds of around eighty.

The 500-mile race celebrated its 100th running in 2016. At that point, I had attended more than half ever run.

I relinquished paying jobs on more than one occasion simply to be there every day the track was open in May.

The stadium itself has aged into a mystical shrine. It is one of a very few places on earth in which spirits of history touch senses once inside. Entry begins through a tunnel, which is the only way in or out by car or foot. The town of Speedway and the city of Indianapolis have grown up around it over almost twelve decades. The race track is the biggest physical stadium in the world. It hosts the largest single-day sporting event crowd of more than 300,000 people. Any attempt to describe size is inadequate except for those who have seen it. The Indianapolis 500 set the template for how most other auto racing and many other sports are presented. Once it begins, every single sense is assaulted.

Sportscaster Jim Lampley, best known today for excellent boxing coverage, once hosted the big race on ABC. His words about the start of the race still resonate. "The Indianapolis 500 does not start. It explodes." The hour that precedes the start is filled with pageantry. Veterans and current military personnel are honored. By the time *Back Home Again in Indiana* is sung, grown men are reduced to tears. From 1972 through 2014, the Hoosier anthem was rendered in most years by Jim Nabors, known best as TV's Gomer Pyle.

The race itself produces complete surprises nearly every year, and scripts are never identical. The track and its most famous event remain the most intoxicating legal, expensive addiction ever voluntarily consumed. There is no cure.

Part III: ROCK & ROLL!

CHAPTER 19

CAREER INSPIRATION LIGHT BULB

Every aspiring star has a moment of absolute clarity along the way. Mine occurred halfway through high school. Priorities up until then included attempting to lose my virginity, staying enrolled at Washington Catholic while simultaneously terrorizing it, and earning enough money to both pay for education AND own a car. All were hit-or-miss prospects.

People I like rarely conform to societal norms. Eccentrics and outright oddballs are among those I remember the most. The first person who served as an unselfish mentor was a few years older, already out of school, and working professionally in radio. Dennis Daily was a Washington resident who lived in the home of his parents and worked at WAOV Radio on the banks of the Wabash River in Vincennes, Indiana. He commuted driving a decidedly red AMC Gremlin.

The intricate mind of Dennis continuously shifted direction, and all were fascinating. If you were able to keep up, he liked (or at least tolerated) you. Twists and turns of the journey were wildly enjoyable.

Among things I found odd but cool were his diet and technical obsessions, but mostly his work at WAOV.

He explained the station's history to whoever listened: "WAOV's call letters were said to have been inspired by the 1900 best-selling novel *Alice of Old Vincennes*, written by Maurice Thompson and set in that locale during the American Revolutionary War. In reality," Dennis claimed with laughter, "they stood for "Water All Over Vincennes" after the Great Flood of 1913 nearly wiped out the town."

His diet was relatively simple. Dennis ate when he felt like it and usually featured just a couple of regular staples. He regularly opened small tins of tuna, then sort of smashed it into a paste before loading a slice of white bread with it and sprinkling additional salt. Pan-fried, salted hamburgers, also served plain on white bread, were always great too. "Got any pickles and mustard, Dennis?" Dennis feigned shock. "Are you CRAZY?!"

Using a telephone in the early 1970s was challenging. Local service came from the Bell system, a monopoly controlled by AT&T. That was about the only choice. AT&T was forcefully broken into pieces called Baby Bells in 1982. Even now, most widely recognized communications companies can trace lineage back to that monopoly. Verizon, for example, was once Bell Atlantic, a Baby Bell spun from AT&T.

A typical monthly bill included rental of corded telephone equipment (devices could not yet be owned and were definitely not mobile) and monthly service. Long-distance calling carried per-minute charges, and pricing varied depending on where calls were going.

Many people still had party lines, shared with snooping neighbors.

Dennis converted the basement of his family home into a newsroom and fully functional broadcast studio, complete with an ability to go on the air if he ever chose to do so. Instant communication was either controlled by AT&T wires, or by broadcasters whose radio and television stations broadcast over the air. News outlets spent a small fortune wiring stations for multiple telephone lines to operate essential equipment such as teletype machines.

Most stations could afford only one content provider for news sourcing, either the Associated Press (AP) or United Press International (UPI). Really big stations used both. Teletype machines delivered news to stations, who provided it to their consumers. Rhythmic clattering was constant in all newsrooms. When these noisy boxes fell silent, verifying whether mechanical problems existed was common.

If bells began ringing, the content was designated as urgent. The more bells rang, the more urgent the story. Richard Nixon resigning or tornadoes on the ground sounded five (the highest number) bells. The broadcasting term "rip and read" refers to ripping a freshly sent story "hot off the wire," then immediately reading its content cold on the air.

Considering the expense and effort it took for even federally licensed broadcasters to successfully operate teletype machines, my jaw dropped the first time I visited the Daily basement while observing both AP and UPI happily churning out news 24/7. "How the heck is this even possible!?" I repeatedly asked. Dennis even figured out a way to re-use the other side of paper fed through the machines. "You HAVE to tell me how you did this." All Dennis ever did was wink.

"And how is it possible to get two feeds into those machines? It's just not possible." The usually chatty Dennis remained steadfastly ambiguous in a nodding way. It is not difficult to suspect Ma Bell, not to mention the federal government, might have taken issue with such a fully operational but completely unlicensed facility.

Dennis worked nights and weekends at WAOV, which was located in really old studios inside an even older building in downtown Vincennes. None of that mattered to me. It had multiple studios and what seemed like a large main studio complete with a lot of soundproof glass, a knob-riddled control board, turntables, tape machines, speakers, and a very imposing hanging microphone.

An intended career path took shape, although I needed to avoid electrocution first. Dennis nearly accomplished that while tinkering away on the WAOV transmitter with a large screwdriver one night. We were the only warm bodies in the station, and he was motionless on the floor. *If I touch him, will I get electrocuted? Is he alive? Who do I call?* Eventually I poked him with a yardstick, and he popped back up with renewed enthusiasm as if nothing happened.

I remained all in except for transmitter maintenance. My entire career path was formed and accelerated based on six months of tagalongs at that small local radio station.

Whenever I had a night off from my real jobs, I latched onto Dennis and began a voluntary, unauthorized internship. He did it all. Tunes from middle-of-the-road musical stalwarts such as Bert Kaempfert and Woody Herman were spun straight from their albums. The New Seekers was about as risqué as the music ever got. He read the news. "Hey Dennis, can I write a story?" He encouraged it, and occasionally read one or two of them. Time and temperature were carefully annunciated. Network programming was joined. I was a sponge.

"Hey Dennis, can I run the board later tonight?" Again, with perhaps some trepidation, he nodded yes. My first few attempts with the knobs, called "pots," or cueing up records featured Parkinson's-like trembling.

Between stooging at WAOV and eventually the hands-on learning approach that VU espoused, my interest in actually doing well at school spiked dramatically. C's became B's, and B's eventually became all A's.

In April of 1973, Dennis asked a random question. "How would you like to head for Washington, DC for the National Association of Broadcasters convention, then up to New York for a day at CBS?" It happened suddenly. "Say WHAT?!" There was barely enough time to pack, much less inform employers or professors. Other than occasional family vacations to Florida, Missouri, or states that neighbored Indiana, an adventure of this sort was unimaginable.

First-time attendance in 1973 of the largest trade show in the business as a young college student inspired wonderment. Seeing the latest technology on display in one place much like room arrangements at an IKEA store overloaded senses. It represented just about everything that would be possible for years to follow.

Dennis chatted up vendors in conversations about their gizmos and how everything worked. I listened and collected bags of swag. One particular piece was a cricket clicker toy, which was a thin piece of metal inside a logo'd plastic case that made noise. Perfect, we thought, for our planned visit to the Smithsonian Museum of American History. A giant Foucault pendulum was displayed inside. Every twenty minutes or so, while demonstrating the gravitational forces of earth, a peg got knocked over by the pendulum. We arrived about five minutes after the previous peg toppled. As the next peg fell, we approved enthusiastically, both using our clickers repeatedly. That failed to enamor us to the staff. "You need to leave now, gentlemen," one of three uniformed docents demanded, pointing to an exit door.

Dennis cultivated broadcasting contacts all over the world. Before leaving D.C., one such friend gave us a private tour of the old Executive Office building, including hidden passageways and several legislative offices. "This is the room where President Nixon gives all his news conferences, and there is one scheduled for later today." Watergate and the Vietnam War were taking a serious toll on Tricky Dick, and our visit to that room was cut short. "Can we stay and watch?" Laughter was the response.

From there it was on to Manhattan.

Three events stood out. Some of his contacts worked at CBS, so Black Rock is where Dennis and I spent the day. The building was filled with studios, and the first one we entered featured a sportscast being recorded for the CBS Radio Network by the late Andy Musser. Instead of merely glancing at us, he asked "Where you boys from?" What brings you two to the big city?" *This is amazing*, as I pinched myself again. Being inside CBS seemed just a little more significant than being inside WAOV.

Dennis also knew the chief meteorologist and primary on-air

weather anchor at WCBS Television, Gordon Barnes. Dennis and Barnes exchanged hugs, and he shook my hand. I knew him from TV. He was on with Walter Cronkite once in a while.

"John, Gordon here is part of the CBS Apollo Mission Television Team, and lets them know if the weather is safe to launch."

"It's no big deal," Gordon protested.

"Gordon also introduced the importance of the jet stream to weather," Dennis continued, "and we know what wind chill factor is in Indiana. Gordon came up with that concept too."

This is just not real. It's not happening. I was in New York for the first time, and in a complete stupor.

Gordon invited us in to the WCBS-TV news studio while he prepared his weather graphics for the evening newscast. "Come on in, you two. This takes me about an hour and it's kind of boring, but pull up a chair." Greenscreens were not yet ubiquitous. Maps and graphics had to be assembled manually every day. Gordon was not allowed to touch graphic components, and could merely point to them during on-air segments.

"We're all union in here, and every different union has its own guidelines," he explained." Tony here puts the numbers and the arrows and the cold fronts onto the map, then takes it all down after the newscast. My job is the easy one. All I have to do is point and talk."

On that particular day, there were entirely too many 5s in the forecast. Temperatures would reach 55, neighboring tri-state areas would also be 55, barometric pressures contained numerous 5s, and so on. WCBS quickly ran out of 5s to place onto maps.

"There is a requisition process to acquire additional 5s," said Tony, the union member.

Gordon looked at Tony and suggested, "Could you go take a peek down in the shop? We must have more 5s down there. It's worth a look, and I'd appreciate it."

While Tony was gone, Gordon made unauthorized substitutions.

"Dennis, John, the revised high temperature is suddenly going to hit 56. And we don't need this many 5s in the barometric pressure."

The newscast and weather portion of it went off without a hitch with Dennis and me looking on from the distant darkness in a corner of the studio. We never found out what sort of trouble ensued over union contract-violating number substitutions.

From WCBS studios, it was back to the CBS Radio Network, and the studio of *The World Tonight* with Douglas Edwards. *Oh my God, this guy is a legend!*

Dennis ran through the history with me on the way in. "Douglas Edwards was the anchor of the very first evening news broadcast on a then brand-new CBS Television Network in 1948. It was a position he held until 1962 when he was replaced on the air by a young reporter named Walter Cronkite."

There were two small rooms. The one from which we observed contained a producer furiously typing away, on a typewriter, neatly double-spaced news that Edwards would deliver. Another technical person sat behind him, splicing leader tape between news actualities for cueing purposes during the newscast. When the producer changed the story order, actualities also had to be changed. The fact they were staggered between two reel-to-reel tape machines complicated matters a bit. A sound technician stood ready at the audio control board, and a director prepared to bring it all to air. None of them were chatty, but insisted "Just have a seat and watch us pull off some magic again tonight."

The other room was a small studio where another producer received freshly typewritten copy through a slit in the glass wall. Text was reviewed and passed along to Edwards. The producer also provided cues for actualities and breaks. Adorning walls in every room anywhere at CBS were identical Swiss Favag clocks, all meticulously synchronized. At precisely 6:00 pm, the CBS Radio Network went live nationwide no matter what. We arrived at twenty-four minutes to six. Everything and everyone were in place. Except Douglas Edwards.

About fifteen minutes before air, the director loudly looked up and asked, "Anybody seen Doug?"

No one had.

"Stu, go check his office really quick. He's not answering."

Stu, out of breath a couple of minutes later, reported, "No sign of Doug in the building."

Favags clicked away a second at a time. Eight minutes to go. No Doug. Panic boiled over. Potential replacement anchors were considered.

My mind exploded. *This is the biggest break I would ever have in my entire life. Raise your hand and volunteer.* I came to my senses, figuring I was lucky enough to just be standing there and wanted to continue doing so. I started nudging Dennis, whispering, "Go for it." He brushed me aside, mouthing "NO!" He would have done a much better job anyway. Dennis eventually became a national anchor for United Press International. The director confirmed the in-studio producer would be the emergency backup.

Nearly full-blown panic expanded as Favags passed the two minutes to go mark. Douglas Edwards casually strolled into the studio with hangars of freshly bagged dry cleaning slung over his shoulder. With only a minute and a half to spare, and the director was frazzled. "Where the hell have you been!?" Edwards, calm as could be, explained, "I had to get my suits from the cleaners before they closed," glancing at his watch. It stopped working at 5:20 pm. Twenty-five seconds remained until he went live nationwide on CBS, and Doug not only was still unseated, but couldn't believe his watch stopped working.

Three pages of copy were completed and passed through the glass. At precisely 6:00 pm, Douglas Edwards began reading copy out of the electronic sounding CBS intro absolutely cold with no preparation. He was flawless. The calm in his studio contrasted with mayhem in our room. Furious typing of copy resulted, literally, in pages being ripped from the typewriter and passed through the glass with only seconds to spare. If there had been no taped actualities or commercial breaks, Edwards may well have had to ad-lib a newscast. We wondered whether it was like that every day.

Fifteen minutes passed quickly. Edwards, still as calm and professional as ever, thanked everyone for their work and invited his guests into the studio. He walked up to both of us, and said, "Thanks for coming in today." Dennis asked if it was like that every day, and Edwards smiled. "More than you might imagine." He picked up his laundry, and pointed at his arm. "I need to go buy a new watch now."

We didn't say much on the way back to Indiana. I couldn't. My brain was in overload mode. *These adventures are too far-fetched to adequately explain to ANYONE.* Mostly all business Skip Sparkman, my mentoring professor, was not happy.

"Son, you missed exams, casually disregarded rules, and you are in big trouble."

Skip offered an out: "Getting yourself out of this means you'll give a formal presentation to the entire broadcasting student group about your activities away from school."

That effort, in conjunction with handing out free swag and taking tests at a time convenient to Skip, alleviated the jam. We both figured that when opportunity knocked, doors should be answered. I prefer believing he may even have been proud of the initiative.

Sparkman and I had an interesting relationship. He believed I had potential. He awarded an A for a film project that could have gotten me expelled. Students were required to produce and direct a three-minute movie that had a plot, told a story, and elicited emotion. Shooting required a 16mm camera from school. I chose black and white to give it the feel of a silent movie. A borrowed idea from high school instructor Standley Falk centered on a sexual tryst between a highly experienced woman and an older, nervous virgin male. It was called *The Rookie and the Veteran* and starred my college girlfriend Shelly along with one of the folks from class, Jim Hayes. There was no nudity per se, but several shots left little to the imagination.

What began as a pathetic depiction of a shy virgin with knocking knees by Jim ended with him as a swaggering, self-confident stud that ravaged Shelly into a disheveled mess. How many students get A's for producing softcore implied pornography? I did. Unfortunately, that particular loop of nitrate is fully decomposed.

Dennis Daily and Skip Sparkman gave me the boosts I needed to start a career.

CHAPTER 20

FRESHLY HATCHED RADIO MAVEN

Two life choices existed in the spring of 1974. I could endure two more years of college at Indiana University and earn a Bachelor of Arts degree, or attempt a grab at stardom. Spotlights beckoned. Self-confidence brimmed because I was armed with both a hot-off-the-press associate's degree in science AND an FCC 3rd Class Radiotelephone License (with Broadcast Endorsement). It was obvious to me (and only me) that I was smarter, more prepared, and talented than just about anyone then working in that business. Money was also scarce, since I had spent the proceeds of my amateur drug dealership to fund academic and motorized exploits, and wooing sweethearts.

Becoming the first in my class to arrange a full-fledged, full-time job after graduation was a deep source of pride. My professional career was about to begin at WCVL, a daytime AM station at 1550 on the dial (all the way to the right) in Crawfordsville, Indiana. The specific employment position was ambiguous. Station ownership launched a brand-new FM station, WLFQ, and they needed a newsman.

They also required someone to be on the air and run the board on WCVL, but only during hours when the signal was nondirectional. For directional hours, I would need the FCC 1st Class Radiotelephone License. They assigned me an on-air name, Jeff Tyler, primarily because their jingle package already contained that recorded name.

Two people managed the stations. Both were highly seasoned radio veterans Rich Hawk and John Payne. They, along with a highly effective ad sales team, turned WCVL into a small-market cash cow. I was paid over $85 every week!

I attempted almost every job at the station over the next few months. Tasks even included constructing program logs, preparing invoices and answering phones. I willingly spent more time at the station than at home. Only showers and sleepovers with Shelly diverted my attention. Still, my first foray into professional life proved challenging because I fancied myself smarter and more talented than anyone around me and was concerned more about the bells and whistles of the business instead of actually doing work.

My primary job was supposed to be newsgathering. That meant drudgery like attending city council meetings in small towns, which I usually shunned. If an event featured important politicians, I might show up to ask the snarkiest questions imaginable. Three months into the gig, boss Rich Hawk, an imposingly large man who stood 6' 5" and backed it up with bulk, grabbed me by the neck and pushed me into a soundproof production studio barely big enough for one normal-sized person. He took that action after I told him I would be unable to cover the quarterly meeting of the county sanitation board that evening.

Rich spent the next ten minutes in high decibel mode.

"When I hired you, I thought you had a work ethic. If you are a newsman, you need to cover the damned news!"

He twisted the knife.

"This is your first job in radio. You may believe you have talent, but you have only hope. You are a pissant who I felt sorry for."

Finally: "Your act had better improve by 100 percent TODAY, or you are out on your ass."

Subsequent attendance at several small-town meetings, grand openings, high school events, and all sorts of other fabric-of-middle-America soirees failed to generate the results Rich desired. I was fired from my very first real job. The gig lasted barely half the year.

Sufficiently humbled and devoid of income, I moved out of a new apartment after the six-month lease expired. I leased replacement lodging for half the price in a second-floor apartment of an old home in town. A mild stroke of luck occurred over a beer with a stranger in a pub, who was also in radio.

"I am leaving my gig at WXUS, man."

WXUS-FM was licensed to operate in Lafayette. It was a loosely formatted, mostly top 40 station. As a matter of fact, this largely emotionless drinking buddy, Dave Clark, informed management he was leaving in one week that very day. He gave me contact information and an address, followed by a suggestion that if I wanted the gig, being first in line might be advisable.

"It's a little weird," Dave cautioned, but was vague on specifics.

I was in the car and headed out to the country the next morning, armed with an audition tape and freshly typed resumes. The striped tie was probably overkill, but first impressions counted. Dan and Corrine Stenson, a young married couple who ran and owned the station, were older than me, but not by much. I found it impressive they actually owned a radio station. I must have made a positive impression because I was hired within two days. There was even a chance to spend the next few days being mentored in their operations by the guy I would replace. Dave painted an even-less-glamorous picture of the station while mostly sober.

Undaunted and forging ahead, I sought silver linings. A WXUS paycheck equaled what I made at WCVL, but my euphoria was short-lived. The station was located in a remote rural area atop a slight hill in the middle of an active cattle farm. The transmitter and the on-air studio were located in a two-room shack that once served as a lighting and communications facility along the approach path for a decommissioned airport runway in nearby West Lafayette.

Next door to the small greenish cinder block structure sat an insufficiently anchored mobile home that housed the only non-on-air employee. Barbara Moore was an affable young lady who sat in the front and took care of reception, program logs, wrote the copy, reconciled commercials, and finagled subsequent billing, as well as all of the accounting necessary to operate. She also occasionally did commercial production. The trailer featured two bedrooms, one in the middle and one in the rear. Between them was the lone bathroom for miles. The middle bedroom was converted into a private office for Dan and Corrine. They were rarely there. The back bedroom became a production studio. Veneered wood-look paneling did not make for great acoustics, so egg cartons were glued to the walls to enhance audio ambiance.

In my brief educational and professional careers, I had already been to WAOV and CBS and worked at WCVL. All three were equipped with relatively modern, impressive-looking equipment that worked most of the time. WXUS had what appeared to be a control board constructed of remnants from a strange concoction of Radio Shack parts, along with pieces of actual control boards that became obsolete. Two turntables were antiques, as was an old Ampex reel-to-reel machine and a couple of tape cartridge decks.

The studio was more photo booth than creative space, but it had an operable door and window. A slanted piece of double-paned glass separated the control room from the transmitter room. The tower stood just outside. An old transmitter was gently used, and it was Dan's pride and joy. He also served as chief engineer and usually interacted with staff only when he needed to replace something while folks were on the air. Because the transmitter required relatively cool air with a stable temperature, its room was the only one of the two that was air-conditioned. Two used window units were installed: one to actually run, and one used as a backup when the other one needed repair.

WXUS hired me in the late fall of 1974. Although days had begun their fall cooldown, the ramshackle equipment inside the studio could generate often-stifling heat within its confined, non-air-conditioned space. As a result, on all but the most frigid days, the door and window remained wide open. The only pieces of equipment in the studio purchased were two very large speakers mounted on the wall. Crystal clear sound was delivered through them and helped those of us on the air entertain ourselves. Because the station was very rural, speakers got cranked up loudly and never disturbed anyone except Barbara in the trailer once in a while.

Loud music consistently drew the attention grazing cows just outside an electric fence that ringed the station. Whenever the control room microphone was activated, speakers automatically muted until the microphone got switched off. Almost every time folks on the air said anything, their eloquence was usually accompanied by loudly mooing cows, likely concerned about where their music had gone. It was funny for a time but between mooing, decrepit equipment, and broadcasting from a glorified broom closet, my career choice often led to personal, skeptical introspection.

WXUS employed three on-air folks, four if you count a strange, smelly overweight guy who ran the board for taped programming. I worked middays, a fellow named Dan Scott did afternoons and a third, Russ Wayne, pulled down nights. From midnight to 10 am and for much of the weekend, the station broadcast taped religious programming. "I follow God onto the airwaves," I proudly proclaimed. The station was once all religion, which explained the call letters WXUS. The stylized "XUS" in the logo was not subtle in reminding the flock that Christ died for us.

The staff and handfuls of potential listeners mostly derided it as W-SUX.

The first order of business every day involved spraying Lysol all over the control room to ease the stench of the odd board operator who squatted there all night. Once the smell was somewhat alleviated, in wafted the fragrance of freshly plopped cow manure. We spent an inordinate amount of disposable income purchasing Lysol before germaphobia went mainstream.

There was no program director unless you count Dan or Corrine asking you not to play a certain song anymore. I used WLS in

Chicago as my guide for a playlist. Much of what they played also got played on WXUS after I purchased 45 RPM records from favored retailers. I usually kept my stash in a cooler so they would not warp in the heat. The other two guys brought their own music as well, and the sound got progressively edgier as the day progressed. It was the early days of FM and anything was possible.

The fun did not stop in the studio. Another component of a radio personality job involved producing commercials when not on the air so that paychecks continued. A production studio is a lot like an on-air studio. Although the trailer was newer and more spacious than the lighting tower, the WXUS production studio offered its own set of challenges. A noisy used window air conditioner had to be switched off while voicing spots. It rarely sounded good while buzzing in the background.

The worst aspect of production tended to involve background music played while voicing commercials. The music originated from one of two turntables. It was uneventful unless anyone entered, exited, or walked around in any part of the trailer. That type of movement caused turntable arms to jump around on records. Hearing a toilet flush while on mic through the paper-thin wall that separated production magic from the bathroom was also regularly amusing.

Adult common sense still had not become a part of my DNA, and eight months into the gig, Dan and Corrine held an all-hands-on-deck meeting in the trailer. Sensing trouble, I made sure plenty of current audition tapes and updated resumes were squirreled away.

The meeting turned out to be a critical, tough love assessment of the on-air sound, an indictment of folks on the air, and an overall lack of team spirit.

Following the group session, the young owners spoke to everyone individually to berate some more. About halfway through their diatribe with me, what little sense and patience I possessed expired.

"How fucking inept and brutally unappreciative can two people possibly be!?" I shouted, rising to my feet. Then, I urged them to "take your little hobby, trailer, egg cartons, cows, religious programming (and anything else that popped into my head at that moment) and shove it ALL right up your asses! I am OUTTA here."

While driving down country roads on the way home, I had a stark realization that maybe having another gig lined up first would have been a smarter play.

As part of the transition into adult life, a concept of debt became palpable. One short-term friend I met while in Lafayette was Will Tieman, then an aspiring sports broadcaster on the local television station. He later achieved amazing notoriety as the voice of Michigan State University sports. For reasons never totally understood, I convinced him to cosign a loan for the first new car I ever purchased. It was needed to replace the lemon I was attempting to drive. The brand new 1975 Ford Mustang II had a sticker price of just under $3,600. Not wanting to let him down, I embarked on an all-consuming mission to find a new job.

Sniffs were had from Indiana stations in Wabash and Kokomo. Neither seemed capable of pointing toward the big time, so making a decision stalled.

Just as my wallet completely emptied, a call arrived from an old-line station I considered a wish-list destination. WBOW at 1230 on the AM dial in Terre Haute, Indiana was interested in putting me on from 7 p.m. to midnight. It was the number-one station in town and they wanted me. I made a beeline for Terre Haute, and my career felt back on track.

The young lady who became my first spouse also began dating me. Life seemed good.

CHAPTER 21

GROUPIES 101

A significant part of any real or imagined rock-star lifestyle, especially for young rock 'n' rollers brutally obsessed with sex, involved groupies. These young ladies were usually devoid of self-esteem and nearly always possessed emotional or other issues. Rational people always steered clear. I was always horny, but rarely rational.

The very first groupie experience of my life occurred while entertaining grazing cows at WXUS and very few others. Night guy Russ Wayne and I became fast friends. He consummated an ongoing flirtation with an attractive young blonde named Lorna Kiley. Russ appeared at the station while I was on the air one day with Lorna and her friend Kerry Miller. Kerry was beautiful—a porcelain-skinned redhead with a few freckles and adorable dimples in her cheeks. She was somewhat shy but very engaging. Kerry smiled brightly without saying much.

Russ enjoyed kissing and telling. I had a feeling this whole groupie thing might just be incredible at some point down the road. By the time his air shift ended that same night, I was already sound asleep in my apartment. The wall phone rang about 11:30. Russ was enthusiastic.

"Get up, get dressed and I will pick you up in forty-five minutes. You are about to get a really nice surprise."

My curiosity centered on what type of surprise he had in mind.

"Kerry wants you bad, dude."

Oh. OOHHH!

A quick shower, fresh laundry, and the stroke of midnight elevated my sudden anticipation.

Russ, Lorna, and Kerry arrived at 12:15, and off we zoomed to Lorna's two-bedroom apartment shared most of the time with Kerry. I made myself at home on the couch, and Kerry sidled up right next to me as if we had been a romantic couple for years. The small talk gave way to Wayne and Lorna excusing themselves to a bedroom. Barely two minutes passed before smooching began. Four minutes in, Kerry seemed downright ravenous as she initiated dramatic activities. I badly wanted to see whether she had freckles elsewhere on her body. As awkward, futile attempts to remove clothing failed, she suggested, "Let's go to the bedroom." Inside, the most prominent feature was a waterbed. Those 1970s relics were never ideal for sleeping, but consistently enhanced pleasures of the flesh.

Raw, unbridled passion of primitive nature took control over the next hour or so. It was the most fun I had ever experienced in my burgeoning carnal life up to that point. Kerry was the polar opposite of my steady Shelly in terms of passionate aggressiveness. I admired Kerry's efforts to the point of sheer helplessness. Our coital timing was impeccable, mutual, and intense. Thinking ahead about gas and electric stoves, I figured it was cuddle time in preparation for another round of the same sort of over-the-top pleasure.

Kerry, however, suddenly began crying. Crying gave way to uncontrollable sobbing. I was confused and attempted compassion.

"What is wrong?" I pleaded.

All sorts of thoughts crossed my mind. *Was she really on the pill? Did she have a boyfriend or husband? Was she not of age? Had she just relived some sort of trauma?*

"Why don't you get dressed and get some sleep at home," Kerry suggested.

Smiling Russ and I soon left. He had no idea why she broke down either, but concluded, based on noises made, that I had "boned her into another dimension, dude."

The entire process inexplicably repeated itself for five or six nights over the next two weeks. Each time, intense passion preceded uncontrollable sobbing that brought evenings to abrupt halts with never a hint as to why. I was determined to get to the bottom of it, not only because it seemed urgent, but also because I was becoming smitten and enjoyed being around her outside of bed as well. She even met my parents, who visited one weekend.

"We need to talk," I told Kerry after a few weeks had passed.

The invitation to my apartment included dinner but had to include serious discussion. She arrived and we shared my attempt at meal preparation along with a little wine. The main question, asked directly, was, "Why does the best, most mutually pleasurable passion imaginable always end with you in tears? What is wrong?"

Kerry apologized profusely. "We should take a long, hot bath and discuss it all there." The old apartment contained an oversized antique claw foot bathtub and I just happened to have some bubbles. MISTER Bubbles. Only the best. It was hotly romantic. The only thing she actually said inside the tub was "I'm afraid." Of what remained elusive. She failed to yield ANY clues.

Following the bath and while still damp, Kerry proceeded to instigate the most passionate intimacy we had yet experienced. Perhaps this special sort of schizophrenia would finally end. It did not. Kerry was reduced to the exact same basket case of tears afterward. Then she was gone, as in for good and without any trace, forever.

Russ remained busy horn-dogging beyond Lorna, and neither of them knew much. Lorna implied some sort of vague family dysfunction, and that the entire clan just packed up and relocated to South Carolina without even goodbyes. One of the enduring mysteries of my life still remains the question of why. It would be nice to understand. Perhaps she knew her imminent departure would end a promising relationship.

Having hit a groupie grand slam, sort of, the first time at bat and despite heavy emotional baggage, my warped mind figured all who followed might turn out as good or better. As previously indicated, WXUS had an audience in which bovine listenership in the field next door mostly exceeded the number of human beings tuned in at any given moment. One of the scarce but evidently most loyal listeners called everyone on the air all day long. Her name was Awanita, a Native American moniker of Cherokee origin that meant "fawn." Awanita preferred being called Anita.

At various points during almost every day, Anita called to chat, and I never gave it much thought. The spinning of vinyl and determining what would be enunciated next took priority. The hygiene-challenged overnight guy who board-operated mostly thirty- or sixty-minute taped religious programming took a week-long vacation. Dan and Corrine asked everyone else to take turns double shifting one to two days to cover. "Something extra will be included with your next paycheck." Ka-ching. The something extra turned out to be station trade at a nice steakhouse. It was the thought that counted.

The biggest challenge about working all night at a radio station in the middle of nowhere, changing a reel of tape every half hour or so, is staying awake. Attempts to do so allowed for more in-depth telephone conversation with Anita, as in for hours all night long. One tenet that remained elusive until later, but perhaps the most important unwritten rule about groupies, is that the degree of sexiness in the voice of a caller is inversely proportional to their appearance and state of mind. Anita had one of the silkiest, smooth, cooing, sexy voices I have ever heard. Sweet nothings whispered through Ma Bell's equipment were downright scintillating.

As hours of praising the Almighty droned in the background, her full story emerged.

"I have Cherokee blood."

"I am thirty-one years old and very blessed with dark hair and large brown eyes."

"I am not too tall at about 5 ½ feet."

"I have really had some struggles."

Predictably, the conversation turned sexual and included lurid descriptions about what she needed to do to me. Her articulation of such potential pleasures, with graphic, explicit detail, even included a little moaning along the way as she described ways in which she was already pleasuring herself.

Anita also revealed she was in the late stages of a futile battle with a form of cancer that began in her liver and spread. All she wanted before checking out was a little more passion. I was as naïve at that age about the ravages of cancer and its often-draconian treatment as I was about groupies who did nothing except call radio stations most hours of every day. My mind concocted a romantic image of a slightly dark-skinned Pocahontas, complete with ponytail and tight-fitting leather attire, desperate to leave the planet fulfilled.

Based upon telephone skills that would shame phone sex operators, I figured this benevolent mission could be accomplished the next day after I got off work. She gave me her address, and then informed me, "I won't be hard to spot in my favorite skimpy light pink negligee." Anticipation remained high for the following eight hours.

I was wholly unprepared for our eventual meeting. When the front door opened, multiple senses were assaulted. A smell best described as a combination of badly run nursing home and astringent chemicals wafted out. Then her appearance became evident. She was disheveled, sort of a greenish color, very large and devoid of entire patches of hair. Some of her teeth turned black. The pink negligee made her appear to be a giant out-of-date Peep that developed mold. The compassionate side of me would have definitely wanted to stay and offer comfort, but such inner compassion had not yet ripened.

My next move was simply turning around and running away. A

glass bottle nearly full of Pepsi-Cola clutched in her hand suddenly became a missile. It winged me on the shoulder.

"Come back here, you cowardly bastard!"

I was nearly inside my failing Chevy Nova when gunshots rang out. It was the second time in my life spent ducking live rounds for perceived sexual impropriety. No actual sex even occurred in either case.

Anita's aim was not great, but she managed to put a hole and a slug into the rear wheel well. Charges were not pressed, and the station's studio lines remained unanswered until Dan and Corrine appeared, demanding, "Answer the damned telephone, John!" a few days later. I had just completed experiencing the two most extreme ends of the groupie spectrum.

The story did not end there. Russ's turn with God on the air and Anita on the phone all night long occurred the following night. Upon my arrival the next morning to relieve him on the air, he was nearly breathless with anticipation. He knew of my Anita visit the previous day and was kind of aware it ended awkwardly. In as serious a tone as I could muster, my advice to him was firm. "Steer clear at all costs, Russ. It is a horror show of incalculable description. Don't believe me? Go look at my car." His equally warped mind interpreted the advice as meaning he should stay away from her because I wanted her all to myself. That made him more eager than ever to proceed.

Arrival at home following my air shift found Russ parked in front of my apartment, drinking hard liquor from a bottle inside a paper bag during the middle of the day. His first words were, "Dude, I will never, ever doubt you ever again." Easily noticeable was a bullet hole in his right rear corner panel. I encouraged Russell to come in, plop onto the couch and sleep it off. Once awakened, he simply looked at me, shuddered painfully, and walked out without any words. Neither of us spoke much about our Anita experiences going forward. Lessons were learned the hard way.

The saga had STILL not concluded. After the fragrant regular all-night guy returned to work, a sexual tryst with Anita was actually consummated. Russ asked, "How could you possibly do that, dude!?" His shallow answer was, "Look, she has no close relatives, and I'm thinking maybe she will leave me some money." At that point, my entire radio career should have been thoughtfully reevaluated. We all hope Anita is peacefully reposed.

CHAPTER 22

BANKS OF THE WABASH

WBOW was the leading radio station in Terre Haute, Indiana for most of five decades. It went on the air in 1927 and featured a long list of folks who went on to bigger things. One of its most famous really early stars was Burl Ives, but each decade featured stars-to-be. It was a real radio station with modern equipment, a cool building, a news department, a sales staff that aggressively sold advertising, and complementary staff in every department. It was the middle of the 1970s, and AM radio was king. The only other station in town with similar ratings was WTHI. They played country music and had older listeners.

From 7 p.m. to midnight, the playlist got edgier. Craig Riley, my chosen alter ego, spent five hours most nights in a high-energy frenzy. Trade tools included a large Gates President console, an RCA DX 77 microphone, and more reverb-laden processed audio than any south of the border. Old Radio Shack cans from gigs past got replaced with higher-end Koss headphones. I can trace my hearing loss directly back to that period.

Craig Riley had his own jingles, and legendary Chicago voiceover artist Gary Gears annunciated that name with voice-of-God authority.

The only real competition was primetime television. Teenagers couldn't watch beyond bedtime. But they could listen. Six request lines lit buttons at the base of the telephone continuously, and I enjoyed answering them once in a while.

Typical teenage girl phone chatter: "Um, um, um, can you play *Run Joey Run*?" Whenever one snowflake flew through the air, it would be "Um, um, um do we have school tomorrow?" Craig Riley was a teen god at just over twenty-one. I shied away from teenagers, primarily because the older I got the more illegal it would be. Any conversation that began with "Um, um, um . . ." was also never promising from a carnal perspective.

The mid-1970s were fascinating. Disco ruled the airwaves, and the remarkable career of Larry Bird at Indiana State University was just taking off. Terre Haute was often dismissed as an unremarkable town that smelled bad, the result of various aspects of the Wabash River, some oil wells, and a badly located wastewater treatment facility. For me, it became the center of a universe where I became an idol for young women. The town provided immense and consistent personal entertainment.

My personal life took a romantic turn as well. Having learned the hard way that taking chances with groupies could be fatal, I decided the best choice might be securing an actual normal girlfriend. I already had one, sort of, with Shelly, but she lived over an hour away. Her idea of romance was confined to shopping for wedding accessories. Marriage to her was not in the cards.

Prior to my dramatic exit from W-SUX, a local woman named Jan Crowder, working with a community organization that provided public service materials, stopped by to record a message. She also had in tow her best friend Suzie.

"John, I'd like you to meet Suzie. Suzie, this is John." Jan played it cool. I did what all red bloods do silently. *Hmmm. Would I? Is she cute? What's she like?*

It was not love at first sight, but Suzie was a genuinely nice, sweet person. Jan knew of both my available and lonely status and figured Suzie might also feel the same way. It took a little while, but Suzie and I soon found ourselves dating and having a great time. Her best qualities were honesty, a straightforward approach to life, commitment to family, and a strong desire for simplicity. We bonded one evening as she suffered through a really bad cold. I stayed with her, providing ample chicken soup, Kleenex, and comfort. Suzie seemed to appreciate the effort very much.

It was soon a steady relationship, and I broke the news to Shelly. She got very angry. "How DARE you, JT!" She stalked away and that was that for a few years.

It was not long before Suzie and I met the other parents and family members and next-level plans considered. She was a joy to be around and there were no complaints about our relationship. But were we ready?

Suzie and her family resided in a small, Mayberry-like hamlet in north-central Indiana. It was a very small town that oozed idyllic charm. It sparkled more than most other similarly sized burgs. The simple attraction was unmistakable. I was incapable of grasping those qualities.

Our relationship blossomed around the time I suggested Dan and Corrine cram it. That put a damper into the nascent relationship Suzie and I nurtured, but love was going to conquer all. It was all going to happen in western Indiana.

CHAPTER 23

THE DISCO ERA AND LARRY BIRD

Terre Haute, Indiana is often derided by outsiders as a backwater town in a red state. For many who lived there, including me for more than three years, it was a wonderful place. It is known historically as the home of Eugene Debs, who led the Socialist Party and ran for president five times. There is also a large federal correctional facility, where domestic terrorist Timothy McVeigh was confined and ultimately executed. During my brief time there, Larry Bird began and finished his remarkable college basketball career at Indiana State University. The disco era was also in full swing.

My on-air shift was 7 to midnight. The competition was scarce, and not even home VCRs were available yet. Folks entertained themselves by watching live television, reading newspapers or books, going to theaters to watch movies, or listening to the radio. I was the homework companion and played the hits, becoming an influential voice for a generation of local teeny boppers. Many post-midnights were spent alone listening to distant signals for inspiration. WLS in Chicago boomed in. On most nights it was also possible to pick up WABC or WNBC in New York.

All were influential, as were many others including WCFL, CKLW, and even XERF in Mexico.

Marriage to Suzie was consummated shortly into the Terre Haute run. She was (and still is) one of the most genuine, sweet, grounded, and sincere people I have ever met. Suzie was saint-like and essentially had to be. Given my youthful but increasingly boorish narcissism and almost total disregard for her needs and feelings, she hardened. Wife #1 did not deserve emotional neglect but always gave it her best. Suzie crafted her life after that marriage not only with grace but fierce determination and spirit. She turned out to be a more remarkable person than I ever imagined.

She adapted to life away from her hometown as well as could be expected. Suzie landed a good job at the utility company. She owned a mobile home that got transported to a well-maintained park east of Terre Haute. Three distinct memories of that first dwelling remain fond. Well, two of the three.

Most important was the arrival of our son John III. He became a toddler in that flimsy, wheeled home and seemed to grow rapidly. He was bright, intelligent, and often introspective. He smiled and laughed a lot. On the day my father passed away, J-III wanted to play, but looked confused about my sadness and grief. I was glad my father got to hold his grandson before passing.

That mobile home was also the scene of an election-night party in November 1976 for some station cohorts, primarily because it was the nicest residence. Suzie headed out of town to visit her parents. None of us got rich on WBOW salaries. We were fans of Jimmy Carter, celebrated his election, and forgot we resided in a hotbed of ultraconservative patriots.

Our enthusiasm was short-lived as prices for everything kept rising.

A single woman named Becky lived across the street. She was gorgeous and I spent inordinate amounts of time fantasizing, gazing out the front window to catch glimpses, and plotting how to seduce her. That was not acceptable behavior for a married father, but local stardom went to my head. Oblivious to life outside my sphere, I had no idea Suzie and Becky struck up a friendship. The way I found out was notably embarrassing.

Early one holiday afternoon before heading for work, I stepped out of the shower then shaved, brushed my teeth, and prepared to get dressed. Suzie and everyone else with a real job had the day off. I figured it was a perfect time for a little amorous hanky-panky.

A novelty towel unfolded in the bathroom featured a Superman logo. Securing it around my neck required a diaper pin. My intended surprise was to "fly" into the living room by running from the bathroom down the hall, through the kitchen, turning left to essentially jump over the dining area and land, hands-on-hips, into the living room sans any stitch of clothing except the Superman towel. Suzie would then be swept off her feet, transported to the mirrored boudoir situated over the rear axle, then get passionately ravaged by her super-powered husband.

Final flight preparations were completed. Anticipation produced an erection from which an anvil could be hung. In my best radio voice, I announced loudly from the hallway to prepare for something "Faster than a speeding bullet! More powerful than a locomotive! Able to leap tall buildings in a single bound! Yes, it's SuperJohn—a strange visitor from southern Indiana who came to Vigo County with powers and abilities far beyond those of mortal men!" As the sprint to her vicinity commenced, I da-da-da-da'd my way through the cheesy television Superman theme song. Everything worked exactly as planned and I perfectly stuck the landing in the center of the living room.

That is where Suzie was comfortably seated, and enjoying a very cordial conversation with Becky from across the street. The toweled cape quickly became a loincloth. The last thing either young lady saw was a bony set of butt cheeks vanishing back down the hallway. Suzie was able to laugh about it later.

Speaking of supermen, Larry Bird lasted about three months at Indiana University in Bloomington under Bob Knight before returning home. Bird was disillusioned by its size, distance, and unfamiliarity. Indiana State University managed to re-recruit him in 1975 from a garbage truck in French Lick to their basketball team, playing for a young coach in a brand new 11,000 seat arena. The rest is history, culminating in the most highly rated college basketball championship game of all time in 1979. It was Larry with his undefeated Sycamores, and Magic leading a tough Michigan State squad. In seasons that led up to that game, locals became quite enamored of Bird and Indiana State basketball. The program reached heights never previously imagined. The vibe in town made it a very cool place to reside.

The disco era coincided with the Bird era, and WBOW made the most of it. The station concocted a great gimmick that promoted "the world's largest disco." Hulman Center, home of ISU Basketball, was converted into a makeshift discotheque with flashing lights, twirling balls, and pre-EDM disc jockeys spinning actual discs.

It was a huge success with thousands of dancing, sweaty youngsters in attendance. Successful enough that many on the air staff were invited back a few months later to open for actual big-time disco acts Donna Summer and KC & The Sunshine Band. Both acts were at their popularity peak. Creativity ruled and possibilities were limitless.

CHAPTER 24

FUCK JERRY LEWIS

Yes, THAT Jerry Lewis. The legendary king of comedy for boomers and their parents nearly scuttled an ill-advised romantic romp with a seductive fugitive from the United States Navy. Perhaps unfortunately, lust prevailed.

First things first. A tall skinny guy named Steven Bowles also attempted to fulfill his radio dreams in Terre Haute. He was, at best, nerdy. Steven worked part-time at WBOW and filled in whenever others took vacation days. He stayed really busy. Steven somehow managed to get himself into a steady relationship with one of the most naturally beautiful women on earth. The usual reaction of peers who knew both of them was always the same.

How the heck is this even possible?! What does she see in HIM?!

Her skin was dark in a creamy, silken way. Long legs complemented an unnaturally perfect shape. She was a Persian real-life Barbie doll with long, flowing dark hair. We guessed Steven simply provided a safe, nonthreatening place to live.

Little by little, small things were revealed about gorgeous mystery woman Jessamyn Fortner. "I sell Toyotas," got worked into conversations. "And I will give you a GREAT deal!"

She worked for commission-only at the local Toyota dealership. Japanese cars then were still full imports, and a very tough sell in middle America among a sea of Chevy, Ford, and Chrysler automobiles. She sold a lot of Toyotas. Her fabulous looks had a lot to do with it.

As I got to know her better, Jessamyn revealed "I am AWOL from the navy." She found her way from California to Indiana and Steven. "I really enjoyed that life, but sailors and officers think you're asking for it if you are young, female and wear the uniform. No one at any level did anything about it, so I didn't go back after a leave. I figured going from the West Coast to Indiana would keep me off their radar. They don't like people just up and leaving." Jessamyn seemed melancholy.

Most important (at least to me) was an admission. "Craig, I am your BIGGEST fan. I LOVE you." Predictably, my charm button was set to high whenever we were together. The middle of the 1970s was a time when men wore Daisy Duke-like shorts too, mimicking young women. I felt downright sexy in them.

Soon enough, groupie grand slam number two was knocked out of the park. There were few tears afterward. A sinister feeling we were doing something dangerous and wrong (we actually were) kept it mysterious. There was also the aspect of blatant adultery, but that got rationalized away. Sexual mores of the 1970s included generous concepts of open marriage or even spousal swapping. It did not matter to me that it was usually a one-way street.

Jessamyn whispered an invitation at the end of summer. "Craig, let's blow town and find a room with plenty of room for us to have some fun without any interruptions." It was easy enough if it involved Sundays when we were both off. The state of Indiana in many ways was not evolved philosophically or in terms of law from 1816, the year it became a state. Blue laws prohibited Sunday car sales. Someone might go buy a car instead of going to church. Sunday liquor sales were also not possible. After all, people might get drunk and then go to church. Sundays were perfect escape days.

The ongoing fight against muscular dystrophy and related insidious diseases that fall under that nasty umbrella is an honorable, worthwhile quest. Many advances in the fight against, and treatment for, neuromuscular afflictions result from generous contributions. Ordinary people commit themselves to help find cures. How can anyone not be a huge fan?

The annual Labor Day Muscular Dystrophy Telethon pioneered by Jerry Lewis funneled millions of dollars for treatment and research. The days-long broadcast celebrated its heyday during the 1970s and '80s. Jerry Lewis was larger than life as its driving force and master of ceremonies. Radio personalities in town dutifully volunteered at a local television station carrying the telethon. We media types took turns both co-hosting local segments and answering telephones during cutaways. Jerry Lewis held conference calls with local stations and segment hosts a few weeks beforehand. Calls became motivating speeches to get stations fired up about the telethon.

My biggest problem with Jerry Lewis was his temperament during our interactions. He acted like a complete asshole. Lewis was a colossal jerk. Following the pep talk, I made what I believed was an innocuous, legitimate request. "Jerry, would you be willing to voice a couple of promos not only promoting the telethon but involvement of WBOW and its personalities?"

That is the point at which his shouting and profanity intensified. He could have easily declined the request respectfully, and although disappointment might follow, an easy move to some plan B could serve as an alternative. "I do NOT do cheesy fucking promos, goddammit! How DARE you ask me for such trivial things." The great one declared, with enhanced volume, "You are NUTS."

What an asshole! I fumed for a long while. It no longer mattered who he was. No one was going to scream at me like that for any reason.

In a defiantly selfish fuck-Jerry-Lewis-and-fuck-his-fucking-telethon phase that followed, Jessamyn and I blew town. A jaunt down US-41 toward Vincennes, Indiana to the once opulent but now completely leveled Executive Inn, and in a brand-new demo Toyota Corolla, seemed advisable the Sunday of Labor Day weekend. Neither of us had to be at work until late in the day on Monday. Suzie was away visiting her family. Perfect.

Our primary problem was that we could not tell anyone. That meant no RSVPing my way out of local segment hosting or phone answering duties for the telethon. On Sunday evening, Jessamyn and I were naked and frisky atop a king-sized bed in the no-tell-hotel. "Do you care if I turn on the telethon, Jess?" She nodded approval, winked and suggested "Turn it up. We may need to drown out the noise." As she and I wrestled, one of the television hosts droning across the room wondered aloud "Where is Craig Riley, and has anyone seen him?"

An empty spot at a table with my name and a telephone became a shot.

Had I let victims down? Guilt crept in later and stayed for a while. Later I decided my absence resulted in zero dollars of fewer donations, and that fucking Jerry Lewis could continue fucking himself for the rest of his pathetic fucking life. Even the Muscular Dystrophy Association eventually distanced their organization from him. When Jerry Lewis died halfway through 2017, guilty sadness replaced emotions wrought of youthful selfishness.

Both Jessamyn and I left Terre Haute very soon after and never made contact again.

CHAPTER 25

A STRIPPER AND THE OLD LADY

WBOW's on-air staff had a strong bond. It was a motley, diverse cast that included an always jovial, friendly, and giggling character, short in stature with two first names (Joseph and Lawrence). There was also the impeccably dressed and always precise Brainy Tom, along with a dry-witted part-timer named Chuckie. A sales guy who could talk his way into or out of just about anything, Lynn Halterman, was also one of the guys. We were quite serious about our collectively chosen crafts. WBOW was number the number-one radio station in western Indiana. We frequently scheduled personal appearances at local businesses and community events. Even if an on-air buddy did not work events, everybody usually showed up anyway.

As recently legal full-fledged adults, we also enjoyed after-hours fun. Before any of us understood the pointlessness of strip clubs, or their potential ramifications, we were consistently enthusiastic about visiting such places. One was aptly named The Body Shop. It was a run-of-the-mill dive, complete with small boxing-ring-like stages ringed with bar stools and poles in the middle, as well as private areas for more intimate grinding. Clientele included everyone from businessmen to bikers. All patrons got along.

Only bared breasts about every third song were allowed. G-strings of the day left little to imaginations, but those particular private parts had to remain covered every day of the week except Tuesdays, when "artists" that held special performance licenses from the state of Indiana could bare it all AND remain within the confines of Hoosier law. The legal reason why such licenses were necessary accommodated traveling presentations of legitimate artistic endeavors inside mainstream theaters. If, for example, the traveling company of the musical *Hair* happened to stop in Indiana, all actors that ended up nude on stage needed the license.

The Body Shop was far removed from anything even remotely resembling legitimate theater. That did not stop management from maintaining the spirit of a ridiculously bent law. On Tuesdays, the main event performers would not simply slither around on poles or hustle dollars and drinks. They performed artistic acts that always involved bared female genitalia in close proximity to the faces of many WBOW staff members seated ringside.

One memorable evening, the chosen artistic approach to another glorified strip show involved audience participation. The stripping artist allowed her nude body to be painted using tempera with small brushes. Brainy Tom actually began work on a meticulous portrait using the ribcage of the performer as his canvas. The rest of us, drinks gulped, quickly grew bored with paintbrushes and began finger painting. Paint splattered digits eventually found their way into the woman until at least three of us made progress converting her fallopian tubes into artistic masterpieces.

It did not take long for a burly fellow in a dark suit to strongly suggest we "Please vacate the premises immediately and return another night, gentlemen." We agreed, slipped him a few tempera-splattered crumpled bills, and bid adieu.

The only reason The Body Shop is mentioned involves a stripper who was the star of the club. Her real name was Caroline. On stage, she was known as Destiny. She was genuinely sweet to all of the youthful WBOW staff who frequented the club on nights she worked. Tall and naturally blonde, very curvy, and in impeccable shape, Caroline was the main attraction. All of us and every red blood in the club desired a date with Destiny.

Back at WBOW, Caroline's dowdy mother was the after-hours cleaning lady. She worked at least three hours every weeknight keeping the building spotless. On one or two nights a week when not at the club, Caroline showed up to help her mother. Those nights also included many other members of WBOW's staff who suddenly decided to work late. It is impossible to know whether Caroline's mother knew how her daughter earned a living, or that almost everyone in the radio station had seen her mostly naked and provocative on several occasions.

All of us dysfunctional males stupidly believed we had a shot. Caroline brought along a friend one evening to assist with cleanup duty. Her name was Carolyn. Caroline and Carolyn. They were roommates in a rented house. Carolyn looked a little rough around the edges. She was mildly attractive, but not overly so, and with a very average Indiana frame. All eyes remained focused on Caroline. Around 10 p.m. that evening, Carolyn entered the studio alone, leaned over the board, winked, and whispered,

"We will be making love by 1 a.m."

I was intrigued by the word "we." Did she mean just me and her, or "we" as in Craig, Carolyn, AND Caroline? It was definitely a chance worth taking. After all, I was a star too.

By 12:40 a.m., Carolyn, Caroline, and I were seated comfortably on the living room couch enjoying cocktails. Carolyn whispered, "I have a promise to keep," and began fondling.

Caroline, you are free to join the fun too! I smiled and winked at her.

The most beautiful stripper in Indiana got up and went to her room.

Perhaps that's where we'll all end up!

Fantasy was not meant to be. Carolyn's before-1:00 promise was unfolding, and she took it seriously. By 12:55 we were naked on the couch. Carolyn deftly maneuvered herself into launch position.

Although brutally irresponsible, I felt that with either or both of those women, adequate sheathing with a durable condom was probably a smart move. Installation dutifully occurred with a minute and a half to spare.

What the holy hell?! Where's her snatch?!

At 12:59 am the reality of a birth defect Carolyn failed to disclose became embarrassingly apparent. I had no idea what it was called at the time, but later figured out she had an imperforate anus. What that meant in flesh and blood terms was that Carolyn did not possess a "taint." In other words, there was little to no perineum up there between her thighs.

Boy, am I glad I didn't use my mouth down there!

Determining where to poke a rubber-sheathed rod proved confusing and challenging. Both approximate spots were attempted, but Carolyn seemed to prefer what was almost certainly the wrong orifice. It did have more elasticity and Carolyn enjoyed it, so we rolled with the flow. Twenty minutes later, additional drinks were badly needed. Carolyn whispered, "Craig, I'm ready for round two."

Caroline burst into the room seconds later. She wore a nothing-left-to-imagination nightgown. I, already naked, was momentarily overjoyed. Her face, however, filled with sheer terror. Caroline ran over, grabbed my cheeks, and looked me right in the eye. Very deliberately, she said "You need to grab all your clothes, follow me to the back door, and leave RIGHT NOW. If you do not do exactly that, you will likely be DEAD, literally, within three minutes."

I began trying to put clothing back on. She growled "CRAIG, JUST GRAB YOUR CLOTHES! YOU NEED TO LEAVE NOW!" Motorcycle engines and rowdy hoots got louder outside. Inside my spinning head, two plus two suddenly equaled four with remarkable and urgent clarity.

Oh, SHIT!

That is also when I figured out for myself how futile attempting to dress while running actually is. Shouted words like "sonofabitch" and "you're dead, punk" began echoing through dark neighboring yards. The pace escalated. Bullets flew. It was the third time I had dodged actual gunshots after fleeing real or imagined sexual misadventures.

At least I got sort of laid this time.

The closest parking spot to the house of Caroline/Carolyn earlier that evening happened to be a couple of blocks away. That was fortuitous. I was naked, literally running for my life, and not slowed by heavy leather attire or a potted belly. What might have happened had they remembered the mobility of their hogs?

Carolyn was hitched to the leader of the local Sons of Silence motorcycle chapter by common law - an "old lady" in Harley parlance. She also failed to disclose that really important nugget of crucial decision-making information before I began poking around her ambiguous innards. Slipping quietly into my car, I drove away in the opposite direction at high speed with no lights, naked, for a few miles. The way back to the station meandered. WBOW had a driveway behind a privacy fence in the rear. That is where the latex came off and all clothing except one shoe went back on. What happened to the other shoe has remained an open mystery for nearly fifty years.

Absolute fear added to paranoia for months, especially when anything with an unmuffled motor and two wheels passed the station. The entire WBOW front facade was glass. Inside, a large lobby was connected to a glass-walled control room and the back of my Koss-clad noggin. WBOW claimed the glass was bulletproof but I never felt like testing it. Those fear-filled months featured an all-new Craig Riley—one with a complete rededication to the craft. The Body Shop never got visited again. Attempts to remain inconspicuous despite local stardom were valiant. I more deeply appreciated having a fake name for use on the radio.

CHAPTER 26

FORMULA RADIO

WBOW was a successfully operated local station with great ratings and a professional, dedicated staff focused on just one market. The group that owned the station hired a New York-based programming consultant to evaluate their stations and recommend ways to make them better. The professional they hired, a fellow named Dean Landsman, was knowledgeable, focused, and completely inoffensive. Had my vastly inflated sense of knowledge and skills been kept in check, I may have even learned something from a guy who could have been a great mentor.

Instead of absorbing valuable new insights into operating great local radio stations, I scoffed at any idea that might change the sound of the station. It seemed intrusive.

In a one-on-one meeting, Dean suggested "Craig, why don't you tone down the screaming on the air. You don't need to do that. Just be yourself. Talk naturally. Your audience will relate much better." It seemed incomprehensible.

I'm number one by a wide margin. Why would I change?! He doesn't like energy. He doesn't like jingles. He doesn't like reverb. He wants me to read LINER CARDS. Screw him. That's not what stars do.

I went out of my way to subvert his efforts. One example involved the song *Ease On Down the Road* by a disco group called Consumer Rapport, adapted from the Broadway musical *The Wiz*. It was a huge hit in New York, but nowhere else in the country. It always sounded great on WABC.

"Dean, why would we not play *Ease On Down the Road*? It is #1 on WABC, and *The Wiz* is the hottest show on Broadway."

Landsman then endorsed the song for airplay on WBOW. It was obviously out of place, and very few stations nationwide played it. I believed in a defiant way that it proved a point about consultants from New York who knew nothing about Terre Haute, Indiana.

*Hell, maybe **I** should be in New York.*

In the end, WBOW became a more consistently programmed station that sounded bigger than its market size. Instead of being grateful and appreciative of newfound knowledge, I became belligerent and willfully offended. Professional maturity not yet realized, I decided again to leave for a place where grass might be greener.

Terre Haute was a medium-sized market with a fair number of television and radio stations. FM radio in the mid-1970s was coming into its own. It was also scaling ratings and revenue hurdles. Theater of the mind continued its evolution.

Program Director Ed Gansmann at an FM station in West Terre Haute was a Craig Riley fan and wanted to hire me away from WBOW. He offered me whatever shift I wanted (afternoon drive) and equal pay. I could transform from boisterous Craig Riley to smooth John T. Howard. Becoming a cooler and more laid-back FM guy, like Clint Eastwood in *Play Misty For Me,* would be on my own terms.

WPFR initially reminded me of WXUS. It was founded by an entrepreneurial radio guy who built it himself and used religious programming to keep the lights on. WPFR stood for Paul Ford Radio, although many local radio peers derided it as "Pussy Fart Radio." The station was sold to a newly formed local group, and that is how a new gig opened up.

Buyer remorse plagued the first few days of a journey to the Wabash River lowlands. That is where the station existed, in spare rooms of an old house. It was dramatically different from WBOW. Still, I felt a new vibe could be created and enjoyed.

Soon enough, the station got moved to new digs inside a very old building in downtown Terre Haute not far from Indiana State. New owners acquired better equipment. Helping during construction phases offered a kind of sweat equity not previously experienced in other jobs. I began feeling invested in the future success of the station. On air at WPFR became more comfortable. Craig Riley got pushed aside as the real John T. Howard emerged.

The self-confidence I always enjoyed was inexplicably shaken one afternoon when the band Styx stopped by the station for concert promotion. Hulman Center, just around the corner, was the site for a stop on their Grand Illusion Tour promoting that just-released album. Everyone in the band showed up, and they were at the peak of their popularity. For the first time either before or since, I became completely star-struck and could not manage more than a word or two. Inside my head was radio gold. There were questions and discussion topics galore.

Tommy, what makes Grand Illusion so great? Dennis, is it our imagination, or is there a medieval theme to this album? Who is "Fooling Yourself" about? How do you guys like being so close to home for a change? J.Y., how surprising is the success of "Come Sail Away?"

As Tommy Shaw, Dennis DeYoung, James Young, and Chuck and John Panozzo sat there around the console wearing smiles and eager to promote their album and sold-out show, their eyes fixed on John T. Howard, what came out of my mouth was "Uh, ummm, aaaa, welcome to the Wabash Valley, guys. Err, uhhh, ummm, what time is the show tonight?"

I was suddenly mute. The mic was on, but only snippets of words came out. That is really bad for someone on the radio.

I motioned for Ed to come over. "Ed here has a few questions for you guys … and welcome to Terre Haute. Their looks included surprise and pity. I ran down the hall into the restroom and puked.

Doubt crept in. Suzie professed a strong desire for moving home (**her** home) and settling down for good. That led to increasingly serious introspection. Suzie made almost weekly weekend visits home, especially after John T. III arrived. It became clear Terre Haute would not be a permanent residence. The career limbo that followed led to the end of what might have been a great marriage, and eventually to much bigger personal mistakes.

CHAPTER 27

DESCENT INTO MISERY

As the 1970s ended, and shortly before marriage to Suzie dissolved, I resumed attempts to resuscitate a radio full-time career. I filled in part-time and on weekends at WAZY-FM in Lafayette, Indiana to keep dreams alive. During daylight hours, a succession of truly awful actual jobs was torture.

The first lousy position involved a full-service Pizza Hut restaurant in Lafayette. My tomato-stained white shirt featured a pinned badge that identified me as manager of that red-roofed brick structure. Previous management allowed the joint to slip to a level of uncleanliness that drove customers away.

The area manager gave me clear instructions. "John, clean this place up. Every nook and cranny. And get rid of any food stock that has gone bad."

The whole place quickly sparkled again. Business began booming, but restaurant management under the PepsiCo corporate umbrella felt ill-advised and potentially disastrous.

Perhaps mercifully, that career phase ended abruptly the evening of the Old Oaken Bucket football game between pigskin rivals Purdue University and Indiana University. Purdue won the game lopsidedly. Locals were happy, hungry, and numerous. The biggest problem involved my being on the air at WAZY that evening after having worked in the restaurant all day. I felt the store was in good hands with both assistant managers and a full complementary staff. It wasn't. Jack Williams, the area manager, called the WAZY hotline about an hour into my shift. Colorful language and vulgar epithets preceded his ultimatum.

"Now look here, you son-of-a-bitch, if your sorry excuse for a manager ass is not inside this restaurant within fifteen minutes, you are fucking fired, and you will be lucky if I do not hunt you down and pound you into next Tuesday."

Human Resources protocols we take for granted today were not as prevalent in 1978. The problem was that you could not just put a radio station on auto-pilot. Even if I wanted to save the crappy dead-end pizza job, it would take far longer than fifteen minutes to find a replacement. One thought crossed my mind.

Screw it.

The Saturday night air shift at WAZY ended at midnight, and I headed for Pizza Hut. It looked like a bomb exploded inside. Dirty dishes sat in piles nearly ceiling high. Food scraps littered prep areas. Sauce appeared in places suggesting it was shot from cannons. All employees appeared to have been whipped into near unconsciousness. The potty-mouthed area manager was also woefully bedraggled. No one said anything to me as the kitchen walk of shame commenced. Termination paperwork was thrust my way. The back door was held wide open. The only thing I did not receive was a swift kick in the pants. "Get the fuck outta here," snarled the area manager.

So long pizza as a career path.

An even crappier, more ignominious excuse for a job followed. Essex Wire was a division of the United Technologies conglomerate. Their primary Lafayette-manufactured products were wiring harnesses for Ford and Lincoln automobiles. The bulky bundles were assembled one wire and connection block at a time aboard moving industrial jigs. Each employee along the line held responsibility for one or two of the wires. Harnesses reached the end of the line fully assembled, taped, reinforced, and ready for efficient installation inside brand-new Fords and Lincolns somewhere in Michigan.

A few problems became apparent. Pay was not bad for the time, but all employees had to join the union that occupied the factory. "Line workers will be well represented," claimed the brochure. Union dues deducted from the not-so-horrible gross pay made net pay relatively lousy. The union essentially did nothing other than collect dues to enrich their leadership. Work on the factory floor was mind-numbingly repetitive. Monotony was the enemy.

Many individual wires were not quite long enough for proper installation. We later discovered it was intentional. Every finished harness had to meet a specific contractually obligated weight threshold. Fractions of ounces mattered.

Despite this handicap, supervisory personnel continuously roamed the line yelling at anyone deemed working too slowly. Near constant attempts to speed up lines compromised quality. The union that grabbed such a high percentage of pay remained passive and rarely intervened. Most everyone on the line felt like prison laborers. Perhaps as in penitentiaries, creative line workers concocted schemes to stop the line periodically. That allowed everyone to catch up. Someone would look up and down the line to make sure no snooping managers were around, then loudly whisper "HEY…step back a second." Then the person would "accidentally" drop a handful of junction fixtures into the mechanical line chain. That enabled an emergency stop sequence. Recovery could take up to ten minutes. Accidents occurred every other hour or so.

During a portion of that dismal career phase, I was charged with plugging one end into a piece of plastic, then routing a bright orange wire around several pegs on a jig, and finally plugging the other end into another piece of plastic. The orange wire was nearly an inch too short. Essex Wire management saved money wherever possible. Miracles were routinely expected from indentured servants along the line. "Speed it up, Howard, you're behind! Smith, why are you so slow?! Jones, you are supposed to be working, not playing!"

The one thought on the mind of everyone was some variation of *FUCK YOU.*

As merciless haranguing for not being fast continued with increasing volume, I eventually devised a way to allow for easy connection of the wire at its terminal end. Once the wire was initially connected and wrapped around the first three of seven pegs, leverage allowed for a forceful, unnatural tug of the wire. That made up the missing inch at the terminal end. It was easy to accomplish, especially considering the degree to which I wanted to physically assault screeching supervisory personnel gnawing at my eardrums.

That bright orange wire ultimately provided illumination of rear license plates on Lincolns. Most states required lighting above rear license plates on every car.

My stretched piece was critical for adherence to state statutes.

Toiling in the hell that was Essex Wire was demoralizing. One day, the suits held an all-hands-on-deck meeting. "Ladies and gentlemen, we regret to inform you that this plant will permanently close in thirty days. Your positions are being eliminated, but you will be paid for forty-five days. The Ford Motor Company desires consolidation of vendor operations and improved quality. You will be given a brochure that has a checklist after this session concludes."

It was over. Snap. Just like that. Later that winter, Ford's Lincoln division sent recall notices nationwide to luxury sedan owners. An issue involving rear license plates not illuminating caused problems for law enforcement. I evidently tugged a little too hard several thousand times in a row.

The only bad thing about the third gig of the period was not the occupation. That was great. The pay was beneath lousy. While in high school, my best jobs were at the Indiana Theater in downtown Washington or the East 50 Drive-in just outside of town. United Artists owned a 1,000-seat theater in Lafayette and a drive-in on the outskirts of town. Technology dramatically improved as well. In the late '60s and early '70s, manually operated carbon arc projection systems were common in most small-town theaters. By the late '70s, carbon arc was replaced by high illumination bulbs and highly refractive mirrors. Reel changes became unnecessary because all single reels of physical film could be spliced together once, and then operated from a single platter that resembled a giant eight-track tape. That design allowed the spinning platter of a 35mm flick to continuously wind itself back to the beginning.

I managed both the movie house and the drive-in.

Responsibilities included accounting for ticket and concession revenues, operating projectors, occasionally working the concession stand, and generally being Mr. Congenial. At the drive-in, more focus on concessions was important, not to mention monitoring the behavior of young people in cars.

It also offered opportunities to turn boredom into sick humor. Consider the Best Picture of 1978, *The Deer Hunter*. It was most controversial for its occasionally graphic depiction of Russian roulette. As the guy who operated and had to regularly monitor the projector, I learned exactly when key moments of the film occurred, because it had been playing in the theater for weeks. Scenes with guns touching temples were tense and suspenseful enough, but I derived sick pleasure from jacking up the volume milliseconds before clicks with no bullets. At least four or five people literally jumped out of their seats every time. It made me smile.

Twisted antics came to an abrupt halt during the release of *Battlestar Galactica*, a movie I always liked better than *Star Wars*. A special sound system was added to boost attendance. The package consisted of several industrial-sized speakers positioned around the theater, a mixing console, and equalization equipment to optimize sound for the movie. Lessons for operating the equipment were provided, which consisted of demonstrating factory presents and instructions not to touch anything ever. Having been in radio, I knew my way around a console and rationalized any do-not-touch instructions did not apply to me.

Audio eventually got to where I wanted it. Other than a few ongoing tweaks, it sounded great every night. Customers appeared in droves.

Tuesday night-late showings were typically not well attended, and that was the case shortly a couple of weeks into the run. Tinkering with the sound system went a bit too far, something painfully realized as several ceiling tiles crashed from the high ceiling onto thankfully empty theater seats below.

The second task after checking to determine whether anyone had been injured was resetting sound to factory defaults. Upper management concluded it was merely a freak incident.

That depressing succession of no-hope jobs was bad, but it could have been worse. I was offered a commission-only sales job for Chrysler, Plymouth, and Dodge automobiles at a point when that car company nearly vanished in a sea of red ink. "John, these are the most affordable cars in America. It's a dream job." I disagreed. It was before Lee Iacocca and K-cars came along. Despite the relative glamour of dealing with cars instead of manufacturing wiring harnesses, I spurned the offer.

The part-time shifts at WAZY kept me sane through a grim litany of day jobs. Rescue came in 1979 from Mike King. He managed operations at WCSI Radio in Columbus, Indiana, and offered salaried daytime air work. I accepted his offer without hesitation.

CHAPTER 28

CAREER DECISION MILESTONES AND WHIMS

My relaunched radio career gained momentum at WCSI in Columbus, Indiana as I resumed higher education at nearby Indiana University. In 1981, I earned a bachelor of arts degree in telecommunications. I wanted to be a program director and began a nationwide search. Armed with a four-year college degree and the usual inflated self-assessment of my talents, the entire country seemed ripe for picking.

Nothing was wrong at WCSI. It was a wildly successful, well-run local station with an on-air staff that brought a bigger sound to local small-market radio. It was way more fun than the preceding few years.

I met my second wife, Stevie Bloom, on September 21, 1979. We said "I do" on February 1, 1980. The world, however, still needed to be conquered and Stevie was all in.

Radio folks then applied for jobs by submitting a resume and a compilation recording of aspiring stardom behind the mic called an aircheck. Most of us believed that was enough. Resumes were not thoroughly checked for accuracy. In many cases, tape on a small reel or cassette tapes weren't even labeled. If they were, words were scribbled from a felt-tip pen. I believed that if effort went into the presentation and included a typed cover letter to demonstrate literacy, not to mention conveying a sense of excellence, prospective employers might give me a leg up. Fancy presentation usually did not matter because those who hired prospects didn't really care. Creative people are rarely detail-oriented outside their own niches. My rationale involved impressing general management, hoping for a higher salary and more important positions.

I spent more money than I had printing professional labels. I placed them onto small reels of tape and cassettes (I sent both to make it more convenient for prospective employers) to complement my fancy resumes. Postage also dented my wallet. I sent fifteen to twenty such packages every week. Occasionally a "no thanks" form letter might arrive later. Usually, I received no response, even after follow-up. The phone occasionally rang, and that justified the effort and expense.

I ultimately considered four legitimate offers. Stevie and I drove to Beckley, West Virginia to interview for an operations manager position at the flagship station of a larger broadcasting group with studio ties to Hollywood. I quickly realized that dreary burg in winter, during a depressed coal mining era, did not align with world-conquering dreams.

That was followed by a flight to New Orleans for a program director interview with an AM/FM combo in Biloxi, Mississippi. Monsoonal rain soaked everything the day I spent there. Views outside dingy station windows near the coast offered stunning vistas of oil derricks. Money was not great either. It was before casinos came along to stimulate their economy. No thanks, Biloxi.

A market-leading news/talk station in New Orleans also called four times, phone interviewed twice, and eventually offered me a job as program director. I was intoxicated by its big-league market size, not to mention the allure of New Orleans. Due diligence revealed management was not too concerned about who went into the position, provided they could keep all legal forms filed correctly. What they needed was essentially a warm body with half a brain for clerical work. Again, thanks but no thanks.

The most intriguing opportunity involved Tom Young, owner of KVON/KVYN in Napa, California. He flew Stevie and me out the same week final examinations were conducted at Indiana University in Bloomington. Personal study habits did not include cramming per se, but time flying across the country and back could theoretically be spent preparing for exams. That was hard to accomplish on a plane traveling west, and impossible on a redeye immediately preceding a final.

We landed in San Francisco and were picked up by the sales manager of the stations. He spent the drive back extolling the virtues of the region and confiding about what a wonderful place it was. No convincing was necessary. The Napa Valley wine country was always among my favorite spots on earth. Once thoroughly explored, it was easy to confirm that place as an extraordinary place to reside.

The widebody landed on the West Coast around 11 in the morning. It took an hour and a half more to reach the valley. The sales cheerleader announced our next agenda item, touring several wineries before meeting Mr. Young for dinner at 7 that evening. It seemed like a great idea right then. The first glass of wine was swirled, sniffed, and mostly swallowed at 1. Lunch at a small roadside bistro an hour later was the only interruption of what became ill-advised overconsumption of several really tasty, fermented grape juices. It would have been nice had insistence about spitting gargled wine into nearby buckets carried more urgency. *What a waste,* I thought, guzzling away.

By the time we arrived for dinner and an important meeting with the owner, standing up was as much of a challenge as speaking coherently. Miraculously, all such feats were accomplished with neither slurring nor excessive peeing. Mr. Young was affable, knowledgeable, and asked tough questions. His status as a pillar of the local and broadcast communities was widely respected. He also seemed smitten with the missus, which did not hurt our chances. The entire party arranged to meet at the station the next morning at 10 when opportunities to tour facilities and interviews with other staff members were scheduled.

Given the three-hour time difference from Indiana, not to mention liters of wine, my body craved sleep. Deep REMs began as quickly as my head hit the pillow. Overnight bags were repacked by 10 am the following morning, just in time for the sales guy to retrieve us. The journey to KVON did not take long, and a tour commenced. Facilities were functional but sparse and somewhat cluttered. The building that housed the stations had been expanded a little at a time over many years. It was a hodgepodge of hallways with offices and studios in peculiar locations.

"This office," they explained, "will be yours. It is presently used for storage, but will be ready for you once these contents get relocated." It was an interior room with no windows.

Mr. Young repeatedly stressed the importance of local focus and being involved very heavily in the local community. That was a concept with which I was gaining new appreciation because WCSI also espoused such focus. Other than a windowless closet office, I was all in.

Their intended position for me was program director of the FM station, a frequency on which they wanted to attempt programming other than syndication or simulcast with the AM station. A private conversation with the AM program director proved eye-opening. His viewpoints and outlook could most optimistically be described as a half-empty glass. He actually warned me: "Think long and hard about coming to work here, John. Tom enjoys being involved in everything you will ever do."

Was owner micromanagement or even meddling cause for concern? I simply dismissed it as negativism from someone who might be disgruntled under any circumstance. Meetings with four other department heads rounded out the day. Each seemed burdened with some interior unhappiness despite easygoing California enthusiasm. No one else mentioned dissatisfaction with Mr. Young, but subtle sniping among the staff pointed toward a dysfunction I may not have been prepared to handle.

Mr. Young's salary offer began in the $13K-per-year range, which I quickly negotiated beyond $16K. That part of the country, even then, was among the most expensive in which to reside. A $16K salary, realistically, seemed like something that was only around halfway there. I promised Mr. Young that I would take a couple of days, wait for finals to get completed, and then give him an answer.

The flight from San Francisco back to Chicago was a redeye, and connection to Indianapolis was tight. If everything remained on schedule, I would arrive in Bloomington with about five minutes to spare before the final. The airport food I consumed prior to boarding attacked my gastrointestinal system on the return, and at least two of nearly five hours of flight time were spent in cramped commodes mixing vile human waste with blue fluid over several states.

I obtained an emergency pink drink at O'Hare, and delayed final squirting until right before the exam. I cracked open the classroom door with fifteen seconds to spare. Nothing about the exam stuck, but the earned grade was a lucky B with a struggle.

During four decision days that followed, something unexpected happened. KIIQ, an FM radio station serving Colorado Springs, Colorado, called. I submitted an unsolicited resume and aircheck package just before our San Francisco trip. The voice on the other end belonged to Jesse Bullet, a person widely admired for accomplishments no one thought possible, including beating the legendary 89 WLS Chicago with upstart FM station WLUP. His Windy City talent lineup included Steve Dahl. Jesse was also the program director during the infamous disco demolition that forced the Chicago White Sox to forfeit a baseball game after an impromptu drunken riot broke out. Bullet's reputation as an FM rock systems guy able to manage offbeat personalities at stations like WLUP and many out west fascinated me. He was also aligned with WLUP architect Lee Abrams, himself a radio pioneer and already a guru. Chuck Dunaway, also a legend, was general manager at KIIQ. The very first thing he said to me was, "John, I NEVER lose."

Jesse offered me a job over the phone, but not program director. "John, how would you like to be our music director with an overnight air shift, then program director of one of our sister stations in either Amarillo or San Angelo, Texas down the road?" He vowed skies as limits and offered as much money as KVON without high costs of living.

"Sounds great, Jesse," I yelped, "but I need to visit you first." Jesse caved somewhat grudgingly, and a flight was arranged for later in the week.

Between the time Jesse hung up and I flew out four days later, I agonizingly evaluated all pros and cons of both jobs. My left brain selected Napa for a variety of solid, sensible reasons. My right brain kept nagging about world-changing possibilities with legends engaged in a rehabilitation adventure, not to mention taking a leap-of-faith career gamble. We could lose everything.

On the evening of the flight west and following a brief dinner with Jesse, I called Tom Young in Napa and turned down his offer. Conversation from the static-inducing nightstand telephone in Room 12 of the La Fon Motel in Manitou Springs was tense. Young called back twice with better offers during the following week, but my decision was final.

Persistent, nagging feelings of "what if" remained for years whenever unexpected career detours occurred.

The same KVON job I turned down nearly three years earlier popped up again in classified sections of trade publications in 1984. I called Tom Young ready and willing to finally make a move further west and began reselling myself.

"*Click.*"

He hung up on me. A post-retirement career as a master winemaker in a beautiful area of the country was no longer probable. That one choice between those two jobs set the permanent direction for my entire career. Had I chosen Napa, a 40+-year career in the same place might have been forged, much like my WCSI mentor Mike King did in Columbus, Indiana. Several friends and peers happily spent entire careers in one town. It had appeal.

Instead, I chose a roller coaster that turned out to be wildly exciting even though it crashed a few times. It even led to an adventurous second career that also featured unexpected twists and turns.

Was it the right choice?

CHAPTER 29

THIRTY-SIX HOURS OF BRAIN-DAMAGED RACISM

Full-time radio employment at WCSI also featured a whirlwind courtship with Stevie Bloom, ultimately my second wife. Both of us were native Hoosiers, but our backgrounds differed in much the same ways as my parents. The traditional protocol of asking her father for his daughter's hand followed. Our marriage that lasted eleven years commenced a few months after we met.

Nuptials were very nearly thwarted. A few weeks prior to vow exchanging, Stevie and I were returning to her house following a Friday night movie. One of the final events was a left-turn attempt onto Central Avenue well after our traffic light turned green. A burly 1978 Buick Electra 225, traveling substantially above the speed limit, swerved around stopped traffic and through a red light on my left. The inevitable collision caved in the left front quarter panel and driver's-side door of Stevie's 1978 Chevy Nova, where I sat wide-eyed behind the wheel.

The Electra won. After regaining consciousness, I recognized blood leaking from my head and injuries to Stevie's left leg. Someone helped us from the smashed Nova.

Six Electra passengers were also injured in varying degrees. All were men of color who worked nearby in the local Cummins Engine plant. It was their payday. The hours that transpired between the end of their shifts and the violent collision of GM metal featured conversion of substantial portions of their fresh paychecks into alcohol, consumed with reckless abandon. All six appeared to be dangerously intoxicated without the slightest possibility of designated drivers.

A helpful older woman who lived on a corner of the accident intersection rushed into the street to help Stevie and me with wet and dry towels until medical assistance arrived. The well-intentioned lady was also a flaming racist. That would not necessarily have been unusual in central Indiana. The Ku Klux Klan at various times in Hoosier history influenced many such locals in small towns throughout the state, and variations of hate-filled stereotypes often trickled generationally.

I have very little recollection of the entire following week, yet my concussed brain managed to grab snippets. The most significant piece of opinion gleaned from the helpful neighbor lady were words she repeated to Stevie, investigating officers, EMT personnel, gawkers that began gathering, and just about anyone else within earshot. According to the neighborhood Good Samaritan, and with relatively high decibels, we had been "hit by a carload of drunk, goddamned niggers."

Three questions wormed their way into my subconscious and lodged in the gray matter, seemingly permanently. I began asking all three out loud almost immediately, and then continued asking the same exact three questions over and over for the next thirty-six hours. The three questions never went unanswered; replies to them simply could neither be processed nor retained.

The three questions were:

1. Were we in an accident?
2. Whose car were we driving?
3. Were we hit by a carload of drunk, goddamned niggers?

A cycle of me asking those three questions, having them answered, then asking again began almost immediately. Stevie did not feel like talking because she was in pain. I am told the same questions were asked of most police officers and EMT personnel on the scene, bystanders, and six men of color who shared an ambulance that was more like a bus. That must have been entertaining.

I was released after a few tests. Back at the home of Stevie's parents, midnight approached. The cycle of asking the same three questions repeatedly continued. Her family locked me in their basement and left. A phone sat nearby and I recalled a few phone numbers of relatives and my boss. Perhaps it was touch-tone muscle memory. I called all of them, repeatedly, with the same three questions.

During that exile, Stevie's father, Lawrence, attempted to talk his daughter out of the marriage. He concluded I was permanently brain damaged and may also have discovered racism. Lawrence also insisted on taking me back to the hospital since I was not right in the head. After being formally admitted, Stevie handed over a notebook with three pages, numbered 1, 2, and 3. Sheet 1 contained the words, "Yes, we were in an accident." Sheet 2 indicated we were driving her car. Sheet 3 said, "We were hit by a drunk driver. You should NEVER use racial slurs." Written answers remained well beyond my level of concussed comprehension.

The hospital admitted me to a room that contained another gentleman I do not remember. He wanted to sleep. I wanted to ask three questions. He was a smoker healthy enough to occasionally locate the nearest stairwell in which to light up. My smoking habit was over by then, but when his Salems were spotted, part of my injured brain decided they needed to be smoked. Every last one of them. It is unclear whether I asked him or just snatched the pack and his lighter. Smoking prohibition inside hospitals or rooms was also beyond situational awareness. I apparently became angry with nurses who removed the lighter and cigarettes. Butts were extinguished, but I am not sure how.

Within two hours overnight, the room telephone was removed, the nurse call button was disconnected, the innocent roommate was relocated, the television was unplugged, and my lower extremities were restrained. They could not sedate me. The staff was forced to ride out my trauma alongside. My desire for cigarettes was relentless. A full pack, a lighter, and a large ashtray were delivered, and the door was shut. Stevie got angry about the smoke the next day, but my asking the three questions died down.

Several days that followed are also spotty from a memory standpoint, but I felt disbelief and remorse when informed about the quirks of a concussed brain. The third question in particular really bothered me.

That word used to be tossed around more casually in society, but never became part of my vocabulary.

Stevie's car was totaled. The driver was not tested for sobriety at the scene because the necessary equipment was not functional. His blood was drawn at the hospital, but results were not readily available. Once the driver was released from the hospital two hours later, police arrested him on suspicion of driving while intoxicated, and then transported him to headquarters. Proper testing was administered, and three hours after the accident the driver still tested well over the legal limit.

Life lessons: Never, ever drink and drive. Racism is really ignorant. Medical professionals and spouses frown on smoking cigarettes in hospital rooms.

CHAPTER 30

K-DOUBLE-I-Q, MANITOU SPRINGS

The whimsical choice of an entirely speculative venture with no guarantee of any success was bound to affect our entire future. Knowing precisely how was impossible. Stevie and I were certain our adventures together were just beginning as the Hoosier State disappeared behind us.

KIIQ-FM and its sister KRTS-AM were located inside a small, one-story steel building near the top of Manitou Springs, Colorado, at 7,100 feet along old US Highway 24. The building today has housed a liquor store for the past few decades, which seems oddly appropriate. Although the state of Colorado led the way in legalizing casually ingested marijuana, that step forward remained decades away in the early 1980s. Despite legal prohibition then, a higher percentage than seemed normal enjoyed recreational pot anyway. Cops tended to look elsewhere when responsible adults enjoyed cannabis. Manitou Springs was often referred to as the place where hippies migrated after Haight-Ashbury went commercial. The small community was home to an eccentric variety of colorful characters.

Extreme right-brain rationalization justified my dramatic career move. First, Jesse Bullet was program director and my primary mentor. That meant the most. Chuck Dunaway was the general manager. He was already a living broadcasting legend, accomplishing significant success at big-name stations such as KILT in Houston, KLIF in Dallas, and WKY in Oklahoma City. Dunaway was even a WABC Good Guy in New York. An opportunity to work beside TWO legends seemed like a rare opportunity.

The air staff included a crew of talented up-and-comers from all over the country. Bob Jacobs did the morning show and arrived following big success in Fort Wayne, Indiana. Kirk Russell was a fixture in Texas and west coast rock radio. Mike Daniels, an affable local guy who moonlighted on television, did middays. Ron Chase worked nights and was a production wizard. Jesse went on the air occasionally, and yours truly settled into all nights and music directing.

KIIQ was part of a then-recently formed broadcast group known as Wiskes/Abaris Communications, a company concocted by two suits. Don Wiskes, a money guy none of us ever met, and Jack Higgins, a red-headed Irish-looking guy from Chicago, whose professional background included real estate and advertising, were the faces (and money) of the company. It was also rumored that venture capital came from other investors, including well-known NBA stars of the period—Magic Johnson, Isaiah Thomas, and Mark Aguirre. No one knew for sure, but we believed it sounded impressive and offered additional street credibility. The promise of something great led every single radio geek to that small, corrugated metal box atop the hill.

KIIQ plagued itself for years with a litany of format changes, indifferent ownership, and little to no promotion. Arbitron ratings were mid-pack at best. Numbers from their most recent survey (rating periods occurred twice annually in that market, which was barely inside the top 100) reached 5.4, just below the middle of the pack. Dunaway, Bullet, and the company had big plans, eyeing double-digit ratings. Local, regional, and national advertising agencies were blitzed with promotional presentations. A budget of $100,000 was set aside for external promotion that included slick local television advertising. A newly created station logo got attached to anything that might carry it, and promotional swag was distributed like candy at parades. KIIQ went all out. It was the best-sounding station in the market and played the hits. High goals seemed within reach.

Working alongside Bullet and Dunaway was eye-opening. Although Chuck was the general manager, he essentially programmed the station. His background at hit music stations ensured a philosophy of tight, relatively conservative playlists, presented enthusiastically by up-tempo folks on the air. KIIQ airways were a continuous stream of promotion. Jesse Bullet always looked for edges that made the station sound less predictably formulaic. I had a front-row seat for much creative tension. One weekday late in 1981, Bullet, Dunaway, and I conducted our weekly music meeting to discuss which songs should be added to or removed from the playlist. My job was to provide a list of nominees. Only one new song seemed worthy of consideration. George Harrison's *All Those Years Ago* was a medium-tempo tribute to then-recently murdered John Lennon.

Bullet liked it. It grew on me but was really only on the list because George Harrison was a name artist. No other recently released songs really deserved consideration. Dunaway hated it. As consideration of the song continued, his mood further soured. Chuck made blunt points, wondering aloud why we would even consider adding a song about "dead fucking John Lennon; it's way too goddamn depressing." As Dunaway fretted over each new observation, his face turned a brighter shade of red. Chuck was a guy who hung out with John Lennon when the Beatles were a touring band.

Dunaway glared in my direction. "Why do we have to fucking add ANYTHING!? Who says we have to do that?" My reply attempted to justify refreshing the playlist and including an instantly recognizable artist. "FUCK THAT! We do not NEED to add ANYTHING!" Jesse was never averse to conflict and seemed to relish pouring gasoline onto fires. About all he got out of his mouth was "Look here old man…" before Dunaway stood up, put the cigarette he was smoking out in the palm of his hand, and threw us out of his office. Meeting over.

Weekly meetings either went like that or Dunaway rubber-stamped whatever we suggested before ordering us out of his office so we could "Get back to fucking work." In either bipolar case, Bullet usually dragged me down the street to the Royal Tavern, a colorful local joint where disgruntled veterans and patchouli-scented longhairs sipped suds together in peacefully tentative ways. Jesse and I tended to make short work of long necks before lunch and heading back to work. His venting and subsequent cool-down seemed critical in a valuable mentoring process.

The results of the first Arbitron rating period under the new regime were not what anyone expected. The numbers did not rise. The final 12+ fell to 4.8. Affront to professional egos aside, dropping nearly a full point meant selling advertising for the stations suddenly became much more difficult. Dunaway was beside himself, absolutely inconsolable. The only thing he kept repeating was "I have never lost." He alternated between depression and anger and remained unable to accept defeat. His course of action was blowing town with a business-minded female several years his junior who headed up all station back-office operations.

The good thing about Arbitron rating periods was the relatively short amount of time before new surveys began. KIIQ had three months to change course. Jesse Bullet assumed components of general management, but essentially maintained control of programming. His primary background was album-oriented rock. He became enamored of a trend unfolding in Southern California that included alternative rock. The birth of MTV also fueled new delivery of music that included video. His idea was to give the traditional top-40-sounding station a kick by including new rock and positioning the station as edgier than everyone else. He scribbled call letters using a magic marker on a restaurant menu one night, and that became an alternative station logo.

As the next Arbitron survey period began, $100,000 for promotion was out of the question. Jesse managed to wrangle almost $60,000 from the Wiskes/Abaris coffers. Once again, the station sounded great throughout the survey period. It was bright and edgy, and promotion was concise. Jesse took me further under his wing and became a great mentor. As management consumed more of his time, additional programming responsibilities were handed to me.

One lesson included dealing with competitors. The monster station in town was an album-oriented rock station with the greatest call letters in the history of radio, particularly in Colorado. KILO. When they gave away baseball caps, they were not merely hats. They were lids. KILO had everything hip covered, and their numbers were impressive. A Bob Seger concert was planned in Colorado Springs, and KILO paid Denver promoter Barry Fey to become the presenting sponsor. KILO air was filled with promotion, always prominently tagged with "KILO Proudly Presents Bob Seger." Lines at ticket locations the day sales began were long. Every location was blanketed with "KILO Presents" banners. My thought was simply that perhaps we would get the next one. Everyone feared Barry Fey but always kissed his ass.

Jesse had different ideas. The morning concert tickets went on sale, my home phone rang. Jesse was angry. He demanded to know why in the hell the entire staff was not at each ticket location passing out donuts and station merchandise. "John, why is there NO on-air promotion of this concert?!" My thought was that it was a KILO deal, and a certain amount of discretion was necessary so as not to alienate Mr. Fey. That was the wrong thought. Bullet insisted "We need to BLANKET our air with "KIIQ Proudly WELCOMES Bob Seger" promos. It costs us nothing, and is the RIGHT way to promote! Barry Fey gets free publicity! We can trade air time for tickets then give them away on the air--no money required." Jesse strongly advocated getting hands dirty every time.

Final 12+ rating number: 2.8. A fall of TWO full rating points. That defeat soon sent Jessie packing for greener pastures in Southern California. In the wake of rock bottom, the station's Herb Tarlek-like sales manager got promoted to general manager.

I officially became program director nine months after walking in the front door for the first time. The stunning, inexplicable ratings plummet deeply affected the entire air staff. All of them departed one by one. Frustration over not making any dents in a relatively small market and ultimately reporting to someone far less experienced proved too much. Bob Jacobs landed at WPLJ in New York, where he was Fast Jimmy for years. Kirk Russell headed west. Ron Chase expanded his status as production wizard and masterminded the first (and still leading) online trade publication, but did so from his native Texas.

The primary challenges of my very first program directorship were simple. Get an entire air staff hired on the cheap, make the sound of the station cohesive, promote the hell out of it with a total budget of zero, and get the numbers up to a level that supported advertising sales.

CHAPTER 31

A ROCK STAR AND A SUPERMODEL. NAKED.

Stevie and I sought a tropical vacation away from the mountains of Colorado as winter got serious in 1985. We selected St. Barthelemy in the French West Indies, a relatively secluded island known for hip people and beautiful beaches. One of the most interesting (and terrifying) aspects of St. Barts was the flight in. Specially equipped small planes were flown by pilots trained for the approach. Food on the island was top notch with significant French and Creole influences, not to mention great wine selections.

Terrain on the island was mountainous and most roads were more like goat paths. Cars were not widely used there, especially by visitors. Most rented Mini Mokes, British vehicles that were part tiny Jeep and part golf cart. All-wheel drive made short work of up and down hilly, rutted paths. They were also relatively fun to drive while dressed sparingly.

Most locals and tourists fostered a laissez-faire attitude about beach attire. Speedo? No problem. One-piece? No problem. Bikini bottom only? No problem. Naked? In most places and cases, fine. Frolicking nude on a beautiful beach was something we desired, but our Midwest upbringing prevented casting fate to the wind among large groups on public sand. Many chose not to be so exposed or had kids running around.

We heard about really small, intimate, secluded beaches where privacy was assured, complete with otherworldly scenery. Specific instructions about how to find such places were vague. The proprietor of the small bed and breakfast serving as our hideaway attempted guidance one bright morning. Directions were, "See the third mountain over there? Traverse it beginning at the base of its west side. Go halfway up. On your left, you will see a boulder on one side and a stake with a tiny red flag on the other. Drive between those two objects and a path will become apparent. Go through the clearing then down the other side of the mountain to the beach. Very private."

No cell phones or GPS devices were available to ordinary folks in the mid-1980s. Hurriedly scribbled directions from a local had to suffice. We managed to find the base of the west side of the third mountain along with a pathway that resembled a road. Almost all the way up, we saw a series of tiny, secluded beaches far below. The boulder and red flag on a stick eluded detection. Worse, we found ourselves grill to grill with another identical Mini Moke. Neither of us could get around the other because the path was barely one lane wide. Down one side was a relatively steep cliff, and on the other rocks, trees and hillside.

A traffic impasse atop a mountain on St. Barts did not incite road rage, just hope for mutual resolution of getting vehicles out and to their destinations. We male Mini Moke drivers stepped out for a chat. The other guy looked familiar, but sunglasses, a hat, and beach attire yielded few clues. He also sought the exact same beach we did, right down to the boulder and red flag on a stick. We agreed to try locating it together. The woman in the other vehicle and Stevie climbed out to join the conversation.

Once back in our Moke, I asked Stevie, "Do you have any idea who those two people are?" She flashed a blank stare. "Ric Ocasek and Paulina Porizkova," I continued. Nothing registered until I told her, "He's the main guy in The Cars, and she is the leading supermodel in the entire world. You know, Paris? Fashion? Sports Illustrated?"

Our trip back down the mountain was tempered with continuous advice for Stevie. "Keep cool and do NOT fawn over them. The last thing they need is bug-eyed fans. Just say hello and move to our side of the beach. Act normal."

The trip down the mountain slowly began. Turning around was impossible, so the only way back down for us was in reverse. Ocasek and Porizkova were headed the right way but still needed to follow us. Stevie spotted the boulder and the red flag about halfway down. We missed those particular landmarks on the way up because no one accounted for brush that was never manicured. Tall growth obscured both the boulder (it was actually a big-ish rock) and the red-flagged stake. The cloth weathered to a threadbare color that was pinker and barely attached to a crooked stick.

Sure enough, a path emerged beyond the turnoff. Ric led the way while we followed from a respectable distance. A gorgeous, unspoiled, pristine strip of sand, bordered on three sides by a mountain revealed itself at the bottom. Crystal clear water kissed our little beach with tiny shimmering waves. Rocky outcroppings punctuated the horizon. Ocasek and Porizkova headed right while

Stevie and I zigged left. We were separated by maybe 35 feet, five times the social distance I actually craved.

Weird thoughts permeate consciousness while experiencing unusual events destined never again to occur. Everyone shed clothing quickly but inside our own spaces. My mind raced. I was buck naked on a beach that also contained an equally naked rock star and the most famous supermodel on earth, also wearing nothing. How could time get slowed down or stopped in order to take in every last millisecond of such an unlikely beach adventure?

Remaining cool was a struggle. It was easy not paying attention to a really thin person later humorously derided as a live-action stick figure with a penis. It was nearly impossible to look away from a completely naked supermodel just feet away. I was thankful for darkly tinted sunglasses resting on the upper bridge of my nose. Ocasek may have even checked Stevie out a time or two.

Stevie tossed a towel and advised, "Hey, stud, you might want to do something about that (pointing toward my groin)." Nature took its course regarding rigidity. Dashing into the water did not help. It was crystal clear, and incapable of adequately hiding toes much less erections. Standing with my back to the other three, I silently cursed as barely perceptible current undulated between my thighs.

Once sufficiently flaccid, we (Stevie) decided it was time to head back. Nods were exchanged. On the ride back I lamented not actually introducing ourselves, talking shop, and perhaps having dinner later. Longer-term hindsight supports our actions. People, especially famous ones, crave privacy and go to places like St. Barts to get it.

CHAPTER 32

SHEER JOYS OF PROGRAM DIRECTING

Another career *what's next* moment arrived. Programming two radio stations suddenly became my job. The only direction to go was up. We had no ratings, no money, no computers, and no tangible resources of any kind. An entire excellent air staff walked away. My legendary mentors were gone. The challenges were enormous.

Replacing the air staff was hit or miss. A big miss out of the gate was a gentleman named Quincy. His full name was John Quincy Adams, the same as the sixth president. All he ever wanted to be called was Quincy, or preferably just Q. Nothing else. He was burly and stood six and a half feet tall, a rare black man in a mostly white mountain enclave. He was blessed with a deep and booming voice. Q's personality was also dynamic, and he had tremendous potential. The all-night gig of Q on the Q lasted just three days.

On Quincy's fourth day a little past 3:00 in the morning, the phone on my nightstand rang. The Manitou Springs Police sergeant on the other end requested my presence at the radio station as soon as possible. "Mr. Howard, we have a serious issue with Mr. Adams, and we need to gain access to the interior of the structure." My trip down Ute Pass took twenty minutes. Stereo 102.7 featured a needle at the very end of the groove on a vinyl album all the way down.

Scratch/scratch. Scratch/scratch. Scratch/scratch. Scratch/scratch.

Quincy's fiery-tempered wife Elveen decided to surprise him. She delivered a late-night meal after her shift ended at 2 am. Elveen arrived to find all the lights in the station out. She probably wondered why an entire Luther Vandross album side was playing, especially since KIIQ did not feature any Luther Vandross songs anywhere on its playlist.

KIIQ's control room faced the parking lot and included a large picture window. There were no blinds or curtains. Several lit candles barely illuminated the interior. Elveen soon determined her husband wore no clothing and was atop a much younger and equally nude lady.

Elveen tried hard to shatter the control room window with granite landscape stones ringing the building. Her futile glass-shattering attempts immediately preceded the splattering of Quincy's surprise feast all over the unbroken pane. Elveen bolted for her car, and Quincy probably had no idea what was next. Would she storm away, or use the vehicle as a battering ram to drive through the front of the building? In a panic, he ran out the front door, still naked, to try and salvage his marriage. Elveen squealed away, spraying Quincy with gravel.

The naked young lady still in the control room, sensing big trouble, put her clothes back on and vanished through a side exit door. That left no one inside the building, and security features included doors that locked automatically. Quincy's keys were in the pocket of his pants, crumpled on the control room floor. Side A of *Forever, for Always, for Love* had just over a minute left on the last track.

A passerby spotted a hulking, naked Quincy desperately trying to reenter the station and dialed 911. Cops arrived quickly and caught Quincy pounding the back door with a large rock. Cuffs and a blanket were next before officers began asking questions. That is when Sgt. Hank Meyer woke me up.

Regular programming was reestablished around 3:25 a.m., with me at the wheel and Quincy freshly dispatched. No one ever told me that cleaning grease, greenish vegetables, sweet potato pie, and a scoop of apple cobbler off windows at sunrise was part of a program director gig.

Most of the rest of the staff that arrived during my tenure worked out better. A personable local announcer named Jack Hamilton joined, as did up-and-comers Lindy Scott and Paul Roberts. Kid Manning arrived from Texas shortly before Jesse Bullet took off. We also took a chance on a local musician with an immense personality who frequented many station events and became friends with the staff. He chose the air name Red Noize. He had no radio experience, but we gave him morning drive anyway. It worked well. Red went on to primary competitor KILO, programmed a station in Grand Rapids, and eventually landed in Atlanta at WZGC, where he died of cancer far too young at forty.

Just one other Quincy-like episode occurred at KIIQ. Was it karma for my own earlier transgressions?

Another personality from the Wiskes/Abaris sister station in San Angelo wanted to move to Colorado. Don Costello was British and preferred being called simply Costello. I liked the way he sounded because his native accent remained. Novelty had to suffice because we were unable to pay much more than minimum wage. The appearance of station owners at KIIQ was rare, but when Jack Higgins showed up it was usually to pound fists on desks. Costello's daily calls begging for a job finally wore me down. He became the third Wiskes/Abaris Texas employee to join KIIQ. Jack yelled at me, ordering that I stop raiding the other stations.

Costello lasted a few paychecks longer than Quincy in the overnight slot. On the way home from the once-thriving nightspot Meadow Muffins in Old Colorado City, I heard an unfamiliar album tracking in the middle of the night. The station was on the way home, so I decided to pop a 2:30 a.m. surprise. The control room was dimly lit but Costello and his female companion were still dressed.

My decibel level was high. "Lady, go home. Costello, we have a format. Stick to it. It does not matter what kind of music you like or that you found a female willing to screw you. Take care of both urges outside this building. You got it?"

He appreciated a second chance but blew it a few months later.

Why did I want to do this again?

CHAPTER 33

MELLENCAMP AND MY SMOKES

Rock stars and most other famous people are still just people. Most of them enjoy the adulation they receive but prefer simply being treated as just another person. My personal approach has always been to respect their space and not become some drooling, bug-eyed fan with a bad case of star-struck. While employed by XM Satellite Radio in Washington, respecting the space of artists was considered official company policy.

My life includes numerous encounters with celebrities, most of them from being on the air. Some are more memorable than others.

During the early 1970s, post-high-school academic pursuits and a thin wallet led me to the Broadcast Production Technology program at Vincennes University in southern Indiana. One of thirty-one other classmates in the program for over a year was pre-famous John Mellencamp. A native Hoosier, he hailed from nearby Seymour.

None of us hung out together. I did not live on campus and worked paying jobs when not at school. All Broadcast Production classes were held inside a former brewery next to active railroad tracks.

The building also housed radio and television studios, and offices for a relatively new local CATV company. It was the cable company before that became big business. For a small price, they boosted distant local signals into customer homes using wire.

Six students in the program smoked cigarettes. A congregation of all six gathered on the front steps of the brewery to fire up smokes between classes. Five of the six smokers always had their own cigarettes. They were dirt cheap then at less than 35 cents a pack. The one guy who never had money or smokes was Mellencamp. For more than a year, at least a few times every school day he attended, John asked the same thing of me (and others) repeatedly: 'Hey JT (or whoever) . . . got a smoke?'

Mellencamp was not a great student and largely uninterested in the finer points of broadcasting. He confided to faculty that his real interest was making music. He intended to make that his career. Most of us were skeptical. Odds of success in the music business were even longer than broadcasting, and we interpreted his unpolished style as a ticket to something far less glamorous. His band played on campus occasionally. They opened for a bigger group, Chase, one night. Their one hit, *Get It On*, recently peaked. Chase was a talented band, but their set confused youthful students. Instead of a lot of *Get It On*-like songs, improvised jazz filled the arena. Great, but unexpected. They lost the crowd. Chase ended a shortened set by playing *Get It On* again. Mellencamp's band was raw, unpolished, and loud, but earned an A for effort. The crowd rallied behind them.

Most broadcasting students lost touch after graduation.

While working at WBOW late in 1976, Mellencamp, then known as John Cougar, called one evening to personally pitch his band's new album called *Chestnut Street Incident.*

"It's pretty good, JT. Can you do anything with it?"

"There are no guarantees but we do have a new music hour on the FM station Saturday nights," I explained. "Let's target that."

Mellencamp happily sent a couple of promo albums in time for the weekend. His music still seemed raw and unpolished, but we played the title track and a couple of more. The album went nowhere.

After Mellencamp's string of hit records began in the early 1980s, I felt happy for him and wondered how far he could take it. Later that decade, I was music director at K-View in Colorado Springs. One of the label A & R folks who regularly called to pitch singles was a nice lady named Katie with Mercury Records, then the label home for John Mellencamp's *Scarecrow* album. It eventually became a big commercial success. Katie pitched other artists more suitable with a record company view of adult contemporary music, but none of it inspired airplay that week. I gave her a hearty "way to go" for Mellencamp's *Scarecrow* album and relayed tales of our brief academic career together in Vincennes.

Katie indicated John just happened to be down the hall in her building that day.

"Hang on, I'll tell him hi for you."

Instead of replying back through Katie, Mellencamp jumped on the line, offered a little small talk, then said, "Come to our show in Denver! I'll ask Katie to arrange it, and I'll see you there."

Stevie and I arrived before the show, were ushered backstage by Katie. Joining us were several people from the regional music store chain Sound Warehouse. John and his band walked into the room and began shaking hands, wedding reception line style. Mellencamp said the same thing to everyone in line. "Thanks for coming and enjoy the show." When John got to me, I said "Hey Mellencamp . . . got a smoke?" He looked at me like I was from another planet, and then said, "Thanks for coming, and enjoy the show."

I had a better conversation with Mellencamp's bass player Toby Myers.

"How's your brother Joe?" Toby inquired. Myers helped produce music for my younger brother.

"When does the tour wrap up?" I asked. "Hopefully not for a while, but we're off in May, and I've got plans" he replied. "Track?" I asked. "Yep." Hanging at the Indianapolis Motor Speedway most days it was open leading up to the Indy 500 was completely normal behavior for native Hoosiers.

"Hey, J.T., don't let John's snub bother you. He gets like that before shows. In a zone. It should be good tonight."

The concert was fantastic. John Mellencamp and I have some things in common, including living in Indiana by choice. He has a much nicer home and plenty of cigarettes though.

CHAPTER 34

SALLY, THE AMARILLO HOOKER

I love the entire state of Texas. It is a treasure chest. My first professional venture into Lone Star country was late in 1982. Managers from each Wiskes-Abaris station intended to gather at a quasi-halfway point for a three-day summit. Once beyond Raton Pass, the drive toward Amarillo turned dull, and us boys shot the breeze.

Spouses were not allowed to make the trip. Stevie interpreted that as a secret code that meant all males in the group were destined for unbridled sex with horny Texas gals. That particular notion of coquetry was not on my to-do list. Getting business accomplished, making contacts, and career advancement were my goals. Stevie convinced herself that temptation would lead to inevitable marital breach, and she was determined to thwart it. We had not yet spent any time apart in our fledgling marriage, and her paranoid certainty that I would stray spiraled out of control.

I hopped out of bed and into a hot shower the morning of departure. That is where I discovered the entire shaft of my penis and much of the surrounding torso was painted neon purple with a permanent-ink wide felt-tip marker. A cropped, well-kept nest of pubic hair that normally surrounded the goodies was haphazardly shaven into a crude maze of crooked stripes. Stevie accomplished her discreet genital vandalism very gingerly as I snored.

She figured that if the package was deformed, I wouldn't use it for adultery. It would simply be too embarrassing. I managed to help her reach an entirely new level of anxiety by reminding her, "You know none of your cute little efforts will matter if the other woman and I just keep all the lights off."

Once inside an old-fashioned roadside motel, complete with a cowboy on the garish neon sign, the phone number and room information passed to Stevie led to repetitive phone calls. She needed to monitor any potentially aberrant behavior.

Stevie's sudden insanity was entertaining to my male traveling companions. All were aware of her neuroses and the crude branding of my private parts. Instead of offering compassion, they located, paid for, and then dispatched a prostitute to my motel room the first night we arrived.

Earlier in the evening, our group ate too much red meat for dinner and then chased the grub with Shiner long necks and line dancing inside a local yee-haw joint. I excused myself around 9:30, not just because I was unwilling to pound a few more suds, but I needed sleep before charging into important meetings the next day.

Repeated pounding on the door jarred me awake a little past 11. I threw on a pair of jeans and a T-shirt before cracking it open. Outside stood a thirtysomething young lady with slight facial creases and a cockeyed smile. She wore a cowboy hat, a red-and-white checkered blouse pulled way up and tied above her belly, denim shorts that were a Daisy Duke level of skimpy, and a shiny pair of pointy-toed cowboy boots. She held what appeared to be a nearly empty bottle of tequila and used her free arm to lean against the door frame.

"You John?" she asked.

"Yep. What can I do for you, ma'am?" I replied.

"You're kinda cute, John."

Don't do it, idiot. DO NOT do it. Wish her well and shut the door. NOW. "Would you like to come in? Uh, sorry...didn't catch your name," I asked, instantly regretting it.

"Sally. Like Mustang Sally. Yes, John, I'd like to come in. Please."

It was autumn, Amarillo was chilly, and she was barely dressed. Sally did not mince words once inside, heading straight for the bed. "John, there are only two things rational people can do in Amarillo, Texas, on a Wednesday night. Drinkin' and fuckin', and I am almost drunk. So whatdya say, John?"

"Who sent you over here?" I asked.

"Does it really matter? I'm over here now."

Sally seemed tired. Earlier in life, I might have accepted her challenge. But it was late, and there were important career items at stake. Plus, the phone was ringing, and I did not want to speak to Stevie while there was an impatient whore inside my room determined to pour tequila and start fuckin'.

"Sally, I really appreciate you stopping by. This is NOT going to happen, though. But get your money's worth. If you really crave more than drinking, the fucking needs to include someone else from the honky-tonk down the street, and that's probably where you ought to go. Give your favorite regular one on the house. But sorry. None for me tonight, sweetie."

She pecked me on the cheek and asked, "Are you absolutely sure, cutey pie?" (*I was never more certain*). After I nodded, Sally departed for buckin', fuckin' cowboys unknown.

The first of many amazing lines by Texans carved itself into my memory. "There are only two things rational people can do in Amarillo, Texas, on a Wednesday night. Drinkin' and fuckin,' and I am almost drunk."

I called Stevie back. Her tone was a few octaves north of snotty. "WHAT have YOU been doing, JOHN?!" "I got woke up from a sound sleep by some hooker named Sally who wanted to drink then fuck."

"Yeah, right. In your wet dreams."

Confident in the actual truth, I also repeated the need for solid, uninterrupted sleep before my big day. Stevie only called three more times before sunrise.

On the way back to Colorado, I heard a second possibly immortal line from the mouth of a Texan. The only obviously open food joint at 11 a.m. on Saturday near Dalhart was an old-school pizza joint, complete with upside-down triangular windows and a bright red roof. Just one person was inside. She not only waited on the only table with customers, ours, but also prepped and cooked the pies.

Her nametag read Betsy, and she had no outward enthusiasm for her profession. She wasn't nasty, just indifferent.

Betsy appeared to be in her mid-30s and conveyed an aura of disappointment. Idle chit chat led to a question from Jesse Bullet. "Betsy, how long have you been here in Dalhart?" Bored and expressionless, she simply answered, "Including today?"

The biggest reason Texas is cool involves people who live there.

CHAPTER 35

KIIQ AND THE RATINGS RACKET

My radio philosophies turned relatively conservative when I became KIIQ's program director. It seemed out of character because I generally advocated trying new and different things. After succeeding two legends who failed by going with new and different, my primary aversion became trying anything new and different.

My directive was to get ratings back to respectable levels, then growing them so that ad sales could support profitability. Being at rock bottom fueled optimism, but lack of money was challenging. When I say no money, I mean NO money. Station bills were not always paid. Employee paydays were lotteries. Not everyone who received a paycheck expected the ability to cash it before it bounced. Musical chairs played out on paydays. Checks were distributed to employees like feed sacks off the back of a truck in the Third World. Recipients raced down the street to the Bank of Manitou, armed with embossed safety paper and hope. Most made it, but some did not and waited a few more days for sufficient funds.

I was either second or third in the succession line for general manager, depending on the day and who was there. The sales manager usually assumed the role, but second in command was split with the chief engineer of the station, Rodger Tighe. General Manager Newell Ledbetter was out of the building most of the time, struggling to drum up cash business.

Rodger and I spent inordinate amounts of time concocting excuses for creditors demanding payment. The most popular played off the vagueness of station ownership. We convinced several creditors that payment funds originated in Saudi Arabia.

"Your money will be released once our financial people there, Muhammad Wiskes and Abdul Abaris, arrange wire transfers. Unfortunately, that process takes a few business days. We are grateful for your patience."

Extreme creditor emergencies meant using a secret checkbook squirreled away inside a locked drawer in Newell's office. It was linked to an external account and only used if stations were about to go dark.

The market of Colorado Springs is geographically unique. Situated against the Front Range of the Rocky Mountains, the city is anchored on the west by the 14,115-foot Pikes Peak. South and slightly east of Pikes Peak stands Cheyenne Mountain. It tops out at just over 9,500 feet. The vast majority of FM and television antennas in the market sit atop the mountain. None of them are very high because they don't need to be. They are already a mile and a half above sea level. More significant than what is on top of the mountain is inside. Cheyenne Mountain was hollowed out decades ago, and it houses the North American Aerospace Defense Command. NORAD can withstand a direct nuclear hit. If that ever happened, broadcasting sticks on top would not matter.

Predictably, access to Cheyenne Mountain's summit was severely limited. Those maintaining towers and transmitters navigated a narrow pathway through a series of locked gates to reach the top. Engineers with warped senses of humor periodically installed stolen road signs along the road to the top. "Bridge Out," "High Water," and "Road Closed" signs were popular. It took a long time to get there, even in great weather.

Newell and Rodger were gone the day a local electric power utility truck pulled into the lot. The uniformed fellow who entered the station was all business and did not care who heard him. He demanded to speak with the general manager. Candy Clark, the shapely blonde receptionist who essentially ran the entire station, called me. Mr. Utility held three large chains with padlocks.

"We have a crew on the way to the top of Cheyenne Mountain right now to physically disconnect power to your station transmitter. They also have chains identical to these to lock down your transmitter facility."

My mind raced, but I could only think, *Oh SHIT!*

"Power to your studios will also be disconnected, and all three exterior doors in this building will be chained and padlocked. We have a court order right here," he said, handing me the papers.

It appeared legitimate, but no lawyer was handy.

"The only way to avert this action is to make immediate payment in full for all amounts in arrears, payment for a service call for sending a crew up the mountain, and advance estimated payment for the next three months. You have thirty minutes, and the clock starts now." He glanced at his wristwatch.

My first call rang Jack Higgins, who was unavailable. So was everyone else. I reached for the secret checkbook and wrote $24,997.14 in the "amount" box. One of two things could happen. Either the check would bounce and we would leave the air, or an all-clear would be issued if the secret account was solvent. The Wiskes/Abaris cushion was $25,000, and I used all but $2.86. Higgins later screamed at me, but there was solace in knowing we could stay on the air through my first Arbitron survey period as program director.

KIIQ employed an enthusiastic, young sales staff that mostly made cold calls and dealt with inordinate amounts of rejection. Many of them burned barter at local joints on any given day, drinking or eating on the station's dime. I joined them on numerous occasions because we were allies.

Only one salesperson consistently delivered cash orders. We referred to Laura Morgan as barroom cute. She wore revealing clothing that accentuated her figure, and her closing skills were unique. Remnants were frequently spotted on her often carelessly buttoned blouses. Occasional hickeys or smeared makeup near her tousled hair was a bellwether for cash orders. It drove the sales staff crazy but helped keep the lights on.

Station trade became my means to promote. Given a promotion budget that had been whittled to zero, I managed to get call letters onto bus benches and city buses by running commercials for the local mass transit company. Our spots ran in local movie theaters before each film because we traded for movie commercials. A local outdoor advertising company placed our call letters on unsold billboards in exchange for advertising their company. Television spots for the station also ran in trade.

Promotion turned creative. Halloween rolled around, so we borrowed a hearse from a creepy local kid who was a little too heavily immersed in goth. KIIQ staff set about crashing parties with our "Cruisin' Coffin." Inside an actual coffin was a variety of traded food, beverages, and party gear, plus plenty of leftover station swag. It effectively generated buzz.

The air staff, and most of the rest of the station, remained in near-open mutiny. They did not like the restrictive format. My choice was to retain a "modern rock" image but to play mostly tried-and-true hit records—in other words, large mainstream hits like *Every Breath You Take* by the Police or *Billie Jean* by Michael Jackson. I rolled just enough Flock of Seagulls or INXS to make it seem hipper.

My research demonstrated listeners consumed the station in roughly twenty-minute increments while commuting or when getting up in the morning and at the same time every day. I tailored the playlist to take advantage of such listening habits. It was too soon and prohibitively expensive for automated scheduling. Only around 200 songs were available for airplay at any given time during non-survey periods. When Arbitron surveys began, I cut the number to ninety-seven. Those songs were the cream of the crop. Playback was structured so that any listener who tuned in for twenty minutes at the same time every day would not hear the same song for six days. At night we might even play the same song twice in an hour and promote it to encourage tune-in.

That was great for casual listeners, but people on the air and everyone else in the building who listened all day believed I lost my mind. When the fall Arbitron rating book was released, the only things that dropped were jaws. Our 12+ number climbed to 5.8, which exceeded the starting point of the Dunaway/Bullet era. We were in the top three in critical demographics, and serious partying ensued. Competitors called to congratulate us, followed by television and newspaper interviews. Life was suddenly good again. I revealed a strategy to get to an 8 rating in the spring, along with double-digit targets for the following fall.

Newell and Higgins will HAVE to pay attention now.

Two things stood in the way of that happy ending. Jack Higgins flew in for the holidays and called an all-hands-on-deck staff meeting on Christmas Eve. Our naïve thinking embraced the probability of back-slapping and perhaps token bonuses for jobs well done. That is not how things worked out.

Instead of mentioning our rise from the ratings cellar, Jack cut loose with a profanity-laced tirade about how underachieving the staff was. "You'd best get your acts together, or you will all be out on the street. That I can promise," he snarled. Higgins called out each manager by name spent a few moments berating each one. His timing was odd, considering Santa already began plopping down chimneys along the East Coast.

Merry Fucking Christmas to you too, clown.

In January of 1983, Newell and I had a loud argument about the Chicago song *Love Me Tomorrow*. I made it part of our 200-song, non-survey period playlist. David Foster wrote it, but most members of Toto, one of our core bands, played on it. It filled a variety gap, and I was ambivalent. Ledbetter hated anything by Chicago and shouted, "I don't EVER want to hear another song by that band on this station. NEVER again. You got me?!"

Who the hell does he think he is?

Anger welled up, then exploded. "Newell, who the fuck is programming this station? You or me? If it's me, you need to let me do my fucking job! If it's you, good luck growing the numbers. I don't tell you how to sell commercials, and you can't tell me what songs can and cannot be played. You got ME?!"

February meant preparing for the spring survey period. On Tuesday after Valentine's Day, Newell called me into his office. "John, I promoted Dave Brull from KILO to program director. We will be moving the station in a different direction musically. We need more album tracks and want to broaden our demos beyond the whole modern-rock thing. We appreciate what you've done, but we're letting you go." It was not entirely unexpected but felt insulting.

By the time Arbitron spring numbers were released, I had become music director at KVUU, a growing station across town. Instead of my planned trajectory toward 8, KIIQ thudded to new lows. 2.4. K-View and its up-tempo adult contemporary format began an ascent that ultimately carried it to the top.

I chose to look ahead, shaping the future in positive ways. Although the KIIQ chapter ended badly following my first big success, I only publicly gloated once. On the way home one evening that summer, Stevie and I detoured through Manitou Springs to stop at Tubby's Turnaround, a convenience store next door to KIIQ.

On the way out with our goodies, I turned to face the depressing aluminum shelled radio station, extended both middle fingers, and took the last laugh.

The very short tenure at KIIQ/KRTS remains the most fondly remembered highlight of the radio portion of my career.

CHAPTER 36

PIANO MAN AND THE PRETENDER

Preconceived notions about certain famous people can cloud judgment of them. Celebrities perceived as assholes, for example, can be completely docile, and vice versa. Such was the case with Billy Joel and Jackson Browne. Stevie and I were invited backstage to meet those artists at two concerts in the late 1980s. We were sure Billy Joel would be a stereotypical New York jerk in terms of attitude. We found ourselves apprehensive before his show because there were only four of us in the green room.

Billy bounded in and enthusiastically greeted us. "HEY, how you doin?!" He was genuinely happy.

"How's the tour going?" I asked.

"Absolutely great, but I'm worried," Billy said. "I jumped off my piano in Salt Lake City two nights ago, and I heard my ankle pop. I didn't stick the landing and twisted it pretty good."

His Denver concert at the old McNichols Arena was also home to the NBA's Denver Nuggets. The team employed a legendary trainer named Chopper Travaglini.

His fame was earned by wrapping injured appendages and erasing any concern about further aggravation or performance. Billy was effusive with praise for Chopper, who spent a lot of time with him earlier that day. "Check this out!" He pulled up his pant leg and showed off his Chopper-wrapped ankle.

"Whatya think, John? Should I try it again tonight?"

He's asking ME?! "If it's part of the show, go for it!"

"Fine," he joked, "But I'm holding you responsible if it goes badly."

The Joel song *Pressure* rolled into my head.

Billy Joel was one of the nicest, most accommodating big names I ever encountered. He executed the piano jump successfully during the show. After landing, he pointed in our general direction while nodding.

Conversely, one might assume that based on his extensive catalog of truly great music, Jackson Browne might be one of the coolest people on earth. That is why Stevie and I were excited to meet him after a show at Red Rocks. For hours ahead of time, I repeatedly advised Stevie to steer clear of any discussion that involved Daryl Hannah. Hannah and Browne became tabloid fodder, and that kind of nonsense would no doubt be the last thing he would want to talk about.

Jackson gave an inspired performance at Red Rocks. That venue tends to bring out the best in artists. It was my hope the vibe would carry over to our meet and greet. When he reached us, the first thing Stevie asked involved Daryl Hannah.

Uh oh. I cannot say with certainty that he was an asshole, but he shot a look that telegraphed strangulation. He turned surly and moved away from us quickly.

CHAPTER 37

BACK ONTO A HORSE WITH A VIEW

The first big success of my radio programming career was KIIQ, despite its off-the-deep-end dysfunction. Goals not reached by legendary radio veterans with a staff of seasoned professionals were actually attained by a relative nobody, spending a budget of zero and using a hodgepodge staff of warriors mainly in it for the joy of simply being there. The reward for that initial success involved being unceremoniously dumped by others who incorrectly believed they could do much better.

Radio professionals are, if nothing else, masochists. The notion that humans should get back on the horse that threw them off led across town to KVUU in Colorado Springs. K-View 99.9. Before my arrival, their own recently arrived ownership began the process of transforming a station that barely had a signal in town. It had no ratings and not much of a format. K-View was paired with AM country KSSS, a local legacy station that enjoyed success. The niche K-View began to fill was essentially Top 40 for adults. Radio labeled it Hot Adult Contemporary.

It featured most of the hits and a lot of impactful, well-researched oldies. K-View heavily focused on the local community and hired staff that fit the mold.

An eclectic gaggle of talent was assembled and led by Bobby Irwin, a Colorado native program director with a rich radio history there and elsewhere. I eventually became music director and assistant program director. After just a few short survey periods, the station rose from near the bottom of the heap to number one in the most lucrative adult demographics, and that is where it remained.

KVUU then occupied much of the penthouse floor of a twelve-story building on the south side of Colorado Springs. Views from control room windows included both the front range of the Rockies and fruited eastern plains. The equipment inside was top-notch. Powerful wall-mounted speakers were often used to jeopardize future hearing. The main studio was so well soundproofed that nothing could be heard in adjoining offices or nearby production rooms. The only part of the room not adequately insulated was the floor, which was concrete covered by commercial-grade short nap carpeting.

Just beneath the K-View control room on the eleventh floor was the corner office and conference room of a partner in a local legal firm. The lawyers were upset with the station because they were beaten to the penthouse after the building began leasing space.

Audio from large speakers in the studio tended to funnel through the floor and vibrate the walls of the partner offices and conference room. Several times every week, one or more of the partners from the firm below visited station General Manager Bill Struck to request or demand that folks in the control room tone it down. Those suggestions were usually offensive to anyone on the air, rationalizing that it would compromise their craft. Never mind that adequate volume could always be achieved through headphones without bothering anyone. It was a matter of principle.

I became part of the morning crew, anchoring sports updates twice an hour. My approach was mostly irreverent about everything but the Denver Broncos. The height of John Elway's quarterback career owned the loyalty of almost everyone in Colorado. An air shift followed in middays from 10 a.m. to 2 p.m. Peak legal meeting time.

Struck walked into the control room around 11 o'clock one morning, looking exasperated. "Please, John T.," he pleaded. "PLEASE turn it down for a while. The lawyers are all over my ass." That is all I needed to hear.

The volume was imperceptible for the next several songs until the all-business attorneys got resettled. With Bill safely busy back in his office, all four speakers were removed from the wall. Each was placed business end down in all four studio corners. It was time to play the Miami Vice Theme by Jan Hammer.

That selected ditty was a piece that featured highly processed drums, boom-box bass, and screaming guitars. Volume was cranked as high as it would go. Two minutes and twenty seconds or so that followed was Richter-scale-worthy. It also became the day legal action was threatened by ALL of the attorneys. Cracking concrete and eardrums was fun while it lasted. Getting hauled into court over loud music, while it would have been entertaining, was not something in which station management was interested. Coincidentally or not, the stations relocated from the penthouse to the ground floor a few years later.

K-View was heavily invested in local events. Station personalities remained busy every weekend making compensated personal appearances. Personal entertainment occasionally went too far. Every Saturday night, the station chose one "lucky" homeowner to host a K-View Saturday Night Party. Food and drinks were catered and, for a time, included a very large hot tub trucked in on a flatbed, provided by a company called "Port-A-Party." Ladders were attached, which enabled fun to proceed. Their relationship with the station lasted barely a summer. The combination of a pool-sized hot tub, darkness, and alcohol often resulted in reckless hedonism. The Port-A-Party folks got really tired of cleaning food and bodily fluids, not to mention articles of clothing, empty bottles, and worse out of their giant tubs.

Several relationships either began or ended at such parties. As supposedly responsible adults, part of our jobs included maintaining order. One Saturday night happened to be the birthday of the guy who did weeknights at K-View, Crazy Dave. He decided to celebrate at the listener residence. That was the last night I ever became brutally intoxicated, and I was thankful teetotaler Stevie kept the car keys.

"Come on, LET'S DO SHOTS," Dave insisted.

"What's wrong, people? Let's do SOME MORE SHOTS!" Dave was on a roll.

Eventually, I asked, "How many shots of whisky have we had?"

Dave slurred his reply. "I dongivafuck ... is my birth *HICCUP* birthday gawdammit!"

How could we lose track of shots? The bottle is about empty!

Losing count is never good.

Food was catered by a local pizza joint not known for easily digestive fare.

I proudly sported a fresh pair of $95 grey suede shoes along with fancy jeans and a polo shirt, an outfit Stevie hand-picked. Stopping shots of hard liquor became a great idea when Dave suddenly removed all of his clothing. Every last stitch. It was his birthday, and he had a suit to match. Dave beelined toward the Port-A-Party, then cannonballed into the middle of it. Stevie and I spent several minutes apologizing for Dave's behavior before deciding to slither away. We missed the arrival of uniformed officers.

The level of intoxication experienced went further than ever before. The twenty-five-mile journey home to Woodland Park, just below the altitude at which vegetation stops growing, effectively lasted until the first sharp curve beyond Manitou Springs.

"STEVIE! PULL OVER!"

All of the Jack Daniels, beer, pizza, and putrid remnants of everything else I consumed the previous few days erupted like Mount St. Helens alongside US Highway 24. My new suede shoes and crisp jeans were worn only once. Both were discarded on the spot. It took one hour and fifteen minutes to get home instead of thirty, and there was no traffic. Frequent stops became less productive in terms of vomit but did not stop involuntary heaving. Our bedroom did not stop spinning until nearly noon the following morning.

Although the K-View staff tended to seek out fun, everyone was dead serious about getting to, and remaining firmly, at the top. More importantly, the staff wanted to generate more ad sales revenue than anyone else in town.

Something fortuitous happened in the mid-1980s, but I had no idea at the time about an opportunity that ultimately changed my entire career.

The age of personal computing was in its infancy. Microsoft was not far removed from being a startup. MS-DOS 3.2 was released early in 1986. A difficult, time-consuming task for program and music directors involved compiling daily playlists for folks on the air to use. Automation of that task was a logical way a small computer could potentially be used.

A leading automation product was called Selector. It was too expensive for K-View management. A Colorado-based company that provided software and hardware for back-office business operations at many other stations also developed a music application that was PC-based. They needed a relatively close beta testing site for a break in the price. Columbine Systems was based in Golden, Colorado, and that became my destination for a few days in 1986.

Although I never considered myself a nerd or had any aspirations about coding, it was very easy to become excited about possibilities. Software could enhance productivity and reporting. I was all in. Being intimidated by computers was common early on. Over the course of the next few months, manual music rotation processes trudged through for years were converted into a relatively sophisticated database with an engine that could schedule all the music for a day. Bobby Irwin eventually came to rely on it, and I became the subject matter expert.

A confident stride inside the radio business had returned.

CHAPTER 38

PAYOLA

I was music director at K-View in Colorado Springs in 1987. The station established a solid reputation as a leading Adult Contemporary station. K-View was a trade reporter for multiple industry publications and the number-one station in a top-100 market. An independent promoter invited me to lunch, where he pitched a new song by Amy Grant. She successfully crossed over from Christian music onto the pop charts with a couple of hits. Her record company heavily promoted a new single specifically targeting Adult Contemporary stations. My thought about the song was that it was overly sappy and probably would not fit the edgy, up-tempo musical approach we chased.

Despite a great working relationship, expression of honest feelings did not endear me to the promoter, especially when I asked what else he was pushing. The only other song he had was more of a featured album cut being promoted to Album Oriented Rock stations by the Grateful Dead.

"Come on. Give it a spin!"

"John, you work at an AC station. Amy Grant is a natural. Jerry Garcia is not. Don't be stupid," he protested. Prodding continued and he relented.

Touch of Grey rolled into my ears for the first time. It had not yet been released.

Industry slang for playing a new release immediately was called "adding out of the box." When I added *Touch of Grey* out of the box later that week, Mr. Promoter called and spent painful minutes harassing me, questioning my ability as a music director, and calling me vile names.

"How in the fuck can you play the Grateful Dead on an AC station, you blithering idiot?! Amy Grant is AC. Jerry Garcia is for KILO. John, you are a damned fool!"

I tried explaining: "Our station is in Colorado. The natives have musical tastes that don't conform to the national mainstream. I live here. You blow in from LA every once in a while. Trust my judgment."

A courier package arrived from the promoter two days later. Contents of the package included just a videotape and a note that read, "Thanks for nothing. Fuck you." I popped the tape into the VCR at home later that evening and was assaulted by a compilation of morbidly obese people engaged in hardcore pornographic acts. My only thought as time progressed, other than laughter, was how wholesome Amy Grant might react to the way her records were promoted.

Before the Internet became ubiquitous, successful and occasionally rich music artists earned fame and fortune with record sales that resulted from being played on the radio. Radio folks were also often rewarded with perks. Treats included concert tickets, backstage access, and just about anything else imagination could conjure. If your radio station was deemed a "reporter" by leading trade publications, you drew attention from record company A & R, or Artists and Repertoire, people. Their primary goal was convincing program and music directors to add music by their artists to station playlists. Selected radio stations reported not only new additions but entire playlists weekly.

Major trade publications then included now-defunct relics *Radio & Records*, the *Gavin Report*, and others, as well as more established print publications such as *Billboard* and *Cashbox*. The more publications stations reported to, the more A & R attention they received.

It was a unique system. For the better portion of four decades, it primarily determined which songs became hits. Airplay drove sales, and record companies loved big numbers. The system began to crack once disruptive players and technologies arrived, from MTV to the internet. Old ways seem quaint today. From the late 1950s through the Reagan years, the fame and fortunes of national musical acts could be made or lost based on songs a couple of *hundred* radio people deemed important enough to play, or at least report they did for trade publications.

Payola described paying off programmers at radio stations that played and reported specific songs with airplay and chart positions. Strictly speaking, it has always been illegal and definitely not ethical. A national payola scandal drew the government's ire in the 1950s and threatened even to bring down Dick Clark. Federal regulations crafted back then remain today. Nearly every station required signatures on official payola documents. Carefully worded paragraphs prohibited taking cash payments for any reason.

That did not mean payola was absent, only that it was subtle and often rationalized into something else considered above board. One station, for example, strictly prohibited acceptance of cash or considerations over $50 from record companies or independent promoters. Some stations allowed loopholes for noncash considerations above $50. A neat workaround might involve interviewing artists and securing promotion for the station by artists.

Stevie and I were once invited to Dallas to attend a ZZ Top concert, then interview Billy, Dusty, and the boys afterward. The band was happy to record a few "you're listening to …" audio clips for future airplay. Those noncash considerations included round-trip airfare in first-class, overnight accommodations in a five-star hotel, plus all meals and transportation. The pharmaceutical industry is big on similarly themed workarounds.

Speaking of pharmaceuticals, nonprescribed drugs could also be acquired as noncash consideration for those with, say, empty nostrils. One popular practice involved listening parties. Promoters might arrange a penthouse suite at a centrally located hotel. Music and program directors from the region got invited to review new music. One room always contained trays of tasty hors d'oeuvres and top-shelf liquor, along with various piles of swag. Another closed room might feature harder substances. I always steered clear of noncash considerations such as hookers and blow, but both could be available for those so inclined. More than one peer fell into such traps. Most label promoters were above-board and steered clear of nonsense, but the practice persisted for years.

Being one of a few hundred people who determined songs America listened to seemed cool at the time, but never really mattered. My actual place in that pecking order was far below my own perception. Attending concerts, receiving swag, and rubbing elbows with rock stars was also fun, but the fondest memories involved the tactics of A&R and promotion folks trying to get their tunes played and reported.

For many radio average joes, extra somethings were practical. Radio employment typically meant ridiculously low wages. I enjoyed visits from promoters, whether they invited me to dinner and then filled my car up with gas on the way back to the station or not. Or those who might deliver a new pair of skis or a parka emblazoned with a band logo. One promoter pushing offerings from RCA once delivered an entire Elvis Presley catalog on vinyl. Elvis was long deceased, and the artist being promoted had nothing to do with Presley, but that was an impressive noncash bit of swag.

The big problem promoters had with my philosophy involved relatively conservative approaches to playlists. My thought was people would really only listen to something familiar, and therefore I was notoriously late most of the time in adding new music. Exceptions included either new music by established artists or music that was so unique or different that it screamed for attention. If you were one of the first to add songs that eventually led to high sales for albums, it was not uncommon to receive framed gold or platinum albums as thanks. Record companies were masters at stroking the oversized egos of people in radio.

Any major hit was often referred to in radio parlance as a "fucking smash," meaning it was a huge hit. One of the most endearing memories about promotion does not involve any sort of payola but of consistently entertaining coercion tactics. The song *Eye of the Tiger* by Survivor was a giant hit, owing primarily to being featured in the movie Rocky III. Survivor recorded on the Scotti Brothers record label. There were two actual Scotti Brothers in charge of the label, Tony and Ben. The company was based in Los Angeles, but the brothers originally hailed from New Jersey, which explained their thick accents.

Almost every week, like clockwork, a call arrived from some member of the Scotti family, heavily promoting whatever was being released that week. The Scotti Brothers label was prolific in flooding stations with excessive numbers of promotional copies of singles and albums. Their pitch was exactly the same every single time. Every song by any artist on their label was breathlessly positioned as a "FICKING SMISH!"

"John, I'm telling you, this new song by Felony is a FICKING SMISH!" They browbeat for anything that resembled any sort of commitment and followed up. When the song did not get added, they did not get mad, preferring instead to move on to their next "FICKING SMISH!"

Scotti Brothers Records is long gone, but even today, when talking music and radio with former peers, we inject the words "FICKING SMISH" into conversations. In a restaurant, for example, we often ask waiters "Please inform the chef that our steaks are a FICKING SMISH!"

CHAPTER 39

HEY, HEY WE'RE THE MONKEES

The Monkees—Mickey Dolenz, the late Davy Jones, and Peter Tork—sans Michael Nesmith—embarked on a twentieth-anniversary reunion tour in 1986. The band made a stop outside Denver in mid-August to play the legendary Red Rocks. A&R folks from the label did one better than backstage access. We were invited to an after-show gathering at their hotel.

As grown boomers who liked the Monkees as younger folks, the soiree seemed potentially epic. Most of the activity at the hotel occurred in its bar area, where Mickey Dolenz held court with several much younger and very attractive ladies. It might be improper to establish a correlation between his behavior and a popular white powdery substance, but he was hyperkinetic. Mickey wanted to connect in some way with EVERYONE, and there were a lot of radio people there. The twitching of his nose and excessive blinking got distracting. Most everyone seemed content to allow him to interact with just his small bevy of beauties.

We did not see either Davy Jones or Peter Tork for a long time, but both eventually appeared in casual clothing to shake hands and thank folks for coming out. They became apologetic about needing a good sleep prior to their next shows and excused themselves early. As Mickey partied until the wee hours, radio folks had a great time talking shop.

The show was actually pretty good, parachute pants and all. It seems ironic that Mickey is left standing.

CHAPTER 40

WHIMSICAL END OF RADIO DREAMS

Early in the fall of 1987, I requested a meeting with K-View's new program director (and son of the new owner) first thing Monday morning.

"Ted, here is how I spent my entire weekend in this building. This project took about eighteen hours, but I managed to completely reprogram the software. Please let me show you how this lines up perfectly with the new format you explained to us on Friday."

I took my weekend action proactively, figuring it never hurts to bolster your worth to new owners and their nepotistic offspring who were gifted important managerial roles. My step-by-step show-and-tell took nearly an hour.

Ted seemed distracted. Just before 10 a.m., he stopped the meeting.

"John, thanks for your efforts. We appreciate it, but we're going to make significant organizational changes and we need to let you go. Here is your final paycheck, which includes two weeks of severance pay. Your service with the company is appreciated. We will give you a few minutes to gather your personal belongings, and we will need your keys and ID cards."

My time with K-View ceased suddenly and without warning. Worse, it felt insulting.

K-View enjoyed a successful trajectory that eventually transformed it beyond an investment of a few hundred thousand dollars by a newspaper group based in Peoria. They intended to make something of a neglected FM station with a bad signal licensed to Pueblo, Colorado, early in the 1980s. Getting a transmitter and tower onto Cheyenne Mountain, and pointed in the right direction, gave those efforts a boost. Halfway through 1987, a family some mockingly referred to as the "Fuckaducks," who owned a handful of stations in the Midwest, decided to purchase KVUU and KSSS in Colorado Springs.

The original modest investment suddenly returned several million dollars for savvy print media folks from Illinois. Selling was wise from an investment perspective. K-View rose from worst to first. It was solidly established as number one in adult demographics and led the market in revenue. Everyone who worked at the station actively contributed to its success and enjoyed a journey to the top.

The Fuckaduck family was quickly perceived, fairly or unfairly, as a group of relatively unsophisticated rubes by a newly nervous staff mostly left hanging. In short order, Patriarch Fuckaduck employed his wife and two sons. Son number two, often mockingly referred to simply as "Turd," became program director. That seemed odd, considering his relative lack of experience, not to mention hints of substance abuse.

Son number one became the sales manager and seemed relatively normal. Turd, however, knew nothing about computers and expressed certainty that ours could not handle the format he had in mind. Once the staff found out what it was and how it might work, I figured quickly reworking software to mirror the new format would earn brownie points. It was a source of personal pride.

I was the very first K-View staff member to get canned. I met Stevie in a city park with my boxed professional belongings. We simply laughed and held hands on the bench.

How could I possibly remain excited about a career that rewarded my two most significant professional successes with unceremonious sackings twice in a row?

Getting pink-slipped from K-View was bad enough. Stevie happened to be five months into the pregnancy of my second son, Jordan. I was also nearly finished chasing a master of arts in business management. The last quarter of the program concentrated on thesis development, the final step toward an advanced degree. Ironically, one of the key thesis hypotheses was a correlation between success and how managers treat staff.

"Stay the course!" Stevie and I decided that was the best approach. Not having a daily job allowed ample time to complete the thesis and reap the rewards. Being a househusband for Jordan's first few months before finding a more worthwhile career seemed noble.

For the first time ever, I received unemployment compensation for almost every week I did not work. A weekends-only gig at KKFM's classic rock station was the last time I ever cracked a hot mic on the radio.

I earned supplemental dollars as a DJ at weddings, school functions, and parties. Cash money under the table nearly equaled what I used to make above it, and I had most of every week off. Stevie's entrepreneurial efforts as an expert in early childhood education funded school and our lifestyle, including furnishing a newly constructed home in the Teller County shadow of Pikes Peak.

My efforts to continue in radio programming were half-hearted. I desired something bigger, but ANY realistic gig proved elusive until early in 1988. Dramatic life events suddenly began occurring simultaneously. Jordan was born. A master's degree was conferred. A simple ad in a trade publication changed my professional trajectory.

I knew I was the only person in the country with the right experience and credentials, and this time I could back it up.

CHAPTER 41

A PROMISING NEW CAREER

The end of my once-promising radio career was abrupt and the timing was lousy. There was no choice about things that happened in the past, but I was eager to mold the future. Meanwhile, my master's thesis was researched, composed, and presented. Stevie gestated. I creatively replaced lost income. Overnight air shifts at a local classic rock station kept me in the business with income too low to threaten unemployment compensation. I milked those sources for the first few months of life for our brand-new son. My services as a party record spinner remained in demand, and cold hard cash came in handy with an infant in the house.

Over the next few months, the freshly parchmented master's degree entered a frame on the wall, Jordan became a gregarious toddler fascinated by trains, and a new career was hatched. House husbandry was a wonderful diversion, but worlds remained to be conquered. A requirement to keep unemployment checks rolling involved serious, documented attempts to secure gainful employment. Job hunting occupied several hours every week, not to mention a fair amount of money for snail-mail postage. None of these efforts were yet possible on the Internet, where many boomers still had only a string of numbers on nascent email novelties such as CompuServe. Weekly trips to the downtown library involved scouring all available trade publications, mostly broadcasting magazines, to copy classified ads. From those ads, customized resume packages were crafted.

Jordan arrived late in January 1988. "Black Monday" coincided not only with the latter part of Stevie's pregnancy but also with my unplanned departure from K-View. Employment was a challenge for anyone, especially in a boom-or-bust state like Colorado.

A trade publication ad I spotted on my birthday in 1988 ultimately changed the direction of my professional life. A great company that also owned several highly regarded stations placed a classified ad. They needed an experienced product manager centered on a newly developed music rotation software application for radio. The job at Jefferson-Pilot Data Services sounded right up my alley. "Advocacy, development strategy, product testing, support, implementation, and training at client sites." I was a perfect candidate because of my radio programming background and because I helped another company roll out a similar product. I used FedEx for the resume.

Then, we waited. And waited some more. I began calling. An entire month passed before Jefferson-Pilot called me back. The ladies doing the hiring were scheduled to visit company stations in Denver one week later. "John, would you mind visiting us at our Denver stations next Thursday at 1 p.m.?"

"Not at all." My palms began sweating. The initial interview went well, and an invitation to broaden dialog with others in Charlotte followed. The entire company mostly agreed that I was well suited for their open position. A new career was born, and southeast was the destination.

Jefferson-Pilot was an insurance company that traced North Carolina roots back to the early 1900s. Jefferson Standard merged with Pilot Life Insurance in 1968. It became the fifteenth largest insurance company in the United States. One of its subsidiaries was Jefferson-Pilot Communications, whose portfolio included a respected, well-managed group of television and radio stations across the country and a regional sports broadcasting syndicate.

Jefferson-Pilot Communications built software to manage back-office and technical aspects of on-air production in their radio and television stations. Eventually, the automation tools became the foundation of a new venture called Jefferson-Pilot Data Services, or JDS for short. By the mid-1980s, JDS was one of three major vendors supplying software and automation to radio and television stations across America.

Primary competitors included Columbine Systems in Denver, and Data Communications Corporation, known by its acronym DCC, in Memphis. Columbine's product offering was a suite of products loosely referred to as Columbine, named partly after the state flower of Colorado and partly after the guy who founded the company, Bill Cole. That word carried a completely different connotation then. DCC differed from JDS and Columbine in that all their computing originated from a large, industrial-strength mainframe housed in a large data center adjacent to the airport in Memphis, accessed by end-users across the country from dedicated terminals. It was an early, crude form of cloud-like computing well before more modern technology became ubiquitous. A fourth competitor also emerged, ironically in Colorado Springs, owned by defense contractor Kaman Sciences. Their product was eventually referred to as Enterprise BMS, or Broadcast Management System. Several much smaller competitors dotted the landscape.

JDS acquired DCC in 1986. Home base for JDS remained in Charlotte, and DCC continued in Memphis. Both companies were remarkably well run and experiencing steep growth trajectories. A merger made sense because DCC licensed many of the largest broadcasters in the country. JDS also serviced many large clients but had a middle-market sweet spot. Columbine became a solution for many middle and smaller market stations.

JDS was staunchly conservative. Men were expected to wear ties to work, and pantsuits for women often raised eyebrows. Casual Fridays were just beginning at JDS in 1988. Even then, business casual still meant no jeans, sneakers, or anything else that might be deemed *too* casual. My tie collection stood at two before JDS, one for job interviews and the other for funerals or weddings. Stevie's father funded a shopping spree at a local menswear establishment that yielded six pairs of pants, six dress shirts, six neckties, and three suit coats. "It's about time you got a real job, John."

Stevie was nervous about selling the Colorado house and decided to keep it. We secured a small apartment in a complex next door to JDS. The company paid for the move, and shortly thereafter, Stevie and Jordan moved in, optimistically headed toward happily ever after.

CHAPTER 42

CORPORATE AMERICA SURPRISES

I jumped into the process of becoming the Autoselect product expert from the very first hour of employment at JDS. The brains of anyone with even remote knowledge of the product were picked to the point of annoyance. Three weeks passed quickly, and I was anointed as fully ready. Only one problem blocked the way.

The woman who hired me less than one month earlier, Donna O'Brien, pulled me into her office and shut the door. "John, brace yourself. JDS sold Autoselect to a smaller company based in Opelika, Alabama, that serves mostly radio stations."

My mind immediately shifted to a mode that screamed *what in the holy hell?!*

"Because your employment was based on becoming the intended product manager for Autoselect, your services were effectively included in the deal," she further explained.

My recently fired mind began racing. *I just got to Charlotte, and Stevie is already in open revolt.*

How is she going to react when I tell her to slow down on the unpacking and prepare for someplace else in rural Alabama?

Donna leaned in and looked around to guard against eavesdropping.

"But this company really appreciates your knowledge and effort, and we do not want you to leave. We are prepared to bump your salary if you are willing to stay and learn our core systems. Travel will be involved, but we do not want to lose you."

In less than a month, I received both a promotion and a raise. That was something anyone could get used to.

It turned out the core business involved much more than just songs on the radio. Two of the most important aspects of operating any radio or television station, or any cable channel, are:

1. Selling enough advertising to support the business.
2. Staying on the air so viewers can listen or watch.

Simple. Or maybe not. There exist litanies of business processes that have become automated in broadcasting. Most of them evolved into even more sophisticated, specialized practices. Broadcast commerce begins with ad sales. Automated tools link ratings, proposed schedules, and anticipated audience delivery together for deal negotiation. Commercials eventually come to life on contracts that grow quite large because they specify entire flights of purchased commercials.

Most ordered commercials contain constraints such as what programs and dayparts in which they can, and in many cases cannot, air. Restrictions can be specific and add additional complexity. Mercedes-Benz, for example, may not want to air inside programming about WW II Germany. General Motors may require exclusivity in programs they buy to prevent Ford or any other auto manufacturer from airing in the same programs. Advertisers may choose to air in prime time, but not in one or two programs in prime time they may find objectionable. Advertising may take the form of sponsorship. Ad sales deals for air usually now include a host of digital components.

Even more complexity results when attempting to separate for products (like cars) or brands. Procter & Gamble may compete with Unilever, but not all brands compete with one another, even within the portfolios of each conglomerate. That is merely an iceberg tip in broadcasting commerce.

When advertising agencies purchase commercial time on behalf of their client advertisers, the only thing actually being purchased is time. Air time may be purchased for commercials from Coca-Cola, but no one yet knows what specific content for each ordered increment of time will be. That is a different business process, managed separately. These processes are referred to as continuity, or simply copy. The Coca-Cola umbrella features a wide variety of brands, including Sprite, Dasani, Minute Maid, Glaceau, Powerade, and many others. Each requires its own continuity.

Commercials and the associated copy must be scheduled to logs (also called playlists), and all placement criteria, restrictions, and other rules must be considered. Logs do not just magically appear. They must be created. This is accomplished by merging templates for programs (usually referred to as formats) with scheduled programming.

Once a skeleton framework is constructed, entirely different "engines" to schedule commercials kick in. When commercials get scheduled, specific brands or the content that will air is rarely known. That information arrives much later in the delivery process. The scheduling of commercial copy is an entirely different 'engine.'

The playlist remains a partial skeleton. For many stations and networks, the purchase of programming rights is an entirely different business process. Specific episodes or movie airings must be scheduled adhering to contract terms, which limit things like the number of plays and even when they can (or cannot) be scheduled. Because programming rights are considered assets that require payment and accounting, entire modules exist to track that.

The scheduling of promos that highlight upcoming episodes or other station messaging also requires unique scheduling processes.

All of these business processes apply BEFORE anything even airs. An entire series of business processes kick in AFTER playlists air. Commercials and their associated content must be verified and validated to facilitate billing. That process is referred to as reconciliation. Agencies need to know when commercials aired and what copy ran with them. Dirty little advertising secret: Many agencies tend to send woefully vague, impossible-to-schedule commercial instructions. Then, when the station or network airs their content incorrectly, agencies contact the station or network and demand either credit or make good commercials to rectify mistakes they themselves actually caused. Millions of dollars in ad sales revenue are lost every year in that fashion. Depending on the station or network, programming and promos may also need to be verified.

Because commercials mean revenue, the reconciled business must be invoiced, and then accounts receivables that result must also be managed.

Along the way, it is crucial for the business to fully understand exactly how much inventory remains for sale at any given moment and must take into consideration both ad sales that have already been booked and proposed business not yet officially ordered. Management needs to know how much revenue they can expect at any given time and how revenue is trending against a host of comparative metrics.

All of those business processes in 1988 required more computing strength than any station or network possessed. Today, most people carry such capability in small mobile devices. Learning processes described in the dozen or so paragraphs above took years to master, and all still change rapidly.

Donna spent ninety minutes reviewing everything above in terms of what I had to learn.

“John, are you ready for the challenge?”

“No problem. I’ll get to work right now.”

“Oh, by the way, John, here’s the number for the corporate travel agent. Ask for Carol, and then have her book a trip to Albuquerque. You are going to KOB-TV to help with a project in three weeks.”

Career number two blasted off.

CHAPTER 43

CELEBRITY FARTS AND THE LAKERS CHICK

My "real" career took off. Literally. Consulting and project responsibilities at Jefferson-Pilot required frequent travel from wherever I lived. The most frequent destinations were New York or Los Angeles.

Donna O'Brien asked me to come in to her office and shut the door once again. Uh-oh. "John, we need you to handle a project at WNEW-FM in New York starting next month. Are you up for it?" I tried to be cool about it, but leaping over the desk and hugging her gave it away.

Very few personalities in radio ever get elevated to a level revered as legendary. The late Scott Muni did. He first made his mark during the heyday of AM Top 40, but that was not how or why he became renowned. Muni was a founding father of progressive FM radio. His gravelly voice was perfectly suited to the genre. Reputation elevation to legend was assured at WNEW-FM, New York, where he became a mainstay for three decades.

As a recently active program director, I missed the action. Leading a project that involved implementing JDS solutions at WNEW-FM in 1989 excited me. Interaction with Muni on issues such as program formats, integration with music software, and other business topics was certainly part of my plan.

It became apparent during the second week of the four-week project that only folks working under Scott would liaise in all such business matters. Business objectives were successfully accomplished, but I was disappointed Scott and I had not met.

On Tuesday of my last week at WNEW, things were hectic. The project was live. Intake of caffeinated beverages was feverish, so I excused myself after lunch. I had to go so badly my back teeth began tingling. Shortly after sidling up to one of just two urinals separated by a small, chest-high aluminum divider in the men's room, in strolled Scott Muni. He assumed his place at the next floor-length porcelain receptacle, then asked in that famous gravel voice, "Hey, how ya doin'?" while looking straight ahead at the wall. Urinal etiquette.

"Much better in about twenty-five seconds," I replied.

Scott snickered and then farted loudly for what seemed like five of those seconds. His combination of urination and gas passing must have felt good. Each fart was accompanied by "Aaaahhhhhhh," as though tremendous pressure was released. We were standing in a small restroom completely covered in ceramic subway tile. Every sound echoed.

Well, this is not how I envisioned meeting Scott Muni, but at least I did.

Farts made sounds first. Then noxious stench followed. "Sorry about that," Muni said in his trademark voice. "I need to never eat that much Mexican food ever again."

As handwashing began at side-by-side sinks, Scott said, "You're John from JDS, correct?"

"That is correct, Scott," was mustered as a reply. Neither of us reached to shake hands because they had not yet been properly sanitized. As the toxicity of Muni's gas began dissipating, he thanked me for being there, finished washing and drying his hands then left.

It was the only time I interacted with Scott. My goal of meeting that particular legend was achieved and included more of the primary senses than seemed proper.

* * * * * *

Another important JDS client on the opposite side of America was LA-based Prime Ticket Network, a regional television network mostly owned at the time by the Buss family. It featured the Buss flagship property on the air, the Los Angeles Lakers. Chick Hearn was the play-by-play announcer employed by the NBA team. He was their broadcast voice for decades. Championship runs during the 1980s helped make Hearn a household name.

The Lakers planned a fitting tribute, making him the guest of honor at a special dinner ceremony inside the Beverly Hilton.

No one at Prime Ticket really wanted to go, and that was problematic. It was a work night. Busy Californians had more pressing items waiting. Those were admittedly first-world problems that might only occur in Los Angeles. Prime Ticket management panicked because not having network folks there would look bad. "It is a Buss-owned property and a Laker event. Somebody's got to go!"

I worked most closely there with a very bright and sassy young lady. Prime Ticket made it clear she should attend the gala and take a partner along.

The companion became me. Leticia Valdez was one of the most physically beautiful women I have ever seen. She was of mixed race, predominantly Mexican (her father) and African American (her mother). Both parents were also mixed race, and her genetic combination molded DNA such that she could nearly stop traffic simply by walking down a street. Leticia looked like a model and carried herself accordingly. Even the word "stunning" was not enough when describing her.

Despite an unreasonable quantity of good looks, Leticia remained grounded in several ordinary ways. She chose not to dress flashy. Valdez appreciated the shock value of belching (or farting) in public. She was also Mensa-level smart.

She flirted passively. Her love life was a mess and featured one flawed man after another. I was on the way to becoming happily and permanently married for a third time. There was no denying lust, but it was never going to happen. As a result, attending a private Los Angeles Lakers party in Beverly Hills with a beautiful woman who stole the breath of others was easy.

Had I actually been her real date for the evening, jealousy or anger may have charged in. Relieved of that pressure going in made meeting every single Laker luminary, past and present, a highly memorable experience. Most of them stopped at two tables; the one at which the Hearn party was seated and the one seating the Leticia party.

Kareem and Magic stopped by. So did Jerry West and James Worthy. It continued that way throughout the evening. None of them seemed interested in small talk with me but spent an inordinate amount of time fawning over Leticia. Especially Jerry West. The Leticia sideshow that brought legends over was surreal but amazing. When not nearly drooling in our vicinity, each legend took turns at the lectern paying tribute to the man of honor.

Chick Hearn strolled by late in the evening. He ignored Leticia, shook my hand, introduced himself, and asked, "John, have you purchased a stake in the Lakers or something?"

My puzzled look encouraged him.

"John, I saw everyone from Mr. Buss to Jerry West stop by THIS table. So, I thought that guy must REALLY be important." Then he winked and said, "I really appreciate you two being here. It is a very special night and I am happy to celebrate it with my work and family friends."

The Laker honoree, star of the show, chose to toy with an out-of-place Midwestern yokel at a celebration in his honor. It was astounding and one of my coolest professional moments.

CHAPTER 44

PLAY MISTY FOR ME

The second act of my career led to planted roots in seven of the United States. Each had plusses and minuses. One that may have been potentially more enjoyable (and dangerous) than all the others is Texas. It never became home, but I was a frequent visitor. Texas has distinctly different regions, but the diversity of its citizenry makes it great. Texans are fiercely independent. They speak what they feel in plain, straightforward ways. It is utterly refreshing. I made friendships that have lasted decades.

Visiting Texas was therapeutic. Work began taking its toll on my private life. My marriage to Suzie collapsed in 1991, well after she left North Carolina to head back to Colorado. I needed diversion badly, but got more than I bargained for.

Misty Horton may have been the one who got away. Perhaps that is a good thing.

Misty managed data operations at an AM/FM combo station in Dallas. Her job included all responsibilities for ad sales back-office functions, placement of commercials and maintenance of program logs, customer billing, and generally being the computer doyenne.

I showed up at the station the same week divorce papers were signed in Colorado with Stevie. My feelings about the way it ended differed significantly from emotions felt when marriage to Suzie crashed. The first breakup involved a painful degree of sadness, guilt, and remorse. The second also felt sad but liberating, although it was way too early to begin any sort of pleasure prowl.

Misty greeted me at the front desk and immediately expressed a strong desire to make the new systems work. That was refreshing. People like me represented change decisions, and almost nobody below top management levels was ever involved. It was no different at the Dallas stations, but Misty was ambivalent about the systems she used and felt ours might do a better job.

The project framework was established within five minutes in the lobby, and that was impressive. She turned and led the way back to her department. Inadvertent notice of her backside was not intentional, but limbic processes hijacked business thoughts. The rational, professional portion of my consciousness shoved feelings of near lust aside, figuring a month or so of hard work was still to come.

If this project was typical, it would take five total weeks scattered over three months. The first three days were designed for setting up the remainder of the project, which would begin nearly a month later.

The Dallas stations were located on the way into town from DFW, just off the freeway. My return flight was scheduled for early in the evening of the third day of the initial fact-finding mission. Misty thought it prudent that I leave a few hours before to avoid heavy traffic and allow plenty of check-in time.

Neither of us had lunch, but we finished by 2:00 pm on the last day.

"Wanna grab a quick bite?" I asked. "Is there anything good between here and DFW?"

Misty said, "Your only real choice, good or otherwise, is Whataburger."

Not much negotiation was necessary. We were fine with the gaudy orange-and-white-striped themed fast-food joint. Their menu included Hatch green chile cheeseburgers, a unique taste acquired during time in New Mexico. One aspect for which many Whataburger sandwiches are known is yellow mustard between buns, often in prodigiously squirted quantities.

A small dollop flew from my burger and landed squarely on my favorite silk tie.

"Don't worry, John," Misty told me. "It'll come out. No problem." She was gone in a flash, then back again with a small cup of carbonated water. "Let's go outside to clean up your tie."

We stood between my rental and her daily driver. Gently but swiftly, she dabbed away every last trace of yellow. "It'll dry in no time, big boy."

Misty did not let go of the tie as I discussed her future. "I'll be back in less than three weeks and will send you a detailed pla …"

What in the hell?!

Misty used the laundered tie to tug my neck close to her face. The lengthy kiss she planted without warning seemed far too passionate. Mostly it was completely unexpected.

Damn…she knows how to use that tongue.

Suddenly, getting to the airport seemed less important. "I am really looking forward to your return, John. Hurry back."

I spent the next few weeks in a conflicted dilemma. I absolutely needed to remain professional and put ANY feelings of lust aside, at least until after the project was complete. On the other hand, I was newly single, and intense compulsion to throw caution to the wind and enjoy newfound freedom counterbalanced the argument. I struggled with an angel on one shoulder and a devil on the other for three weeks.

I was nervous about returning next time. When I did, Misty pulled me into her office almost immediately.

"John, she said, "Look. I'm married. Whether I am happy or not isn't relevant because I made a commitment when I took those vows. What I'm trying to say is that we should stick to business."

I had kind of become a fan of adulterous trysts. They seemed easier. Her words made me selfishly disappointed but also relieved. No potential romance would be one less complication. The stress was lifted.

For a month before it began, I constantly warned her: "You need to be prepared for a lot of late nights, potential overtime, and hard work. You will be maintaining two systems." The project at Misty's station went more smoothly than most. Late nights were infrequent, but every night already had a built-in budget of extra time. She never really wanted to go home.

Misty happily joined me for dinner a few times a week, and I always bought. Sharing a hot meal over a white tablecloth in places where waiters wore white gloves was much better with a companion. It beat the hell out of Subway at 11:00 p.m. alone. Those evenings always felt like dates, especially when we did romantic things. Horse-drawn carriage rides at night through downtown Dallas may have been a little over the top, but became a weekly ritual.

Our mutual hands-off policy became a little too challenging. We nearly gave in about halfway through the project. We remained clothed, but every stitch was badly ruffled.

The project finished on time and under budget. The client was happy, and so was I. On the last Wednesday of the final visit, the end of our daily interaction arrived.

"Why don't we get a nice dinner and eat it on the balcony in the upgraded suite Marriott gave me?" I asked. Misty seemed sad. "John, I REALLY want to, but I am VERY afraid of what might happen." We remained frustratingly chaste but spoke several times a week during the months that followed.

Later that year, a new project took me to Bangor, Maine. That one was not as smooth. Even worse was the timing of their system go-live day, which was the Monday following Thanksgiving. At least I did not have to worry about lust. A few staff members at the station were already sleeping with one another and everyone was unhappy to see me.

The station chose the nicest accommodations possible. A Ramada Inn stood fairly close to work, and the rooms were comfortable. I was literally the only guest in that hotel on Thanksgiving Day. No one from the station invited me over for dinner. No restaurants were open. My dinner decision began to involve choosing which flavor of convenience store burrito to microwave. Then, the room phone rang. The manager and her husband opened the hotel restaurant just for me.

A turkey dinner with all the trimmings was ready and waiting.

"Mr. Howard, just think of it as the house special, and it won't end up on your bill." It was bitter cold in Bangor that Thanksgiving. Being outside for any reason was not advisable. One gracious act, and perhaps sightseeing throughout the region on weekends, were the brightest spots of the project.

My best buddy (and later best man) Keith Woodard back at JDS also called me in Bangor over the holiday weekend. We discussed business, then he casually mentioned, "Did you know Misty's husband died?"

"Say *WHAT*?!" I was startled.

"Yeah, he fell asleep and never woke up. Sounds like a heart attack."

I obsessed about how she was doing, and balancing sympathy with lust was unnerving. A mission to purchase a heartfelt sympathy card commenced. Writing it was arduous. Words were inadequate.

As winter passed, I wondered whether Misty also felt the same thoughts bouncing around in her brain.

It's no longer adulterous.

My only direct experience with grieving widows involved my mother after dad passed away. A couple of married gentlemen in town wanted to take advantage of her vulnerability and went for it. That seemed vile. I decided to play it cool and allow Misty whatever space she needed.

A few months later, Misty experienced a technical problem with JDS software and called me directly. "John, I can't produce any program logs." That was a worst-case scenario for clients. In most cases, problems were resolved by guiding intelligent end-users through specific commands on their green screened dumb terminals. That involved bending code on the fly. Every statement had to be precisely typed to avoid potential damage to the software. JDS mandated the use of the military alphabet to assist clients.

One of the final resolution steps involved confirming logs were present. That geek-worthy command was MULTISTA LOGCFM. My instructions were always the same and spoken slowly and with overly deliberate annunciation. "M-U-L-T-I-S-T-A L-O-G-C-F-M, as in Charlie Foxtrot Mike." Users were always requested to repeat each command BEFORE hitting the enter key. Misty repeated, "M-U-L-T-I-S-T-A L-O-G-C-F-M, as in Come. Fuck. Me." I logically assumed that Misty's period of grief had concluded.

HOT DAMN!

That support distress call was taken on a Friday morning in Charlotte, North Carolina. At 5:30 that evening a previously scheduled TWA flight took me to St. Louis and on to Colorado Springs for a weekend with the kids. Every moment I spent with them was precious. But instead of returning to Charlotte on Sunday, I flew to Dallas after requesting a last-minute day off for personal business.

Misty picked me up from DFW. We spent the next 24 hours in a hotel room exploring every pent-up feeling suppressed for nearly a year. It felt dangerous. She began opening up about her life and feelings.

"Jack worked in a factory making car parts. Blue-collar all the way. The older he got, the more of a redneck he became. He wasn't very motivated, grew a belly, and mostly wanted to stay at home. Laying around."

"Did you love him?" I asked.

"Oh sure, he was a sweet man but had no ambition, and I wasn't satisfied. I can be a real bitch, and took a lot of things out on him."

"What's next for you?" I was curious.

"Right now, John, I am attracted to you. You are a breath of fresh air. White-collar, motivated, a future, and you are cute as hell."

"What if we fell in love, Misty?"

"No way," Misty cautioned. "That would be too dangerous. I've got issues, and I can't have kids. It's easy for me to spread my problems, and you really don't need that."

Warning flags or not, the single most remembered thing about Misty is the amazing physical compatibility we had. Men and women come in all shapes and sizes. How truly compatible are most people physically? With her, it was perfect. Still, she remained timid and continued alluding to what might happen if/when she lost complete control. As long as it did not involve murder or genital mutilation, I was probably game.

The next few months were strange. I made side trips to Dallas a lot; nearly always attached to a business trip. Our frequent visits were intense. She never accepted offers of airline tickets to visit me once in a while, and that seemed odd.

A few months later, a radio convention was held at the Anatole Hotel in Dallas. My room included a large Jacuzzi tub. Misty refused to even enter the room. "I will lose control and am really scared of what might happen." Fear did not prevent her from impulsively letting inhibitions run wild after dark outside on the 16th green of the Anatole course. Or again inside the rental car parked outside the hotel. We even managed the act atop THE grassy knoll very late one night. I cannot imagine there were no security cameras catching unbridled, mostly naked lust that surely entertained fat security guards in some darkened room, but it wasn't just Misty that lost control.

The annual JDS client conference was held in St. Petersburg's Vinoy resort the following Spring, and Misty could hardly wait for her rare road trip. Hot tubs were standard in rooms both Misty and I were assigned. "No. No. NO," she warned. "We cannot go inside either room together. Bad things will happen. Water makes me lose all control."

Now we're getting somewhere.

"Let's go for a midnight stroll on a beach," I suggested. After dark and on a public beach near Treasure Island, Misty lost control, but I survived.

Misty letting go completely involved many nature-defiant acts I had only heard about. It happened only a few times, the last inside a Marriott near Ft. Worth. Consulting began for a television network owned and operated by Southern Baptists. Every afternoon at 1:00 pm the entire building congregated in the cafeteria for daily worship and prayers, and each day of that week they thanked the Lord for my presence in their midst. My heathen ways waited until after hours.

Misty and I continued enjoying dinner dates and moonlit strolls. I bought flowers, sent gifts and handed her teddy bears when I got off planes. More than one Texan saw me and action and exclaimed "Now ain't that sweet?"

She always insisted on emotional distance. "I'm no catch, John," she was fond of saying. I never fully understood. She seemed possessed when she lost control. Misty purred exactly like a cat. It was physically wonderful but emotionally intangible. I had strong feelings for her, but she talked me into being scared. Her past was checkered. She had a problem with alcohol. She could not have kids. Her roughness around the edges was just sexy enough, but what would she be in ten years?

Every once in a while, she snapped and say something mean. We passed a Neiman-Marcus while on a walk, and she wanted to stroll through. "Hey John, I've never been in a Needless Markup before...let's see what they have." As we looked at one aisle of overpriced merchandise after another, I confided that I got a thrill whenever I found a real bargain at T.J. Maxx. Misty looked at me with disgust. "There's a big difference between frugal and fucking cheap, John."

Maybe she really isn't a catch.

The intermittently intense relationship eventually cooled as casually and suddenly as it began. When I found myself falling in love with Annie, who is still my wife today, I simply told Misty, "The woman I need to marry has entered my life and there is no room for anyone else." There were neither tears nor regrets.

A short time later, Misty continued a relationship with a peer, and eventually married. I was happy she found someone, especially that one, because she also became a mother against all odds. Our experiences in Texas and elsewhere (mostly around water) are permanently etched.

CHAPTER 45

LONE STAR ADVENTURES

Fortunately, there was much more to Texas than just Misty and rebound lust. I was dispatched to Austin before that city became as cool as people believe it is today. Our client's television station was then owned by Lady Bird Johnson, the wife of the one late president I find more fascinating than any other in history. I even took a class about Lyndon Johnson while in college. My personal library at home contains just about every book ever written about him.

The station was rather ordinary other than its location in an older building near the state capital. Overnight digs in the historic Driskill were great as well.

My station group worked one floor below the top. The upper floor had its own button in the elevators, but nothing happened when it was pressed. Wondering what was up there became a minor obsession. Stairwells were located, but doors were locked except for those coming the other way.

A graceful older woman in the department relayed over lunch one day that she worked on LBJ's ranch years before, during, and after his presidency. Gracine Franklin told many stories. She became an involuntary best friend for a few days, but conversations had to be navigated carefully. I was there to manage a project and not interrogate locals about LBJ.

"Lawd, Lyndon chased the women as much as Kennedy ever did," Gracine confided. "Not only that, but he flaunted 'em right out in the open, even at the ranch and even with Bird at his side." Several photographs exist that show Lady Bird on one side of Lyndon and some mistress on the other. "It went with the territory, John. Bird wasn't gonna do nothin' to jeopardize that gravy train."

The single most important piece of information Gracine relayed was that "Lyndon kept a private residence up there on the top floor. He could take care of family business and also his needs with the ladies, too." No wonder it was off-limits.

I desperately needed to see it. "Please, PLEASE, *PLEASE!*" I often literally begged. The poor woman was cajoled until she let me know she had access and would let me see it. "John, I'll take you up there, but only after hours on a Saturday or a Sunday."

Once that door finally opened on the third weekend, there was very little that impressed me initially. I saw just a few desks and computers along with a sign that said Texas News Network. They were only there because no other space was available for them on lower floors.

Around a corner, my jaw dropped. It was as if time stopped the day LBJ left earth. The wallpaper (a silver and yellow pattern) and furnishings were original. LBJ's desk sat in front of a very large window that perfectly framed an unobstructed view of the Texas State Capitol Building. A large deck just outside provided dramatic views of Austin. Even the bathroom was unchanged, right down to pastel-colored porcelain. The toilet seemed way too small for a man of LBJ's stature. It seemed similar to visiting Elvis Presley's Graceland home before it was remodeled for tourists.

That floor was not a museum, although it should have been. It was history frozen in time. Another dream came true in Texas.

* * * * * *

The opulent Four Seasons Resort outside Dallas was chosen for the JDS annual client soiree in 1993. Conferences involved a tortuous degree of work for staff that went. Preparation efforts for planned user sessions took months. Meals and other activities were carefully choreographed, and JDS people were assigned accordingly. Endless meetings while not in sessions made for very long days.

Learning, griping, or discovering were not the only reasons clients went. Spring break level partying with reckless abandon was inevitable. They were far away from their homes and occasionally bad relationships. We needed to accommodate potentially hedonistic behavior as well as business and tried our best to remain professional.

My assignment one fateful evening involved looking after a group of five managers. That quintet held identical management positions at regional locations of a national cable network. All were in their late twenties or early thirties, and most were either married or otherwise committed. Really young women no longer stimulated my imagination as they had before reaching my late 30s. Misty was in her mid-30s. So was another lady named Lorna Daniels from Portland, Oregon.

She and I were introduced on the first day of conference registration.

Conference night three featured no formal events. My national network account of five youthful administrators and their new friend Lorna, a professional athlete in a physically grueling sport, designated me the official party-their-pretty-little-heads-off-night chaperone. None of them had a car. Sensing this type of moment and feeling prepared, I upgraded to the largest Cadillac Avis had available at DFW.

Each woman possessed natural beauty and charming personality. "John," they cooed, "would you mind taking us to the west end in Dallas? There are some cool bars there we need to check out." It was mostly just one large building locals referred to as an entire mall of just bars. Each was themed differently. Cowboy. Blues. Techno. You name it. It was there. The ladies seemed eager to sample each one.

An evening of glorified babysitting dragged on, and Lorna and I became fast friends. We were close in age. She was physically imposing and very pretty. Lorna was as tall as me and very blonde. Her physique featured a highly defined muscular structure. Her sport demanded peak physical condition. Sitting behind a desk at a television station was her day job. Lorna was also unhappily married to a recently retired Army intelligence lifer who was not only emotionally abusive but alcoholic.

Damn, John - you certainly know how to pick 'em.

Lorna and I spent the evening mostly teetotaling. I nursed Diet Cokes, and Lorna sipped Chardonnay. The younger network ladies preferred shots and chasers in a repetitive fashion.

Shortly past midnight, Lorna and I began corralling wasted network operations ladies.

The Four Seasons is a pretty long way from here. What am I gonna do when one of these girls starts puking? Are the others going to puke too?

The odometer read 000187 miles. Four of them were angled shoulder to shoulder in the back seat. I worried a lot about a potential vomitous chain reaction. Then yours truly would have serious explaining to do, both at the rental return counter and on a company expense report.

The girls survived but demanded that we make a stop on the way back. "John, we wanna see the Mustangs at Las Colinas. Turn here." Sculptor Robert Glen designed a series of life-sized bronze mustangs galloping and jumping across a river, or in the case of that particular art, a large fountain and pools. That is the centerpiece in the middle of numerous tall office buildings. Weeknights at 1:00 am there were downright tranquil. No one was around. Lighting at that hour provided just enough eerie dimness to emphasize the fine details of the sculptures.

The mustangs are, in fact, remarkable works of art. All five intoxicated network managers jumped out of the car and announced, "LET'S GO SWIMMING!" Taking a dip with the sculpted horses was precisely the kind of impulsive act someone that age would try while drunk. But they did it one better. It was not just a swim; it was a skinny dip. In short order, all five were as naked as the sculpted horses and jumping around in the pool with them. While my eyes bugged out of their sockets, the mind behind them was trying desperately to concoct a story for the police. They HAD to be on their way out. Meanwhile, Lorna surreptitiously slipped out of her clothing and mounted the lead mustang. She became Lady Godiva and wasn't even that tipsy. As the girls splashed and continued motioning for me to join them, I could not keep my eyes off Lorna. She began mimicking a very slow and seductively nasty gallop atop the lead stallion, completely naked with long, blonde hair unfettered and covering her breasts.

Suddenly being shoulder tapped by a uniformed security guard caused me to bolt up from a concrete wall. He apologized profusely for startling me. Then, and this is another example of why people from Texas are the very best anywhere on earth, he introduced himself, shaking hand extended. His name was Lester, and he flatly stated, "I am damned glad to meet you, John. Not too much ever happens in the middle of the night here at Las Colinas," he explained. "Now, John, I cannot tell you how much I am truly enjoying this spectacular view, but we are only going to be able to enjoy it for another five minutes or so. Then I will have to call the law because y'all are technically trespassing. I could lose my job if I do not act quickly, even though I am currently experiencing significant ethical and moral dilemmas."

I began waving frantically, signaling naked women to get dressed so we could make our way out. I was roundly ignored. Lester produced a whistle and said, "John, looks like you could use this." Shrill decibels echoed off nearby buildings. That drew their attention. I pointed at Lester and his uniform. All six ladies got dressed without drying off. There were no towels anyway. The new car smell inside the Caddy transformed into a scent vaguely like a swimming pool at a by-the-hour motel.

The precise arrival moment at the Four Seasons valet stand with soaking wet, haphazardly dressed clients tumbling out and leaving puddles everywhere, coincided with that of the company President. He returned from a late dinner with non-hammered clients, and his glare was icy.

Lorna whispered, "Do you need some company?" I didn't. My first 75-minute session later that morning was supposed to follow a mandatory 8:00 am breakfast. I failed to inform Lorna I did not need company. "Room 1426. Give me half an hour or so."

As Lorna freshened up in her own room, I wanted a quick shower, but even those plans changed. This time it was a JDS consultant. A married female coworker. Myna Whitmore was normally extremely reserved, dignified, and all business. That night she was intoxicated beyond the point of being able to stand upright. Myna also sobbed hysterically right in front of my door. I keyed it open and asked, "What's wrong?" She leaped into my room, plopped backside first on the bed, and lamented the fact that one of the largest company clients jilted her. Sobbing, Myna confessed: "I'm secretly in love with Peter and thought tonight might be our night. He's in the room across the hall, but so is that bitch slut Melinda. He's, like, her BOSS! Isn't that an ethics violation or something?" Peter and Melinda were making noises that meant only one thing.

Where do I even begin?! She's a married woman about to commit adultery, and she's talking about ethics lapses? How can I get her out of here gracefully?

Normally I would lend an empathic ear and encourage talking things out, but Lady Godiva was on her way to my room. The other significant distraction was Myna's resort bathrobe. It was wide open, and she didn't care. While I appreciated hitting the naked women jackpot all night long, I needed naked Myna somewhere else besides that room atop my bed in full snow angel position.

Lorna arrived and began knocking.

How the hell am I going to explain a completely different naked woman lying spread-eagle on my bed?

Honesty is probably always the best approach. Myna was nearly passed out. Lorna moved past the initial shock as the whole love triangle situation was explained. She graciously offered to get this fine coworker, who would remember none of this, back to her room to sleep it off. It took Lorna less than ten minutes to safely tuck Myna in for the evening.

Lorna and I soon found ourselves clad only in fluffy resort bathrobes on the balcony outside my room. Embraces and kisses gave way to anything goes. I was with Lady Godiva. The moon was full and clouds were sparse. Bright stars provided ambiance. We were oblivious to everything else, including the hotel architecture. Many rooms like mine had balconies located outside the end of horizontally tiered hotel floor hallways, separated only by large windows. Walking down that hallway toward us as Lady Godiva neared full gallop was the company president, again. I want to say he saw nothing, but the window was eight feet tall.

"Why don't we move this party indoors," I whispered. "Ahh, do we have to?" she replied.

Say what?! I've already earned two strikes tonight.

"We probably should. I know of two definite reasons why I could be fired on Monday."

Lorna gently pushed me inside to the recently vacated bed.

Friday was a very long day. One hour and twenty minutes of sleep was not enough for my stressed body. Functioning coherently was a challenge, and I had consumed no alcohol. It was the wrap day, however, and sleep catch-up became my only weekend goal.

* * * * * *

Texas meant more to me than hedonistic behavior. As a young child, JFK's assassination was as traumatic for me as everyone else. As a teenager, I bought into mainstream conspiracy theories. There HAD to be more shooters. After defiling the grassy knoll with Misty, I felt some retribution was owed to the memory of John Kennedy. His time in that vicinity, after all, was not as pleasurable as mine. Misty lost control, and part of me was horrified, though not enough to suggest she stop.

I often thought of disciplinarian fourth-grade teacher Mrs. Renner breaking down. EVERY adult in the country broke down, and that was frightening for children still in single-digit age brackets.

The events of November 22, 1963 eventually became much more than a clearly defined set of facts composed by a bunch of old politicians. Skepticism was natural. The assassination and Warren Commission excerpts became voracious reading later in life. Movies like Oliver Stone's *JFK* fanned conspiracy flames

I held alternate views until the first time I visited the former Texas School Book Depository building. That landmark now houses the Sixth Floor Museum. In addition to chronicling the tragic events of that day in 1963, museum visitors see the shooter's view from the same window one floor below.

Filmed or photographic evidence and video re-enactments always fail to easily show how close to JFK's head the building actually was. When my own eyes took in the actual view, it was far easier to embrace a lone nut conclusion. That revelation has not dampened an ongoing interest in the subject. Touring the entire area broadened my viewpoint and added context not possible before visiting. Everyone should.

While you're there, absorb the culture, find some slow-smoked brisket, and throw back a Shiner or two.

CHAPTER 46

FAKE SPACE TRAVEL WITH BUZZ ALDRIN

Ten or so CJDS consultants made a business trip from Denver to Orlando in 1996. We attended a conference for broadcast financial management professionals. It was a nice respite from an extended winter that became dreary, but most of us didn't want to go. The NHL team that relocated to Denver from Quebec was playing for the Stanley Cup, and Avalanche fever swept the region.

Duty called. There were worse places to go in the winter than a resort in Orlando. Universal Studios was closed to the public early one evening to accommodate our conference. After dinner, our entire group of peers and clients had free run of the park. It was a great way to enjoy Universal attractions with no lines.

The keynote speaker for dinner was astronaut Buzz Aldrin. I am positive his speech was compelling. The only problem involved being in a well-known amusement park that was all ours for a night, and alcohol was being served from open bars. What could possibly go wrong?

Fortunately, nothing did. Acting younger than we were was fun. It was not every day a major attraction closed exclusively for a relatively small group. No attraction in the park had any line. One of the most popular Universal offerings was enjoying the high point of its popularity. Back to the Future was a motion simulator that sent riders through an imagined space/time continuum aboard a DeLorean mockup, using IMAX technology. It was supposed to be pretty great in its day.

A client and I decided to give it a go. We were immediately led to the back seat of a fake DeLorean. The ride operator indicated it would only be a couple of moments before the ride started and explained that a couple of additional passengers would be joining us in our DeLorean. The two eventually seated in the front seat of the DeLorean were Mr. and Mrs. Buzz Aldrin.

My mind began racing. I was about to fake travel through fake space in the same fake DeLorean with a guy who actually DID travel through REAL space, landed on the surface of the ACTUAL moon, and then followed Neil Armstrong down the ladder to WALK AROUND ON IT.

Somehow the ride was not as impressive as it might have been otherwise. We tried enjoying it, but when Buzz Aldrin made small talk less than an arm's length away, and one of the things he related was, "Wow! This is much more comfortable and un-cramped than the lunar module was," how could anyone possibly enjoy the fictional journey?

We remembered nothing about our imagined trip through space and time. My most vivid memory: *Hey, that's the back of Buzz Aldrin's head! What the hell is going on inside of it?*

There is no way that ride compared with actually flying to the moon.

I tried it again a few years later solo but still could not enjoy it.

Gee, thanks, Buzz.

CHAPTER 47

CORPORATE STOOGE

My radio top dog dream withered, but enthusiasm for a fresh career phase took root. The dawn of the corporate computing era arrived, and JDS was a market leader. Competition among a handful of similar companies made everyone better.

Travel for business began almost immediately. Leading diverse projects in far-flung locations was actually enjoyable. The pay was much better than radio, and none of my own money got spent while traveling. The road also provided separation from internal politics that might come with being trapped in an office filled with southern, conservative business people.

One thing still not completely understood inside my hard head was the relative value of working for a stable company. JDS had long-term contracts with many high-profile media clients. A merger shortly before my arrival brought together two of the three largest companies in broadcast technology. JDS in Charlotte acquired Memphis-based Data Communications Corporation, whose BIAS product was deployed in most major markets. It made the merged company the biggest and strongest in the business well into the following decade.

Over the course of the next twenty-eight years, I flew more than four million butt-in-seat miles on commercial airlines. Travel eventually included all fifty states and all but two continents. The work was consistently stimulating, and those experiences shaped these stories.

Grueling travel for long periods at a time extracted a brutal toll on family life. Adventure and life on the road stimulated me, but the failure of two marriages involving young children forced melancholy regret every day. Father of the Year trophies will always prove elusive, and I always wish my parenting skills were better. Despite frequent absence and lousy role-modeling, all three of my children turned out great and remarkably well adjusted.

JDS, owned by a financial and insurance conglomerate, was a great place to work. The company was operated and staffed by decidedly deliberate southerners who possessed quaint charm and strong work ethics. JDS peers ran through walls to consistently deliver reliable products and services. Everyone pitched in whenever required.

I remained too oblivious to appreciate how great that situation actually was. The biggest competitor at the time was Columbine Systems of Golden, Colorado. Almost every project I led at JDS involved the displacement of Columbine products for those of JDS. Columbine was almost always replaced without any approval or buy-in from people actually tasked to operate replacement systems. That meant consultants like me were forced into awkward situations. Human nature being what it is, line-level staffers were generally reluctant to change their routines in any way. We were continually barraged with complaints along the lines of "…no one ever asked us what we wanted to do."

JDS was forced by circumstance to demand support and diligent effort, despite critical decisions being made above pay grades by people who would barely use such systems. We were nearly always held in contempt before even entering buildings.

Clients inevitably compared our systems to what they already had, and almost always in unflattering ways. Most consultants could only take it for short periods. The combination of out-of-town travel for extended periods and a lack of enthusiasm or cooperation for our efforts could be daunting. These eventually became challenges I relished.

Happy endings occasionally resulted. In Waco, Texas, one television station held a "funeral" following its successful conversion to new systems. The "service" consisted of their staff donning safety goggles and helmets. Obsolete equipment from Columbine that originally cost thousands of dollars was destroyed with sledgehammers in their parking lot. Most projects did not end in such fun ways.

A belligerent client in another southern state complained almost every waking minute of her project. Each observation was usually prefaced with snottily articulated words such as "Well, on Columbine we do it this way." She was utterly incorrigible and well beyond annoying. At times she was actively subversive. Maintaining a professional demeanor was difficult. A small measure of pushing back subliminally involved taking creative liberties with underlying COBOL code that formed the foundation of the JDS software applications.

Nightly data backup routines were forced upon users. If any step was not completed, software became inoperable the following business day. That was by design even though most clients yelped, "This is STUPID." In the event of a crash, data could be recovered to the last transaction. Strict backup protocol helped make the software nearly bulletproof. Most end users disliked spending an extra forty-five minutes to an hour waiting for screen prompts that guided them through loading additional discs or backup cartridges. During the routine, current commands and status lines appeared on screen momentarily and then disappeared. Other prompts stopped the screen every few minutes. Users were required to answer messages after taking the required backup steps.

Most relevant statements remained on screen for less than one second. Users tended to watch screens like hawks so that stop messages could be answered as quickly as possible. All of them wanted to go home quickly. Some days were more frustrating than others. On the worst days, I surreptitiously accessed underlying code related to the backup routine to add brief, temporary messages that went away nearly as quickly as they appeared. Each passing day featured increasingly vulgar subliminal messaging deleted immediately after end-users left.

Flashed messages began as simple taunts. "Well, on Columbine, sterility usually results." By the end of a couple of weeks, which is usually as long as it took to convince end-users the changes we were making might actually enhance their jobs, messages took decidedly juvenile turns. "Well, on Columbine, users end up as crack whores blowing old men in dark alleys."

The belligerent lady complained to her management about vulgar messages on-screen she claimed to see. When asked about it, I simply printed out the underlying code to walk them through the routine. It was plausible deniability and cleverly positioned the complaining end-user as either paranoid or crazy. It was admittedly mean-spirited but provided an effective antidote for rebellious behavior. Offensive messaging always vanished without a trace. A sense of humor helped move projects forward, especially since we always made someone cry at least once during every single project.

CHAPTER 48

WHEN GREENER GRASS IS ACTUALLY WEEDS

Whimsy often deluded boomers like me into believing any job we had was less substantial than at other companies. If nothing else, our demographic stayed restless. Our silent generation parents worked for the same companies for decades, then usually got pensions. My generation mostly switched career directions every three to five years. Hindsight is always an effective way to judge critical decisions that changed career trajectories.

JDS was a great company, but I was fidgety. During much of my time there, the company experienced a high degree of growth. JDS also inherited an ambitious Australian entrepreneur who founded a similar company that JDS purchased. He was tapped to head marketing and other executive-level functions at JDS. Wayne Ruting was a driven, successful individual, and his idea seemed to involve transforming JDS into something that extended beyond North American boundaries. The company suddenly became "The World's LARGEST Supplier of Media Software." He carried with him a core group of peers who arrived simultaneously. We called them his posse.

Company growth included other corporate acquisitions and a roster of clients that kept increasing. Then, just as suddenly as Ruting appeared, he and his entire posse disappeared. At the time, we suspected the organization's trajectory was not aligned with the far more conservative approach favored by ownership. Day-to-day management at JDS was the responsibility of a DCC lifer named Doug Rother, who, as COO, epitomized the conservative nature of the corporate parent. Philosophies of Ruting and Rother seemed at odds. Shortly after Wayne's departure, Ruting and his posse assumed management of the primary competitor of JDS, Columbine Systems.

1990 and 1991 were unusual years. My marriage to Stevie ended. JDS decided to shutter their Charlotte office to combine operations with DCC, the company they merged with a few years earlier, in Memphis. I remained on the road around 80 percent of the time but found the time for a Memphis move.

By the end of 1993, I finished five years listening to just about every new JDS client regale me with their certainty about how much better Columbine was than JDS. When that Colorado company formally recruited me, I listened. I had, after all, enjoyed a good professional experience as a client while in radio. Their reputation seemed solid. I would be based in Denver and much closer to two of my children. It seemed logical to consider joining a company that had suddenly become "The World's LEADING Supplier of Media Software" under Ruting. I jumped ship to begin work at Columbine Systems on January 1, 1994. They paid for my move to a new apartment inside the turret of a castle-like structure in Denver's Capitol Hill neighborhood.

Week one enabled brimming confidence about what a great decision I made. Week two and beyond included nearly fifty more weeks of nagging, unrelenting doubt. My big fear was that I joined a cult whose intentions were impure. Although their products were adequate, clients who used them were forced to operate precisely according to Columbine's inflexible set of rules. The structure was rigid and left little to no room to accommodate operational nuances every single client had. It was one of the reasons their clients were generally smaller stations with less sophisticated needs. JDS products could be either customized or creatively bent, and I had become a master of doing precisely that.

The relative inflexibility of Columbine's offerings was frustrating. When combined with shoe-on-the-other-foot taunting by new clients about how much better they believed JDS was, I began questioning post-radio career choices in general. People responsible for producing and maintaining Columbine products were largely unwilling to walk through walls for clients, although most of those who joined me on front lines were diligent professionals. Management made excuses or blamed clients, and that was easier than working toward solutions.

Toward the end of 1994, something strange happened. Wayne Ruting at Columbine hired his former nemesis at JDS, Doug Rother. Between mandatory product support in a call center and odd travel to really small markets, I decided to investigate the possibility of a return to JDS. The single brightest moment of 1994 was marriage to my happily-ever-after spouse Annie, who still worked at JDS in Memphis.

Skip Sawyer, the leader of corporate sales efforts at JDS, wanted me back. "John, I want to create a new position for you that involves the management of our most critical accounts. Newer clients are getting far more sophisticated, and we need to keep up with it."

My wife was heavily involved in creating a revolutionary next-generation technology product code-named I-40 because it linked Tennessee and North Carolina, like the interstate highway of the same name. It combined the most talented resources from both DCC and JDS and brought those two one-time competitors together. Destined to change the ballgame, it was 85% complete.

As 1994 concluded, I resigned from Columbine. Doug Rother pulled me aside, "That's a really bad idea, John. I think you are making a big mistake." He probably knew where I was going, but I did not tell him.

"Thanks, Doug," I replied on the way out the door and back to Memphis. JDS paid my moving expenses again. Annie and I made an offer on a new house in a historic neighborhood and set about preparing to close.

My first day back on the job at JDS was a breath of fresh air. No longer relegated to a cubicle, I had my own office. Plans for the position were grand. Life was good again, and I dove in headfirst. The pressure was off. I was out of the Columbine cult.

On the SECOND day back at JDS, Skip and I were seated outside the building as he enjoyed a smoke. Mid-drag, we spotted Wayne Ruting, Doug Rother, Columbine's human resources director, and other important people walking toward the building. I was speechless, and my mouth opened. Skip managed only a hesitant "uh-oh."

We looked at each other and simultaneously uttered: "Oh, shit." Skip looked me in the eye and promised, "As God is my witness, I know nothing about this."

A hastily arranged mandatory company-wide meeting included a joint address by the management of both companies. "JDS and Columbine have been acquired by a company operated by Paul Hobby of Houston, Texas." Hobby spoke next. Each successive portion of the announcement became more ominous. "Wayne Ruting will head the combined company, to be called Columbine JDS. We are closing the Memphis facility in ninety days. Operations and personnel will relocate to Denver, and we will meet with each of you to cover logistics. We have decided to shelve the I-40 project and devote all resources to a new Columbine initiative called Paradigm."

Had I committed career suicide? Fear of that was palpable. Skip continued apologizing, and just about everyone in the Memphis office needed days to grasp what happened

CHAPTER 49

SIX LONG WEEKS IN MALAYSIA

Early in 1995, I signed up for a project in Kuala Lumpur, Malaysia. A new client intended to go on the air with a brand-new national television station—the very first nongovernment-operated channel in the country. City-TV was launched by a youthful entrepreneur descended from a Malaysian royal family. The Columbine team referred to him simply as "the prince," primarily because none of us could spell, much less pronounce, his full name.

Never well-versed in geopolitics, I just wondered, *Malaysia has a royal family?*

Our site team consisted of three people. Frank Hu, a Columbine peer of Chinese descent based in Denver, was responsible for all ad sales and back-office components. Brian Chavez managed all finance/accounting aspects. My responsibility was the rollout of a module called Program Control that managed all programming assets, including scheduling.

The program content of any channel is dependent on actually owning programming rights. In other words, if a channel wanted to schedule and air specific movies or sitcoms or most any other recorded form of programming, it first had to contractually acquire the rights to do so, then fulfill the terms of such deals. The primary problem for City TV was a powerful and fully funded government. They proactively acquired exclusivity rights to essentially all available programming content from every source around the world for their channels. Government-operated channels had no intention of actually airing most of the programming. Their objective was simply keeping content off the airwaves of their new competitor.

That put us into a predicament. When a channel owned the rights to zero meaningful programming, the relatively expensive component of the software suite managing that part of the business was not really needed. Tap-dancing around that sensitive issue was daunting enough, but the prince mistakenly believed WE were somehow responsible for the lack of programming availability on his channel. I attempted to make processes appear normal. The only real programming the channel could acquire was a lot of free public domain material such as really old *National Geographic* documentaries produced well before there were cable channels anywhere. This content was only slightly more advanced than grade school educational movies that required clackety 16mm projection for threadbare film. Bean counters back in Denver were fond of frequently reminding all of us on the other side of the globe that "We need to recognize this revenue now. There can be no delays."

I compromised our relationship with the prince the very first week we arrived. He provided opulent and extremely comfortable housing accommodations across town in a residential district. The building was called Su Casa. It was a long-term corporate apartment/hotel combo. Su Casa was spacious and featured a remarkable breakfast spread that started every day optimistically. Traffic in and around Kuala Lumpur was a nightmare, so the prince provided a shiny new chauffeur-driven Peugeot sedan for weekday transportation to and from the building that housed City TV. As slightly stretched sedans were concerned, it was well appointed with soft leather and tinted glass. There was no bar inside because the Malaysian population is predominantly Islamic.

The return to Su Casa at the conclusion of day three featured an unfortunate mishap. The sedan rolled to a stop atop the covered cobblestone driveway of Su Casa, but I failed to wait for the driver to open my door. He was on the other side of the car helping Brian with a package. Previous hours spent getting into and out of automobiles on my own inspired confidence that the task could be handled solo.

I failed to check the driveway before flinging the rear passenger door open, just in time for it to get unnaturally bent backward all the way into the front driver door by the stout bumper of a large delivery van leaving the driveway from the outside. Brian began laughing. The driver scowled. I assumed the unintelligible words he yelled were Malaysian profanities.

A profound lack of programming and a significantly damaged royal sedan earned us, and especially me, a place atop the shit list of the prince for the remainder of our stay.

The replacement sedan was not as luxurious but still very nice. It got us from home to work and back every Monday through Friday, and I discontinued operating doors by myself. We were on our own every weekend. Malaysia is a remarkably diverse country that is highly tolerant of other cultures and beliefs. Native Malay people are largely working class. Residents of Indian descent generally occupy professional roles in disciplines such as medicine or law. Business and commerce facilitators, whether above board or not, are often Chinese.

Brian and I buddied up to a taxi driver named Lawrence Li. We befriended him on the way to Su Casa from the airport immediately after we retrieved the luggage. "Can we call you Larry?" Brian asked. Despite minor difficulty with the English language, Larry was all in. Frank was fluent in several Chinese dialects and acted as a translator during important moments.

None of us were familiar with Malaysia, and we did not know what interesting sites should be explored on weekends. "I can help you explore," Larry insisted. It only took three attractions to figure out his game and call him on it.

He always had a tourist suggestion. We went to the pewter factory. Then it was on to a leather tannery. We eventually toured a batik facility. In every location, Larry was spotted with some sort of site proprietor, and money changed hands. Larry received kickbacks from those who ran sites we visited. Near the conclusion of our first weekend day in Malaysia, we invited Larry into the spacious lobby of Su Casa and ordered a cold drink for him.

Frank translated our sentiments: "Larry, we do not want to spend the next five weekends getting hustled. If you agree, we will make up for any potential lost revenue by excessively tipping you every day. Sound good?" All three of us had generous per diems that included ample funds for transportation.

"How much do you propose?" Larry asked.

"That depends, Larry. How much do you get every time you

drag somebody into the batik factory?" The answer was ten to twenty dollars, depending on how many people he brought. "Fine, Larry," Brian responded. "We'll give you fifty bucks a day over and above the fare to take us wherever we want to go." It was only around sixteen a day for each of us. Easy.

Larry was flattered and appreciated it, and a trustful bond developed that made the rest of the stint enjoyable. Mutual trust afforded all sorts of opportunities facilitated by Larry, who had a devious sense of humor that nearly matched ours.

While not an Islamic state per se, much of the population there is Muslim and are guided by its values. As a result, easy shopping in other places, like purchasing hard liquor, could be challenging. At dusk of the second weekend, Brian asked Larry where he could buy some Jack Daniel's whiskey. Larry jammed on the brakes, looked carefully in all directions, and then nearly whispered, "I take you there." "There" was a dark alley that contained a block of windowless cinder-block structures. Larry stopped next to one of them. Its only distinguishing feature was a really heavy iron door in the middle. Brian and Frank prepared to accompany Larry through it. "Stay and watch the car," Larry ordered.

Huh?! What?! Me? Here?!

About ten minutes later, Brian exited with a small brown paper bag. He was laughing hard. About what, I did not know. It was easy to be spooked in an unlit alley in a strange part of Kuala Lumpur. He hopped into the cab and told me, "You HAVE to go in there, JT."

"OK, but DO NOT leave without me." They couldn't. Larry was still inside, most likely commiserating. On the other side of the iron door was a retail liquor establishment more well-lit and stocked than any comparable facility in the United States, completely operated outside prevailing rules by Asian entrepreneurs.

"I take you there" became our running joke. Larry procured everything we needed that was difficult to find. Just as the running joke was wearing out, Brian asked Larry, jokingly I think, where he could find, "A Filipino hooker that specializes in anal pleasures." Again, Larry brought the car to a sudden halt, looked around in every direction, turned directly to Brian, and said: "I take you there. But I get to watch." It appeared he was either dead serious or had an equally deviant sense of humor.

Near the end of the project, Larry drove us to the largest Hindu shrine outside India. In order to enter the Batu cave complex, we had to climb almost three hundred steps to an entrance on the side of a small mountain. On the way up, macaques attempted to snatch any container that might hold food or valuables and then run away. Larry was hip to thieving monkeys and effectively thwarted the theft of a really expensive camera strapped around Frank's neck. Once inside, we were amazed by the intricate art that lined all of the cave walls. In the cathedral dome of the main cave, Hindu men performed a purification ceremony that involved smashing coconuts. It was fascinating.

Brian and I were eventually asked to leave. Devout Hindus did not take kindly to Brian and me whistling. *It's a Small World After All* in a nearly continuous loop as we navigated art-filled passageways in the cave.

The final ten days of the project were especially challenging. City TV had no significant programming, no advertising, and the BBC veteran they hired for finance and accounting wanted to mimic the mind-numbingly complicated accounting practices she used in the UK. The relative complexity of doing so drove most everyone batty. The prince was well beyond agitated. His seed money vanished rapidly in chunks every day.

In hindsight, the palpable fear I felt was probably ridiculous. The prince told us over dinner one evening that Malaysia had a zero-tolerance policy for drugs, and their customs officials were particularly diligent. The prince nutshelled his interpretation of the law. "If someone gets caught with a specific quantity of drugs or over, that person is considered a dealer. A trial is held. Most are found guilty of dealing drugs. Dealers usually face the death penalty. It is very harsh. You Americans are way too lenient. Here, executions occur swiftly. Two or three weeks from the verdict."

The prince continued: "If a person is caught with under a certain quantity of drugs, the courts see the person as an addict. Most of the time, those people are sent to rehabilitation, which can take years." His words were chilling. Nervous feelings ratcheted up a notch when the prince asked whether we would like passes to a series of executions while we were there. "Strings can be pulled," he said very slowly, mostly looking directly at me.

I tried to stay busy by helping Frank and Brian, but because City TV had no ad sales business and no programming, we were mostly relegated to either thumb-twiddling or trying to look busy. Internet access there at the time was neither fast nor reliable, and mobile devices were not yet ubiquitous. In the entitled mind of the prince, his plight was our fault. It felt imperative that I leave the country before the planned nine weeks were up. Our welcome wore out early.

Immediately prior to leaving Denver for Kuala Lumpur, I visited a doctor and had blood work performed. While in Malaysia, I was informed that my cholesterol levels and blood pressure were dangerously high. My total daily prescription medication intake up until then was zero. My excuse for leaving Malaysia turned out to be a health warning I positioned as life or death. I feared a possibility that illegal substances might find their way into my luggage without my knowledge and then get discovered in customs while leaving. My only paranoid question was whether the prince wanted me to spend the rest of my life in a Malaysian prison or be dead within two weeks. Fears turned out to be unfounded. *Whew.*

As time passed, my memories of six weeks on the ground in Malaysia became much fonder. In many ways, it was a third-world nation finally breaking through to first-world status. That was evident one afternoon as Brian and I strolled in the vicinity of then brand new but not yet open Petronas Towers, which eventually became the tallest buildings on earth. The sidewalk under us consisted of concrete slabs with vented holes. Those slabs covered troughs that guided raw sewage. Even in the modern office building that housed the television channel, restrooms were essentially glorified portable toilets that sent human waste into the ground.

All citizens we met, regardless of ethnicity or religion, were extraordinarily welcoming. It would be easy to return and explore all other parts of that diverse nation without any employment pressures.

CHAPTER 50

A SUDDEN RETURN TO COLORFUL COLORADO AND VARIOUS PORTIONS OF THE FREE WORLD

Any company that merges with, acquires, or gets absorbed by a competitor is not experiencing anything new. It happens all the time in corporate America. Executive management and shareholders usually end up enriched. Mergers are generally not as great a deal for many whose lives get uprooted.

When competitors Columbine Systems and Jefferson-Pilot Data Services were joined, things got a little weird. Moving from Memphis to Denver for born-and-raised mid-Southerners was difficult. Many spouses had careers, kids in school, relatives, and a host of challenges. A lot of locals chose not to move. Many more that moved eventually became dismayed with the distinctly variant corporate culture at what became Columbine JDS.

Seesawing between companies did not get me fired. As a matter of fact, roughly the same corporate coffers paid for three moves across the country within one year.

We were forced to give up our dream home in Memphis one week before closing on it.

There was no shortage of work. Because many mission-critical employees did not move west, a lot of time was spent working on JDS projects outside the office. Between 1995 and 1999, however, Columbine's corporate culture eliminated most traits that made JDS exceptional. The Columbine next-generation product was not intelligently architected and only minimally developed. It was aggressively marketed anyway.

Before on-screen channel guides became ubiquitous from every television service provider, most viewers relied on just one. The TV Guide Channel provided program listings in local markets. It used to be a very large business, including a complex and very impressive IT infrastructure. They signed a contract for the Columbine JDS next-generation product, dubbed Paradigm.

One module of Paradigm was Proposer, a front-end ad sales tool that promised to craft and keep track of proposed business and seamlessly make the technical transactions to actual business. It was also positioned as fully integrated with all other components and capable of a myriad of data collection and reporting.

Its biggest problem was a profound lack of underlying code that could validate most of its marketing claims. My peer Bob Von Kohorn and I were dispatched to New York. The mission was to spend two weeks rolling the product out to TV Guide. Our skepticism was understated. CJDS also sent explicit instructions about which parts of it to use, and more importantly, which ones NOT to use.

A potential problem that never occurred to architects, developers, marketers, or ANYONE at CJDS was any sort of necessity to hide selectable on-screen functionality that did not yet contain full, partial, or *any* code. Nearly 80 percent of the product was underdeveloped in that manner. CJDS, however, needed the revenue, so off we traipsed.

Among the first things smart clients wanted to do involved exploring all the cool functionality the product was supposed to offer, just like they saw during the PowerPoint demonstration. "John, it's here on the screen. Why doesn't it work? It should work. It worked in the demo." Attempts to follow the CJDS script failed immediately because the script had very little to do with how TV Guide actually conducted its ad sales business.

Bob and I were asked to leave on the third day. The client was snippy. "Do not come back until you can bring us a complete product. You just wasted three days of our time. That's not acceptable." That was a big problem for CJDS. No revenue was realized. Once back in Denver, we were summoned onto the executive management carpet.

"John, Bob, you failed to adequately manage client expectations."

"Actually," I retorted, more than slightly annoyed, "the only thing that client really expected was software that did something once the enter key was pressed. You know, ANYTHING besides throwing fatal errors."

Any notion of running through walls and continually striving for bulletproof, impactful product offerings failed to penetrate their deaf ears.

It was easier to blame others who had nothing to do with development for developmental issues.

That is the way it went for most of the next five years at Columbine JDS. My tenure managed to last that long at the merged company only because my services managing projects for JDS offerings were in demand. One such adventure took me to Singapore for a few months to help launch MTV Asia. Even JDS was destined to be a square peg into that round hole, but the challenge intrigued me and we made it work.

An example of a problem that demanded creative solutions involved variations of identical programming within different Asian nations. The MTV Asia coverage footprint covered countries as diverse as Australia to more restrictive nations such as Malaysia. The MTV program *Beavis and Butt-Head* usually contained between twenty-one and twenty-two minutes of program content. The remaining time was used for commercials and promotion. JDS easily accommodated that. The problem with many countries involved censorship. Some nations employed censors sanctioned by government entities. Their primary job was reviewing all programming in advance to determine what portions could or could not air. In Indonesia, for example, a strict set of rules applied to sexual situations. Any hint of words or actions remotely related to sex was forbidden.

Poor *Beavis and Butt-Head*. The portion of the MTV footprint that covered a specific country might end up with a version of that show containing just seven or eight minutes of approved content. That seemed odd. In most cases, violence was acceptable. Evening news broadcasts in many of the same countries often led with footage of bloodied, dead victims involved in fatal automobile accidents. Violence was fine, but sex? No way. Rules varied significantly from country to country. In almost every case, special circumstances were accommodated by bending JDS to allow for them.

Assignments like that were like vacations. All expenses were paid. Accommodations included an entire upper floor of the Westin Stamford. Evening company at the eighth-floor outdoor hotel pool often included female MTV VJs from Europe, there to host segments on the new channel. Because they were on television, they were not unattractive. They also possessed the relaxed sensibilities (with no moral entanglements) of many European countries, and all were usually at the pool sans any clothing from the waist up. Most evening meals were consumed poolside. The view was amazing.

Most of the time, however, Columbine JDS career limbo, complete with shoddy development, out-of-touch management, and over-the-top marketing of many products that did not even exist, continued unabated. The company signed the first television entity not owned or controlled by the government in Belgium. Preparations to roll Paradigm into the channel began in 1997. In 1998, a team of CJDS people moved into apartments, where we resided for nearly a year. The apartment building, Lambermont, featured a private bar for its residents. That service was required nearly every day.

Brussels became home in 1998. My inner racing fan was thrilled watching Formula 1 at Spa in person despite hard rain most of the race day. Traveling companions and I visited castles in Belgium, Germany, and Luxembourg. Weekend trips to places like Bruges, Belgium, to bike around town, or to Amsterdam in the Netherlands to soak in culture were fantastic.

From a project standpoint, the TV station was no closer to going live at the end of 1998 than they were at the beginning. That painful process was a direct result of flaccid products and tepid support for it. Having a team on-site with software not yet functional cost a small fortune. Suits in Denver remained either blissfully insensitive or downright oblivious, despite carefully crafted documentation of all issues. My team became a futile conduit between clients who needed to vent and management not prone to listening. Belgium is also known for its great chocolate and even greater beer. We appreciated both, although rarely at the same time.

During 1998, I made ten round trips across the Atlantic for that project. An eleventh trip sticks out more than most. Early in September 1998, I flew to Denver from Brussels through Cincinnati on Saturday morning. Sleeping at home most of Sunday was inadequate preparation for an endless stream of relentlessly pointless meetings on Monday.

Shortly before 9 on Monday morning in downtown Denver, I got called into the boss's office.

"John, we need you to attend a meeting at noon tomorrow with a client."

"That's fine," I said. "Just tell me who and where."

"Brussels. You know the client."

I made a mad dash home, stuffed an overnight bag, then violated speed limits to Denver International for flights that arrived in Zaventem around 8:30 a.m. Tuesday. I was met by two executives who worked in global sales but not in development. The meeting consisted of the client screaming about nonfunctional software, out-of-control expenses, and casual indifference from CJDS. The suits spent a great deal of time apologizing, promising progress, and even upselling. My contribution was less than a dozen words. Dinner later was followed by sleep at an airport hotel, then right back to Denver at 8:00 Wednesday morning.

The first meeting Thursday morning back in Denver involved my boss, her boss, and me. Lack of progress on the faltering Belgium project was positioned as my fault.

"John, we are placing you on a Performance Improvement Protocol. You will remain in PIP status until progress is made in this project. If there is none or not enough, you could be pulled off the project or could lose your job. Do we have an understanding?"

It was nothing more than glorified disciplinary probation. I was blamed for a number of breakdowns elsewhere in the company for failures completely beyond my control.

"Perhaps I should either learn how to code or subcontract a seventh-grader to do it," I smirked.

My attitude dramatically slipped from professional norms. I required new challenges.

CHAPTER 51

ADIOS, PARADIGM-SHIFTING PETER PRINCIPLE MORONS

I should have had it made. I was living close to two of my young children in Colorado. My tenure with multiple iterations of the same company that stretched back to Charlotte exceeded ten years. The money was good. Why would I even consider working somewhere else? Here's how.

Boomers weren't like generations that preceded them. We were restless. We invented an entirely new language of business, then asked ourselves what we did and why. Fluid ownership of Columbine JDS changed about every year, finally becoming merely a page or two in the portfolio of private equity firm Thomas H. Lee Partners.

As Y2K neared late in 1999, my vision of an exit strategy began taking shape. One pointless meeting after another listening to youthful climbers attempt to out-buzzword one another made me want to sledgehammer railroad spikes into my own ears. I could not stand listening to any more pontificated nonsense.

"We intend to achieve the synergies we've generated through our organic growth, enabling benchmarking ourselves against all of our competition here and abroad. As we globalize, our mission involves leveraging core products to facilitate business process reengineering in nontraditional environments. Risk factors aside, we have a great deal of intellectual capital to exploit, and employing best practices ensures steady revenue growth."

What?! WHAT?!

Bottom line: The company was unable to produce software that did what it was supposed to do. That made clients unhappy and put me and everyone else on the front line in the middle of unwinnable battles.

I knew the end of the road arrived after Thanksgiving weekend in 1999. CJDS used the start of the new century to upsell every client not already using IBM's AS/400 mini-mainframe and positioning potential catastrophe if they did not. Selling software AND hardware was a lucrative business. Those conversions were technical in nature and required on-site supervision and consulting, which also enriched coffers.

I intended to spend a trouble-free, working holiday weekend in Europe. First up was a radio network in Newcastle upon Tyne, England. From there, it was on to Lisbon, Portugal, for an identical upgrade and brief consulting at a television network. Finally, a stop in Brussels would wrap up the journey. With any luck at all, I would slumber in my own Colorado bed by Sunday night.

I arrived in the U.K. late Wednesday afternoon. Updates were arranged with management for overnights after business hours. Whenever system errors occurred during updates, three potential recovery options usually appeared on user screens. Option 1 attempted to go around errors and keep the update going. Option 3 ended the program and assumed underlying problems would be solved in the meantime, allowing the update to pick up where it left off when restarted. There was also an Option 2, but the one thing drilled into heads from day one at JDS in the 1980s was to never, EVER, E-V-E-R select Option 2 under ANY circumstance for ANY reason at ANY time.

In the case of CJDS's Paradigm offering, selection of Option 2 unleashed strings of mayhem into already ghastly executed and poorly conceived code. Recovery, if possible, took developers hours to diagnose and repair. The real problem with Option 2 was that it was even an option. For average users, the innocuous description of what Option 2 would do if selected after an error seemed to imply it was the most logical choice, and in most cases, did not constitute any problem from an IBM standpoint. Because Option 2 prohibition was reinforced repeatedly to me, I also reinforced it to system users.

That did not stop a supervisory manager in Newcastle from selecting Option 2 while my body loudly disposed of unpronounceable local cuisine and trans-Atlantic airline "food" aboard a bidet-equipped porcelain throne behind bathroom doors. CJDS software spiraled out of control, much like my overactive bowels. Only worse.

"John, I know you said we should never use Option 2 when a halt message appears, but it seemed to make the most sense, so I did."

I called the 24-hour CJDS support line at around 11 p.m. local time. That meant it was the end of the workweek the Wednesday before Thanksgiving in Denver.

"Uh, John, your problem will have to wait a few days."

The Thanksgiving holiday weekend in America is neither recognized nor celebrated by anyone in England or Portugal, and folks in both nations work that Thursday and Friday. Waiting a few days was not an option.

Escalation effort reached C-level before assistance was grudgingly approved. Resolution took fourteen straight hours. My body was weary after having flown across the country, then across the Atlantic, then more or less straight to work. Sleep deprivation followed me to Portugal.

In Lisbon, language differences created additional barriers. Spanish classes in college did not help with Portuguese in Portugal much. I believed my repeated warnings to the client about avoidance at all costs of Option 2 during error messages were understood, especially since they repeatedly nodded their heads up and down. About four hours into their upgrade, I left the system console to retrieve lengthy validation reports from a printer in another room. At some point during my four-minute absence, the systems person in Lisbon selected Option 2 when an error message popped up.

"No one told us something bad would happen," the IT person snorted.

"Actually, that is the first thing we tell everyone, then repeat it more often than the word *birthday* in the song *Happy Birthday*. It's also in the margin of nearly every page in your Operations Manual." I no longer smiled.

That inadvertent screw-up occurred at 10 a.m. the Saturday morning after Thanksgiving. Once again, escalation efforts that began late in the day at headquarters resulted in sixteen hours of disgruntled mumbling by on-call developers whose weekends were disrupted simply because a user chose Option 2.

At that point, nothing mattered. All I wanted was my own bed for twelve straight hours. Sleep was deep and refreshing once it arrived. Option 2-related delays postponed a return flight until Monday. Return to the office on Tuesday featured nearly continuous haranguing from a number of out-of-touch management levels who were inconvenienced over the holidays. Most were able to squeeze in turkey and trimmings with family and friends. I consumed vending machine potato chips in successive overnights across Europe, usually in the company of people who possessed fragrances that were a bit too ripe. Every encountered problem was positioned as my fault.

Columbine JDS became a corporate hell. I guzzled New Year's Eve champagne on hiatus between professional gigs.

CHAPTER 52

A PRIVATE LITTLE COMPANY ON THE FRINGE

"Claude, PLEASE get me out of here."

The first call made after I woke up from the CJDS European Thanksgiving nightmare was to Claude Morris. He was the JDS sales executive responsible for renewing the Post-Newsweek account earlier in the decade at CJDS. Claude and I built a professional relationship based on mutual respect and trust, enhanced by re-signing Post-Newsweek. He left Columbine JDS in 1997, and then became chief operating officer of a much smaller company based in Springfield, Massachusetts. Claude and I occasionally danced around the possibility of joining his new company at some point. We decided the future arrived in 2000, and I would start fresh, just like the new century.

Video Communications Incorporated, VCI for short, was launched more than a decade before Y2K by an outwardly nerdy, but really sharp, gadfly named Lowell Putnam. Lowell's father (also Lowell) owned television stations, among other diverse interests.

Lowell, Jr., whose appearance somewhat resembled Jeff Bezos only with more hair, favored offering marketplace computing alternatives that did not require forking over six-figure capital expenditures for mainframe hardware and software.

His notion was well ahead of its time. Lowell and a small team built their first DOS-based system and deployed it inside their own stations. The small company grew. Software that ran aboard off-the-shelf hardware was sold to external clients. Technology Lowell envisioned finally became capable of accommodating advanced features and reporting-rich software.

Lowell's problem was not software or vision. His ability to see clearly five or ten years into the future and steering products in that direction was consistently remarkable. He was simply not great at managing growth. Despite a growing client base and increasing revenue, most deals were of the napkin sketch and handshake variety. That failed to result in consistent, ongoing revenue streams, ultimately leading to profitability. VCI needed someone who could operate a business and generate profitable recurring revenues, enabling self-funded organic growth. Claude Morris became that person.

During the late 1990s, VCI became the new professional home for many former JDS peers disillusioned by CJDS. Among them was Skip Sawyer, the person who created a position for me at JDS immediately before its ownership change. The presence of people experienced in working within a professional environment was the main reason to accept the VCI challenge.

Once again, we packed our belongings and moved across the country, arriving at VCI roughly the moment meaningful business activity took off. Our newly acquired clients were larger and far more complex. VCI was willing to bend over backward to make client relationships successful. It was a refreshing throwback to the inspiration I felt when my JDS career phase began.

Large-scale projects were lined up at the cable networks of NBC. Further north, the CHUM group in Toronto began an acquisition and startup binge and looked to replace dated and increasingly obsolete JDS products. Thirty-two channels were slated for VCI automation.

The magic returned. People at VCI were willing to run through walls to solve problems. Smart people with industry experience worked together. More than one former JDS peer confided that it felt like home.

The most unusually entertaining corporate aspects experienced at VCI were occasional shouting matches between staff members and Lowell. At Columbine JDS, any raised voices, particularly with executives, generally resulted in one-way tickets out the door. Discourse of any type was fully encouraged at VCI. No one held hard feelings, and products tended to improve as a result. Everyone in the small company had a voice and were encouraged to use it.

The corporate experience in western Massachusetts was satisfying. The only problem involved being on the road more days than at home. That was exhausting. Even after accepting a promotion to manage all consultants and supervise all implementation projects, my services away from the office remained in high demand. One personal specialty involved dealing effectively with hostile clients, and I was dropped into more than a few corporate war zones. As annual conventions and client conferences were added, heavy travel seemed brutally inevitable. In the aftermath of 9/11 and subsequent economic hard times, airline travel began its race to the bottom in earnest. Every year of business travel brought new lows.

Nearly six years after walking through VCI's front door and despite rediscovering magic that inspired career passion, major career direction change again seemed like a good idea.

CHAPTER 53

THE NATIONAL BROADCASTING COMPANY

JDS grew significantly during the late 1980s and early 1990s, and their client roster began including blue-chip networks. Viacom's MTV channels occupied a significant chunk. That project took most of 1991 in New York and required an entire team of JDS people.

JDS also began automating cable channels launched by NBC—initially CNBC. NBC also partnered with Cablevision in the late 1980s and launched SportsChannel America, eventually intended to compete with ESPN. Cablevision successfully operated a series of regional sports channels across the country. Many eventually aligned with either Fox or Comcast. At the time, JDS helped automate regional channels in cities such as Boston, Philadelphia, Chicago, San Francisco, and Los Angeles. Consulting led me to all of them.

When SportsChannel America launched, JDS was selected as its business automation vendor. Because the channel was essentially a startup, a four-week project plan was presented and approved.

We were going to share floor space and staff with CNBC on a middle floor in Rockefeller Center that once housed NBC's Standards and Practices Department.

NBC employed a large staff of IT professionals but was not yet referred to in terms of information technology. Computer experts at NBC in the late 1980s also did not have direct experience with proprietary IBM mini-mainframes like the System/36 or AS/400. Very few customers, regardless of size, did. As a result, people like me also became hardware experts, in most cases installing the mainframe and all connected workstations with bulky twin axial cable. All were dedicated, dumb terminals with green or amber displays. Primitive by contemporary standards, they were reliable and mostly bulletproof in their day.

Technical personnel at NBC had little desire to include an IBM mini-mainframe in their data center because it would mean they would have to support it. They possessed neither budgets nor staff, much less technical expertise, to accommodate that. An air-conditioned closet was provided for the SportsChannel America mainframe on the same floor as the staff that used it.

The first day on site of the four-week project was also the day I learned about NBC's bureaucracy. Six dumb terminals had to be physically cabled together and ultimately attached to the small mainframe, and work had to be completed by union electricians in the building. On day one, a union supervisor handed over and explained requisition forms required to complete the cabling job and said "My estimate is it will take four and a half weeks."

I tried hiding a look of incredulous frustration that made my brain throb. *This asshole is out of his mind.*

I protested. "Uh, the project began today and is designated for four weeks with a firm go-live date in less than one month." His response was curt. "You should have thought of that before you got here. It's not my problem." He finished with a shrug and walked away.

I should throw this AS/400 at his pompous ass. Or head.

My project plan featured chronological milestones that had to be checked before moving to the next steps. Days of preliminary meetings laid everything out. Management and operations staff were on board. Scuttling an important company project because workstations could not be cabled within a known timeframe would never fly. Still, no one seemed willing to take on the bureaucracy, much less the union.

I had spent almost my entire life to that point defying authority, and decided to incorporate some feisty rebellion inside 30 Rock. *Fuck 'em,* I thought. *Bastards aren't going to sabotage MY project!*

Late on the first day, I scavenged a large supply of oversized paper clips, duct tape, and binder clips from supply cabinets. I did not intend to knock holes into any walls. All were hard plaster and might be impossible to penetrate. Another bureaucratic group inside the building indicated that no cables were allowed on any portion of any floor. "John, those are OSA safety violations, even if it's duct-taped, covered, and marked." My after-hours hack on day one consisted of using primarily binder clips and duct tape. I attached cable to existing conduit along the walls. Bent paper clips attached cables to acoustic ceiling tiles, bound for six workstation locations below. No known rules prohibited cable hanging in mid-air next to desks.

Predictable howling commenced the following day about hacked cable installation and total exclusion of union personnel. An emergency meeting was demanded that included upper-level management from both internal organizations. At least three departments were represented by ill-tempered silo keepers who spent half an hour taking turns yelling and berating while waving fingers through the air.

During minute twenty-nine, my boiling point was exceeded. I slammed both fists hard onto the conference table.

"Look, my solution is TEMPORARY," nearly yelling as I stood up. "Permanent installation can take place ANY time after the system goes live and I'm gone. Stop trying to derail the project by overcomplicating it. Other than the political nonsense being forced in this room, the entire thing is smooth sailing. Now please excuse me. We still have a lot of work to do, and it won't get done in here. Carry on without me."

I walked out. The Six Sigma note takers had no idea what to write down.

The same argument continued for all four weeks, but nothing was going to impede progress toward going live.

The date that was supposed to happen was the end of November 1989. A memorable week unfolded as the project began. Standards and Practices previously occupied our space on the floor. Although relocated, the floor still contained monitors that provided glimpses into all active NBC studios. Whenever something interesting happened, it usually drew the attention of folks at their desks. Many of those interruptions were far more interesting than posturing over hanging cable.

We noticed the Eurythmics on Wednesday of week two. Annie Lennox, Dave Stewart, and their band were scheduled for *Saturday Night Live* that weekend as the musical act. Their rehearsal was about to begin on the SNL stage. The operations person asked me, "How would you like to run down there and check it out for a few minutes, John?" Despite the workload, we headed for Studio 8H and were one of about six lucky people who enjoyed an impromptu short concert.

Pretty sweet gig you've got here, Johnny Boy.

On the way back upstairs, we shared the elevator with Chris Evert, the celebrity host of SNL that week.

They never do this on the tours.

A short meeting with the director of engineering was also required that week. Technical aspects of the SportsChannel America playlist needed fine-tuning. One delay after another delayed any sort of meeting. Sam, the engineering guy, was busy all day, every day. He finally summoned us to a location where he was already doing something else. "Come on down to the Nightly News studio. Brokaw's out this week. Paula knows how to get here."

The Berlin Wall was about to fall, and Tom Brokaw was in Germany. The wall actually began falling the same time our engineering meeting began. That meant breaking news, which also meant our location inside NBC's primary news studio suddenly became an awkward place for business chit-chat. Garrick Utley manned the NBC Nightly News desk in Brokaw's absence, and he rushed into the studio a few feet away from us. Seconds later, the room went hot. Utley was on the air live. We had no time or way to escape. When that room was live, no one was allowed entry or exit. As the Berlin Wall collapsed, three of us stood ten feet away in complete silence from the man delivering that news to the nation. I was afraid to breathe. Once Utley completed, Sam whispered, "Let's relocate this little soiree."

It was the beginning of several colorful off-and-on adventures at NBC that lasted sporadically over fifteen years. SportsChannel America eventually disappeared in underperformance and red ink, and other channels sprouted in its place. One of them was MSNBC.

For the remainder of my career, my involvement with NBC entities continued in a variety of locations, from Ft. Lee and Secaucus in New Jersey, to various office buildings in Manhattan, even to Hong Kong immediately before the British handed it back to China. NBC launched NBC Asia, which required two months of my life in Asia early in 1997.

I believed my professional NBC assignments ended in late 1999 after joining VCI. Claude Morris and Skip Sawyer, however, were on the verge of signing NBC's cable networks to long-term deals. The fact that I already had a relationship with NBC helped get me hired at VCI. Those networks became my first large project at VCI. Technology and politics advanced exponentially there in just a few years. What was once a four-week project suddenly became twelve weeks and involved entire teams from both organizations.

The business of back-office and ad sales automation, whether in a small market radio station or a large national television network, is still often unrealistically dismissed as mere clerical work that almost anyone can do. That prevailing attitude was far too cavalier, considering every cent of ad sales revenue, hundreds of millions of dollars, flowed through business systems we provided and managed.

The general lack of respect for people hired to do those jobs was palpable.

In the weeks that followed 9/11, NBC became a victim of anthrax attacks launched against several media outlets and politicians. Mailed spores infected several people and killed five. My last major projects at NBC occurred as operations of several acquired channels, including Bravo, SyFy, and USA Network, were integrated into what eventually became NBC Universal.

Most departments that used VCI's business systems were consolidated to the second floor of Rockefeller Center, space previously occupied by NBC's mail facility. That was the location in which anthrax-infected mail was discovered. NBC folks that moved in were fond of claiming not much effort went into tidying up afterward. They often lamented the bureaucracy that inevitably relegated them to lowly clerical classes.

The lengthy NBC adventure involved several memorable people through decades of engagement. 30 Rock provided consistently interesting career milestones.

CHAPTER 54

TWO DISASTERS IN THE SAME DAY

As winter gave way to spring in 2001, I managed an implementation project at KOMO Television in Seattle, then owned by Fisher Communications. My previous experience at that station during the late 1990s involved Columbine JDS. At that time, KOMO occupied an old, nondescript building near the Space Needle in downtown Seattle. No one enjoyed the building, and no real sense of pride about it existed inside. Plans to replace it were in the works.

By early 2001, the old building vanished. A brand new five-story building right next door opened for business just days before, and KOMO was the first tenant in what eventually became Fisher Plaza. Their master plan included a proposed, nearly identical six-story building adjacent to it within the footprint of KOMO's original building, which was demolished and removed. The building that housed KOMO featured ample parking underground, five stories of it, and parking was no longer an issue. The new building would also feature five stories of underground parking.

The scene was surreal. We worked on the fifth floor of the gleaming new tower, but the view out the window was a giant five-story hole in the ground right next door. KOMO was a significant signing for VCI, and we displaced a mostly futile attempt there with the Columbine JDS Paradigm product. It was a rare venture that included significant enthusiasm and diligence by rank-and-file folks, despite the fact many of them worked double duty while maintaining two systems.

The go-live date rapidly approached, and the staff was hard at work late in the morning of February 28. Shortly before lunch, the new building began shaking violently. The Nisqually earthquake lasted for nearly a minute and tipped the Richter scale at magnitude 6.8. I was discussing an issue in an open hallway with the person in charge of technology when it began. As shaking intensified, standing became unwise and not really possible. We hit the floor along with everyone else. Tape cartridges flew off desks. Hanging fluorescent fixtures swayed so violently that many illuminated tubes popped out and smashed. Peter, my floormate, went pale. Barely audibly, he said, "This is the big one. Jesus Christ."

My own thought at that moment involved the brand-new building we sat in, frequently touted as "highly resistant to seismic events common to the West Coast."

I know this building is brand new and "earthquake-proof," but there is a five-story hole in the ground less than five feet away, and we're probably headed there any second.

My previous earthquake experience occurred a few years earlier in Palm Desert, California. The shaking in that one was not bad, and the staff there actually heard it coming. That one sounded like a large truck backing up to a loading dock, only the building contained no loading dock, and no trucks were nearby. It only turned out to be a 4.5. In Seattle, the shaking was akin to being inside an out-of-balance washing machine. The sound it made was deafening, as if bowling balls got tossed into the washer with us.

The shaking subsided, and we needed to assess the potential damage.

"LEAVE THE BUILDING IMMEDIATELY," a loud voice repeated on an intercom.

I took five flights of stairs, two steps at a time. Several cracks in the walls of stairwells appeared. On the sidewalk outside, folks were happy they had ridden it out, and tentative high fives were exchanged. The director of commercial operations suddenly began cursing loudly, something very out of character for her.

"FUCK! FUCK! FUCK! Why now?! F-U-C-K!"

"Why the anger? I'm feeling pretty lucky at the moment," I offered. Paula simply answered, "Makegoods." Local stations suspend all programming to cover breaking stories, sometimes for hours afterward. Commercials do not run when the news is live, and they must get rescheduled so the station won't lose revenue. Of course, that is easier said than done on a station that enjoyed considerable commercial success.

"We'll get through it. I promise." There was no other choice.

The earthquake felt oddly like severe airplane turbulence. I still get anxious when any plane I am on begins bouncing around in the air.

In Seattle, genuine disaster was averted; physical damage was significantly less than it could have been, and injuries were minimal.

Imagine segueing from one potential natural disaster to the remnants of another. Coincident with the quake, KOMO was the presenting sponsor for a traveling exhibit that featured artifacts recovered from the Titanic. That was no small feat, considering most were scattered for nearly a century on the deep floor of the North Atlantic. The exhibit was not yet open to the public, but a special closed KOMO preview had been arranged for February 28. The museum suffered no damage, so the preview went forward despite aftershocks.

Special commemorative cards were distributed to patrons upon entry. Females were given cards representing female passengers aboard the ship, and males received corresponding male cards. No one knew whether they lived or died until the very end of the tour. I did not survive.

The exhibit was spectacular. Most were amazed by the artifacts on display. For my money (free but with a generous donation to the museum), the one thing that inspired awe was the ability to touch a very large section of the ship's hull that was recovered and displayed. If patrons were so inclined, their palms could be placed directly onto an actual section of the Titanic. Duly mesmerized, I did.

I am one of a select few who can claim survival of a major earthquake and touching the Titanic on the same day.

CHAPTER 55

9/11 FROM OUTSIDE THE BORDER

By September 11, 2001, a project to automate thirty-two channels operated by the CHUM Television group in Toronto crossed its halfway point. VCI kept four people on the ground in Canada. Those responsible for operating channels mostly worked in a large, open bullpen ringed with large television monitors to sample not only CHUM's offerings but all competitors. An entire wall was devoted entirely to news programming offered by both Canadian and American networks.

No one paid much attention to what was described as a small plane crashing into the north tower of the World Trade Center. By the time the second plane impacted the south tower on live television, everyone in the bullpen simply stopped working while staring silently with slackened jaws at the wall of monitors. No one moved except for those who knew people that may have been in the vicinity.

Prospects for actual work going forward that day seemed slim. Reverent silence was broken only by the shrill voice of the director of the department. "Get back to work! We're not paying you to stand around!" she shrieked shortly after the second tower fell.

They did, but neither hearts nor minds were engaged.

Some of us were scheduled to leave Canada that week, but travel across international borders simply ceased. We were on our own. The upside involved enjoyment of tasty beer, poutine, and many samples of Canadian cuisine. The awful reality of mayhem, death, and sadness south of the border put a damper on life. We eventually crossed into the USA a week later. It required a car in the middle of the night when the lines were shorter.

CHAPTER 56

HELLO, OLD FRIEND. RADIO. FROM SPACE.

The originally scheduled launch date of XM Satellite Radio was September 12, 2001. Tragic events on the previous day in New York, Washington, and Pennsylvania postponed a game-changer. The service eventually launched two weeks later, and its push to attract subscribers intensified. Television commercials featuring music legends like David Bowie helped drive initial customer interest.

Traditional radio hated it. It made radio no longer free, and XM's music channels had no commercials. It was possible to listen to the same station anywhere and all across the country. The first few years were rocky, and startup costs were extreme. It cost millions of dollars to launch one satellite into orbit, much less four. XM also spent lavishly, gut remodeling a century-old building that once housed printing operations for *National Geographic*. The shabby northeast quadrant of Washington, DC, had just begun experiencing gentrification. Modular, acoustically neutral studios sprouted all over the building, and every piece of equipment inside them was top of the line.

Management paid well above the market rate to attract the most talented people in radio. As a result, living legends wandered hallways and occupied cubicles at XM. They crafted a big splash, but success was dependent on people paying for the service. Unfortunately, the number of subscribers XM expected failed to materialize as rapidly as projected. Predictably, multiple rounds of layoffs commenced a couple of years later as earnest attempts to balance expenses against revenue became a priority.

Near profitability seemed well within reach by 2005. Subscriber counts climbed rapidly as technology changed and additional OEM partners agreed to include XM in new cars. Legends still plied their trades. The trajectory of XM Satellite Radio remained positive, despite new direct competition from Sirius Satellite radio, launched after XM.

In 2005, XM Radio began stressing the importance of ad sales revenue as an additional stream. It might pale compared to subscriber revenue but could generate millions every month and bolster their bottom line. Opportunities certainly existed. XM carried every single Major League Baseball and National Hockey League game, for example. Non-music programming had plenty of room to accommodate commercial time. XM brass decided to get serious about that part of their business.

A serious courtship began with them halfway through 2005. I paid attention for a number of reasons. The two most important were compensation, which was higher than seemed probable, and the job itself. The director-level position was part of the Programming Department led at the top by Lee Abrams and *not* sales, finance, or IT. Their reasoning was that up to 25 percent of every programming hour contained commercial or promotional content. The sound fell under the purview of the department they wanted me to lead. The quality of anything that occupied XM air had to be consistent with the overall sound to which Abrams and crew strived. It was a tough challenge to pass up, even though VCI grass was never greener.

The downside about XM was the business system that supported scheduling efforts, Paradigm from Columbine JDS. That company evolved from CJDS to Encoda under new ownership—this time defense contractor and broadcast equipment supplier Harris. I laughingly surmised that perhaps the product evolved beyond marketing during nearly six years away from it. It also did not hurt that the person leading my recruitment effort began work with XM well before their launch. She also successfully implemented the system in multiple locations around the world as a former peer at CJDS. Travel would likely be limited only to New York.

Travel, in general, transformed me into someone I disliked. Because I did so much of it, a feeling of entitlement festered. On rare occasions that airline seats, rental cars, or hotel rooms were not upgraded based on status, I felt slighted. Frequent delays and additional restrictions seemed to make the timing for a switch seemed right.

Radio dumped me for good in 1987. Or so I thought. Turns out it was a part of my DNA. I tackled the business side in 2005, but almost everyone I looked up to as an aspiring star twenty years before actively crafted imagination-provoking theater of the mind right down the hall. It was a refreshing deviation from rapidly homogenizing traditional radio.

Even with palpable regret about leaving VCI, I negotiated a firm deal with XM Satellite Radio to begin employment in October of 2005. Their offer included a hefty signing bonus and help with moving. There was also the matter of a preplanned weeklong vacation at a resort on Kauai early in November. No problem. XM brass approved a week away after only three weeks on the job as a condition of employment.

The start of that vacation could also have meant the end of my life. Annie and I wondered whether it was an omen. After all, air travel that included millions of miles over twenty years included a few close calls. A Delta 767 once lost cabin pressure at 35,000 feet, forcing the most rapid descent I have ever experienced, complete with oxygen masks. A TWA MD-80 had a problem one of its two engines between St. Louis and Colorado Springs and was forced to land urgently in Kansas City while thunderstorms raged. The most extreme turbulence I ever felt occurred approaching New Orleans aboard a Northwest 727, prompting many of my seatmates to begin praying in unison. Another Northwest flight aboard a DC-9 swerved off a runway outside White Plains to avoid a deer standing in the middle of it. Clear air wind shear forced a regional jet on final approach into Colorado Springs into an unnatural angle that forced a diversion to Denver. An American Airlines 727 once took off from DFW into a thunderstorm and took a direct lightning hit. A prop plane from Chattanooga to Atlanta once flew through a violent hail storm. I lost count of missed approaches or takeoffs early on. I consistently remained unscathed.

The most humorous, potentially dangerous air travel situation occurred after Columbine and JDS merged. The company chartered an antique 737 from a private charter outfit, then on the verge of bankruptcy, and now long gone. Viscount Air (probably rhymed with discount) was hired to fly the company from Memphis to Denver for orientation meetings and house hunting. The castoff 737 had seen far better days. Its interior featured duct tape on walls, windows, and more than a few seats. The captain was the spitting image of Ernest Borgnine in his later years, only more drunken-looking. The first officer resembled Yaphet Kotto. Copilot Kotto was spotted midflight, walking from the cockpit toward the rear of the aircraft with a large hammer. We were unable to see what he did, but we heard loud pounding from the hammer onto some hard surface. Passengers refrained from asking what could be broken enough to require forceful use of a hammer during flight. The plane either must have been flown until fuel tanks were nearly empty, or their credit was shaky. The plane landed in Salina, Kansas, to refuel and have a tire changed on the return flight from Denver to Memphis. At the time, peers darkly feared the merged company found a way to radically downsize in a definitive way.

That was then. My brand-new gig at XM was solidly underway late in 2005. Annie and I began the first leg of a journey that would take us from Hartford to Cincinnati on Delta, where we would connect to a Honolulu non-stop in first class. Hawaiian Air was supposed to shuttle us on to Kauai. As a frequent flyer, I was excited our Hartford flight was aboard a nearly retired 737-200, one of just a handful of that model then still flying commercial routes before being parked in a desert, ripped to shreds, and recycled into beer cans.

At roughly the moment the takeoff roll reached V1, a flock of birds at the liftoff end of the runway met the aircraft. Many fowl quickly became sprayed pate. Aborting takeoff was not possible without dire consequences. Given abnormal engine pitch, sputtering, popping, and smell, actually flying was iffy. The pilot climbed to an altitude that made a really sharp turn possible and landed the aircraft within minutes. Emergency vehicles met the aircraft as it stopped. The captain advised passengers to remain seated until damage and fire threats were assessed. Once given thumbs up, the plane was towed to a gate.

Travel disruption was not horrible. We were flown to Atlanta instead, and although no upgrade was possible to Hawaii, we were each given an entire row in coach. A free unplanned night on Waikiki beach became an added bonus.

I was never more ready to become 9-to-5-ish desk jockey once back on the mainland. We moved to suburban Washington, D.C., and dove in head first.

CHAPTER 57

JOAN BAEZ AND HER FLAT FACE

This is a really short chapter, and for good reason. The less said, the better. The Northeast Washington, DC, headquarters of XM Satellite Radio-inspired audio magic that continuously flowed from the old brick walls at Elkington Place. The structure incorporated a rear entrance used primarily by employees parked within a fenced lot in the rear. To enter or exit meant using a heavy, windowless steel door. It opened outward from a security vestibule that required guest check-in. Another nearby rear entrance was primarily used by celebrities because they could get into and out of the building and studios with minimal steps or fanfare.

My professional reputation was steadfastly one of mostly nonconfrontational tranquility. I have been referred to as a smiling, even-tempered diplomat more than once. It seemed easier to seek peaceful, creative, and preferably win-win solutions to most problems. High volumes of abuse could generally be shrugged off, and my fuse was long. My rare occasions of lost temper went largely uncontrolled and seldom ended well. Tantrums tumbled downhill in a paroxysm of bright scarlet, high decibels, and bulging neck veins.

I began having many more composure lapses after Sirius gained control of XM.

I REALLY needed to vent outside the building on one such occasion, and an urgent quest to get there exploded. Unbridled rage was nearly nuclear once my clenched fists hit the bar of the steel door that led to fresh air.

My teeth were clenched. "Motherfucking cocksuckers …" I mumbled audibly as daylight hit me.

Unfortunately, standing innocently just outside the shiny slab of hardened metal was the graceful, ageless, legendary singer Joan Baez. Her meticulous appearance and shiny gray mane lent a classy aura that reminded me of my maternal grandmother and distinguished aunts. That inspiring vibe failed to prevent an unfortunate mishap. I inadvertently whacked her beautiful face with the cold steel of the heavy door.

I think I broke her nose. Oh, SHIT!

Thankfully, Joan remained nonplussed and reassured all in the vicinity she was just fine.

"I'm fine, dear. Don't worry about me."

Then I felt mad AND guilty. I don't remember what I was mad about but will forever remain remorseful for nearly flattening Joan's mug.

CHAPTER 58

RADIO MAGIC REDISCOVERED, THEN CRUSHED

Holiday season, winter of 2009: "John, your position at Sirius XM has been eliminated, and today is your final day of employment. We have logistics to review, and Kim will go over those with you. Here is your final regular paycheck. We have also prepared a separation agreement that describes your proposed exit package, and you have three days to review it, sign it, and return it. Please leave all key fobs, ID badges, and workplace equipment with Kim. You may remove personal items from your office area, and I will accompany you to let your staff know. We wish you the best of luck going forward, and it has been a pleasure working with you."

Once I settled in Washington at XM Satellite Radio in 2005, the simple joy of that part of the profession returned. It was an extremely cool place to earn a paycheck. Not only did traditional radio folks become peers, so did rocket scientists. Literally. The master control facility for every channel, a set of rooms where satellites were also monitored, closely resembled the bridge of the starship Enterprise, complete with a captain's chair. No physical media existed.

Everything was digital, stored in rows of racks holding storage devices, each capable of storing audio in designations of byte levels never previously encountered.

It was geek heaven. It was also impossible to determine who you might run into inside the walls of XM. Willie Nelson, Snoop Dog, Bonnie Raitt; it could be anyone at any time. Paul McCartney once asked a random XM person for directions to a restroom. James Carville and Maya Angelou had a lunchtime conversation at a table next to mine in the building cafeteria. One minute they discussed politics of the day (with Carville loudly accusing Maya of being "full of shit" at one point), then traded turkey casserole recipes the next.

A favorite lunchtime diversion was attending studio recordings of an XM series called Artist Confidential. Up to thirty people were seated just feet away from artists who were interviewed and performed for small, gathered audiences. Special interviews also occurred on weekends. Finding people to show up could be difficult, but taking advantage of such opportunities was occasionally magical. A few months before his death, George Carlin stopped by one Saturday to promote the book he was writing. Rather than a formal interview, XM allowed Carlin to speak about any topic on his mind. The two-and-a-half hours I spent just listening to that particular legend was astounding. His passing in June 2008 touched loyal fans around the globe who appreciated the sharpness of his wit.

The expansion of XM's ad sales business brought additional operational challenges. My staff of direct reports eventually grew to fourteen talented people. Software used to manage the ad sales business needed improvement. I encountered resistance because custom components specifically engineered for unique technical purposes were unavailable from any other vendor. Despite pushback outside programming and sales areas, an RFP effort was crafted to evaluate alternative solutions that might enhance ad sales business processes.

These were processes I managed at vendor companies for years. Months of meetings were conducted. Internal support outside Programming and Sales remained tepid. Efforts to kill the RFP process by a few entrenched individuals in technical areas failed to derail slow progress. Finally, a workable and relatively cost-effective solution was crafted.

During roughly the same time period, a dreaded "merger of equals" was announced that paired XM Satellite Radio and Sirius Satellite Radio. The government was concerned. In a relatively new business with limited competition, there would suddenly be NO competition. Officials from both companies disagreed, citing the speed at which technology spurred brand-new streaming offerings and other over-the-top alternatives. Besides, neither XM nor Sirius had ever been profitable, and profit was more in reach within a merged organization. Sirius bet its farm on Howard Stern. XM Radio invested heavily in Major League Baseball, Oprah Winfrey, and other high-value marquees. Most behind-the-scenes financing was accommodated by Liberty Media, a quiet but heavy hitter with a great deal of influence.

"Merger of equals" was a misnomer. Management of the new Sirius XM Radio was essentially Mel Karmazin and his team from Sirius. Four years in Washington are often enough for politicians, and it appeared I was also destined to be a one-termer. Shortly after the Sirius takeover became official, almost every executive-level person at

XM vanished. The following year became a gut-wrenching bloodbath.

A large, open bullpen work area that housed my scheduling operations team was situated between the larger programming area and the main entrance to the building. The quickest way out the door from programming was directly through our workspace. One by one, the most talented and creative people in radio, including a few legends, met ignominious fates nearly every day. We were usually the last people in the building to sneak goodbye waves to them as they toted file boxes containing personal contents of desks on their way out, always accompanied by two uniformed guards.

No one can doubt Karmazin's business track record, but his path toward short-term financial success involved strategic nuclear options while slashing to the bone, then purging bones deemed nonessential. Initially, that meant my team was moved from Programming to Finance. Mel tended to dismiss the back-office flow of commercial operations as something akin to clerical work that just about anyone could do. By the time his team worked their way to our level to trim the fat, an entire year had passed. One of the first things they discovered was that most line staff got paid more than industry norms.

Meetings with programming legends to discuss how everyone in the room could continuously improve the sounds of each channel by owning all the content for which they were directly responsible ended. They were replaced by stressed-out staff members fielding calls from Gary Dell'Abate because Howard Stern did not like the way specific pieces of live copy were written.

As a part of the XM programming team, a case against airing, say, Ashley Madison spots on certain channels out of that particular target demographic could easily be won. The same argument about the same client under Sirius management would be summarily dismissed. "John, they're paying big money in advance. Cash is king. Period."

Migration from previous business systems occurred, but not to XM selected vendors. Systems already in place at Sirius were used. Corporate America suddenly became unappealing. Given the economic collapse of banking and markets around the time of the merger, there were palpable fears even the merged company might be finished permanently.

Late in 2009, I was summoned to New York by my boss. "John, we are eliminating redundancies. You need to pick nine out of fourteen members on your team for immediate dismissal, and we need your list tomorrow." Those nine people were to be let go the week of Thanksgiving. Human Resources issued an official script, which I was to commit to memory. Firings were to occur one by one in a Human Resources conference room and would include me, a human resources person, and the person losing their job. Once I made my "Sophie's Choice" selections, the litany began. The speech was filled with official-sounding rationalization, essentially advising their jobs had been eliminated and good luck in the future. It was gut-wrenching. Thanksgiving was not celebrated that year. There was little about which to be thankful.

Additional meetings in New York became somewhat regular occurrences. "John, would you consider relocating to New York to lead the entire team from here?" Yes, I was interested.

"John, would you be willing to take a 20% pay cut?" No, I was not interested.

As 2009 ended, I was summoned to Human Resources. In the room sat the same HR person who assisted me with the evisceration of employee redundancy before Thanksgiving, and my New York boss, a Karmazin lackey who believed she knew it all. She monotoned "the speech" with all the warmth of an undertaker. I already knew all the words anyway.

This is so predictable, yet still so incomprehensibly stupid. I am so tired of dealing with morons.

My reaction was neither sadness nor regret. I was prepared for it and offered little more than relief-filled chuckling. Yet another career in radio met a premature end. Shortly after my departure, every other member of my team met identical fates.

The severance they offered was not bad, so I chose relaxation over panic. I cashed out all of my company stock almost immediately and reinvested it elsewhere. Retirement funding was also rolled over, and benefits related to unemployment insurance were happily accepted. The most difficult part involved selling an expensive home in suburban Maryland, and it lost equity. Still free of panic, we purchased a foreclosed home in suburban Indianapolis for cash, located 342 yards from Gate 7 of the Indianapolis Motor Speedway. Gut remodeling paved the way for becoming our primary home base. A "me" project was the only therapy I needed.

CHAPTER 59

GRIZZLED VETERAN STATUS ACHIEVED

After I left XM, a few odd-job consulting adventures kept career fires stoked, but carrying my own accounts receivable did little to enhance personal daily cash flow. Private consulting soon led straight back to VCI, which I probably should never have left in 2005.

My former boss Mary Blair pitched an idea late in 2009. "John, we are creating a brand-new business intelligence product suite. We REALLY need qualified people for the design, testing, and rollout, and we want it ready for market by Christmas of 2011."

Sweet! Sold.

A small group of peers and I managed to reach final milestones in advance of product release within one year. My contract with VCI was also for one year. Mary pulled me into her office in September, 2011 and shut the door. "John, the company has decided to convert your status from contractual to full-time effective January 1, 2012. Are you interested, and what kind of salary will it take?

Wait. I'm not fired? You appreciate my work? How is this possible?! Surely you jest.

Mary was serious and enthusiastic, and so was I. On the way to that happy new year, however, VCI was acquired by the new king of that market segment mountain in October of 2011.

WideOrbit is a San Francisco-based software and business solutions provider. That company was less than one year old when my tenure at VCI began in 2000. In just ten years, it grew to become the largest and most market-dominant company in that business, handily surpassing every other competitor. A combined Columbine JDS held that position in 2000. By 2010, CJDS was a shadow. Under Harris ownership, most legacy product offerings vanished, from JDS to BIAS to Columbine and Paradigm. The company still exists today under different ownership but is now known as Imagine Communications. It has diversified far beyond its original niche.

My role as a JDS consultant in the early 1990s began hitting its stride. A couple of assignments took me to ABC-owned KGO Television in San Francisco. Professionals leading management and ad sales efforts there appreciated the functionality JDS provided but were impatient and wanted much more. They were one of a very small number of clients that held more expansive viewpoints about what could be possible with the right technology. Instead of simply spouting pie-in-the-sky wish lists, they telegraphed how my company could actually get there. Compared to almost any other ad sales executives, they were atypical. That attitude pervaded their entire organization. KGO, for example, was an early adopter of digital video technology. I appreciated and was excited by their fresh outlook and committed all I could to documentation. Not everyone at JDS was willing to consider a vision KGO was more than willing to share. In business, not paying attention to aspects of the future deemed important by your biggest clients can eventually topple even the biggest and most important players.

A couple of KGO folks even indicated they intended to start their own company to facilitate the type of technology advancement they envisioned. I wished them luck, felt their optimism, and recorded the outline. I also skeptically wondered about the odds.

During the decade that followed Y2K, brand-new systems from WideOrbit, created by former KGO dreamers, were pollinated with not only the best philosophical features of successful competitor products but also new development that took standard processes steps further. They began seeding their new company with talented folks from legacy companies and clients. WideOrbit forged unique development partnership deals with large media operators. It worked, and until the next big operator steps forward (a few always try), the market belongs to them.

The contract I had with VCI was not included in the WideOrbit acquisition, which dropped the project we had nearly finished. A door to employment had not closed, but nearly as quickly as that merger unfolded, a new player reached out.

Broadway Systems was also relatively new, touting excellence in an extremely narrow niche. The specialty of that privately held company included product offerings designed specifically for cable television networks in the United States. They were the first company that fully engineered their products from ad sales inception seamlessly through all transactional gates that followed, with no clunky reverse engineering.

That is admittedly geek-speak, but it seemed remarkable even though it was raw.

The one single aspect of that small Grand Rapids-based company that provided the most inspiration was a small staff willing to run through walls for clients. It harkened back again to both JDS and VCI. The following four years were happily spent working with clients and projects, based mostly in New York.

The seemingly inevitable happened again during October of 2015. Broadway Systems was acquired by an Israel-based company, Sintec Media. Leadership of that organization was on a buying binge, intent on becoming the unquestioned king of the mountain. Their strategy was not to grow mostly organically, as WideOrbit had, but to purchase their way to market dominance.

The products of the new guys were not well suited for the North American marketplace, did not function that well, and very few of its people (scattered literally around the world) were willing to break down many walls for clients. They also intended to kill Broadway Systems.

Retirement became a lot more than a casual desire after a young guy I began mentoring at Broadway and I began openly referring to a new female supervisor with an attitude and facial tics as "Winky Blinkencunt." Cynicism was one thing, but my attitude devolved into something potentially toxic. All signs pointed toward career sunset as the most viable option.

Frustrating?! Yes. I finally reached the point where I really am more knowledgeable than ANY of these people, yet they believe they have all the answers. Do it! Retire! NOW!

The 100th running of the Indianapolis 500 was Memorial Day weekend in 2016. That historic occasion seemed, at least in my mind, to coincide with a path to retirement. I pulled the plug on my second amazing career on my own terms. The time finally arrived.

My journey through corporate America was occasionally perilous, but I got really good at what I did and remain proud of my body of work. There are no professional regrets. It ended without much fanfare. No gold watches. No cake. No formalities. Not even an exit interview. I was suddenly Warren Schmidt, Jack Nicholson's character in *About Schmidt.* I was completely fine with ALL of it.

I remain a proud baby boomer. Our final stretch involves wrinkles, gray hair, and grandkids. We are worldly, but the world does not seem all that interested in what we have to say. That never stopped us before, and we intend to continue enjoying the adventure for as long as we remain upright.

EPILOGUE

KICKED BACK (IN A GOOD WAY)

I no longer fret over definitive employment goals, and that has inadvertently become the most refreshing aspect of boomer late adulthood. The way in which technology continues evolving still fascinates me, and I admire and respect peers creating their own successes. All I really want now is increased and meaningful interaction with my family. My years on the road took a severe toll. I want to become a much better parent, grandparent, and husband than I have been.

It is an uphill struggle. My oldest son chooses not to communicate with me, primarily because I was not around for his youth. Work and swashbuckling stupidly seemed more important at the time. That also means no contact with two of my granddaughters. My other son works way too hard in the oil fields of northern North Dakota. My daughter is a single mom raising her daughter in Colorado. I still don't see them enough. The Ozzie-and-Harriett world I grew up in no longer exists. Harry Chapin's song Cats in the Cradle is relevant.

Advice to generations that follow can be easily dispensed but may never be considered. If boomer kids and grandkids follow the lead of my generation, they won't take life advice seriously until they are well beyond forty. Too late? We'll see. My feeling is to go where life leads you and work hard at whatever you choose to do. Save all the money you can and invest it wisely. You will need all of it and then some eventually. Stop and smell roses earlier than you otherwise might. Above all, avoid becoming some narcissistic jackass. Help others before you help yourself. Family, blood relatives or otherwise, is the most important thing in life.

Here is hoping for an equal number of years as a happy and healthy baby boomer retiree wasting time figuring out Medicare and a bunch of its parts.

Friends often ask what happened to certain people or places along my journey. Folks tend to come and go in life. Sometimes that's OK, but I really miss others. Almost all of them are remembered fondly.

My two brothers and two sisters are alive and well, and our immediate family is closer than most.

Nadine McDougal, the childhood hussy who stole my innocence, is presumably wrinkled and similarly retired. Hopefully, she smiles if she discovers this book. The same goes for the rest of the neighborhood gang, Allen, Caroline, Ricky, and Ellen.

The young adults like my parents in the middle of the 1960s who forged their own sexually free paths are presumably deceased or at the very end of long lives. Cyrus, Marta, the Drake repairman, Mrs. McDougal and the other young mothers of Lawrence all remain young and wearing funny pointed eyeglasses in my memory.

St. Lawrence is still there, but those who educated us are well beyond pearly gates. That includes gruff Father Conan, who left many of us with a memorable approach to pleasures of the flesh. Speaking of spiritual contributions, the makeshift stained-glass windows I created for a chapel at WCHS remained for forty years.

No word on what happened to Nicky Traylor, Moose, or his next girlfriend, Darla Klingenfus. It is probably best. Becky Newsom and Darlene Woodman are distinguished, mature ladies. Both remember our trysts with clarity, and I regularly share smiles with both.

I recently made a list of all the cars I have owned since my first, the 1953 Plymouth Cranbrook in 1970, just for fun. There are twenty-two in all, including all the unusual iterations of the big three. Most are rusted away in scrap yards now. My current daily driver is a fully loaded SUV with all of the safety bells and whistles. The two favorite long-gone cars are the Plymouth, originally bolted together a year before I arrived on earth, and the 1962 Pontiac Catalina. Not only were the cars classics, but so are the memories from inside them.

My high school best buds are still around. Joe Buck was a curmudgeon in high school, but we did not mind. He was a great but serious friend. We interacted a few times as adults, and he centered his professional career around internal combustion. He is enormously successful. Alas, he unfriended me on social media. I am apparently just not serious enough. Mike McKlain regularly blames me for leading him down wrong paths, but not enough to unfriend me.

Delores Schwartz became Sister Grace and married Jesus instead of some horny Hoosier kid. Her slutty friend Lori not only pleasured Joe Buck in my Opel but eventually fooled around with my youngest brother a time or two, and in the strangest twist of all, became Shelly Scott's roommate at Vincennes University. Indiana is a relatively small state.

The first memorable love of my life, high school girlfriend Janice Richards, is as beautiful today as she was in 1971. She is also a grandparent, retired, and is leading a remarkable life. Social media enables connections with the long lost, and that's what happened with Janice. She lives in Indiana, and one of these days, I'm going to go have lunch with her.

Shelly Scott re-entered my life by way of social media. She is a healthy, retired, happy grandma and probably does not realize that memories of her remain fond. Social media also connects me with Misty Horton and Lorna Daniels, but both of them fly beneath the radar. I still arrogantly believe Kerry Miller's tears were driven entirely by natural ecstasy.

The ladies who shared various degrees of marital bliss (or close) with me in the 1970s and beyond are hopefully all still around. I know a few of them are, including my two ex-wives. Suzie remains in the same small Indiana town I fled when our marriage failed. Her story included a happily-ever-after marriage and no other children. Stevie replanted roots in Colorado and married her permanent husband there. These days she splits time between Florida and Aspen, loudly praises Jesus, and buys into every whacky conspiracy theory ever concocted.

Rebecca Bosch got away but probably shouldn't have. I lost her phone number. Back then, they had to be written down. The slip of paper with the number vanished. I thought I remembered it, but the thirty or so people I called in the vicinity of what I thought the touch-tone sequence was were not helpful with my search. I probably should not have waited six months to visit her apartment, but when I did, the new occupants had no idea where she moved.

The Indiana Theatre in Washington is still there, but it wasn't for a long while. It was always managed by Karl Kalvin or a relative. Karl ultimately died, and the chain that owned the theatre shut it down about the time that the supercenter-ization of small-town America finished decimating downtown areas nationwide. It was eventually rescued by a regional entrepreneur who set about rescuing shuttered theatres in small towns to help revive not just main streets but historic legacy theatres on them. The East 50 Drive-In did not fare as well. It was used as a cornfield for a while but is now the location of a farm implements dealer.

Neither of the two Williams Rexall Pharmacies where I worked in high school remain. The downtown location where we found opium on the second floor is now a parking lot. The Highway 50 location burned down while I was in high school but rebuilt and served the community for additional decades. It ultimately became a Family Dollar, but the Williams family of pharmacists and health care professionals have always been entrepreneurial. They grew well beyond drug stores and now operate a large regional pharmacy and medical supplies group.

The guy who inspired my entire professional career direction, Dennis Daily, is also retired and again living happily in southern Indiana following East Coast adventures and residencies out west. The broadcasting program at Vincennes University held an all-class reunion to celebrate fifty years of the program in 2018. There were two of us representing the class of 1974, along with Skip Sparkman, the teacher who jumpstarted my career. All of us reached elder statesmen status. Lynn Halterman, my buddy from VU and WBOW, and I remain good buddies. An entire book could be written about adventures shared with him and his beautiful wife, Mary Kaye. All of us trace our friendship back to 1973.

Speaking of mentors, Mike King, the guy who rescued my radio career in the late 1970s, is also retired and is an occasional lunch companion in Columbus, Indiana. Radio is a small community. I stay in touch with at least one or more peers from every station that employed us.

Most of the friends I had while married to Stevie are still around but mostly invisible. The ones still in touch don't take sides other than occasionally whispering things like "Is she fucking nuts?" For the record, I still like Stevie but give her plenty of elbow room.

My lifelong obsession with the Indianapolis 500 continues, and I attended my fifty-fifth one in 2021. I prefer seating in the B-Penthouse these days.

Professional work makes for nostalgic memories but is not missed. I enjoy seeing people I worked with succeed and feel really good when I was able to help.

Take the keys, Generations X, Y, Z, and beyond. For better or worse, it's all yours. Do not forget to ALWAYS respect your elders.

www.ingramcontent.com/pod-product-compliance
Lightning Source LLC
Chambersburg PA
CBHW071548030726
47593CB00001BA/79

* 9 7 8 1 7 3 6 2 8 2 0 0 7 *